Directing Amateur
Musical Theatre

Directing Amateur Musical Theatre

A Practical Guide for Non-Professional Theatre

Dom O'Hanlon

methuen | drama

LONDON • NEW YORK • OXFORD • NEW DELHI • SYDNEY

METHUEN DRAMA
Bloomsbury Publishing Plc
50 Bedford Square, London, WC1B 3DP, UK
1385 Broadway, New York, NY 10018, USA
29 Earlsfort Terrace, Dublin 2, Ireland

BLOOMSBURY, METHUEN DRAMA and the Methuen Drama logo
are trademarks of Bloomsbury Publishing Plc

First published in Great Britain 2024

Cover design: Ben Anslow
Cover image: Old vintage wood background (© Jirapas / AdobeStock);
Vector set of chalk elements (© oleskalashnik / AdobeStock)

A catalogue record for this book is available from the British Library.

ISBN: HB: 978-1-3503-9876-4
           PB: 978-1-3503-9875-7
           ePDF: 978-1-3503-9877-1
           eBook: 978-1-3503-9878-8

Typeset by Integra Software Services Pvt. Ltd.
Printed and bound in Great Britain

To find out more about our authors and books visit www.bloomsbury.com
and sign up for our newsletters.

For my husband, Ben, who I met in amateur theatre and has spent the last 15 years hearing 'I can't, I have rehearsal … '

Contents

Illustrations

Figures

Tables

About the Author

Dom O'Hanlon is a director with over 15 years of experience directing and working within amateur musical theatre in the UK and USA, ranging from university and college productions, summer camp and summer stock, and educational and TIE musicals. He has worked in a range of capacities on productions with amateur performers of all ages, in all manners of spaces from traditional theatres to outdoor arenas and converted swimming pools, on a range of work from classic to new musicals. He holds an MA Distinction in Text and Performance from RADA and Birkbeck, University of London (UK).

Acknowledgements

I would first like to thank the team at Methuen Drama for commissioning this book and working so hard bringing it to fruition. My fearless editor and wonderful friend Anna Brewer has improved this book no end, championing it from the start and encouraging me to write from the outset. Her generous and essential corrections and suggestions have made this a thoroughly collaborative experience, although I maintain any mistakes are my own. I want to extend my thanks to Aanchal Vij, Margaret Bartley and Elizabeth Kellingley for their parts in bringing this project to life. I'd also like to thank Ben Anslow, a visionary designer who I'm lucky enough to have had work on this book.

My life-to-date in amateur theatre has been challenging, enlightening and inspiring and I have too many collaborators to thank across many years of projects who have all fed into this book in one way or another. I would, however, like to specifically thank my 2023 cast of *Nine* – Stewart, Elise, Fenella, Charlotte, Sarah, Kerry, Jo, Julie, Carole-Anne, Caroline and Milo – which I was rehearsing throughout most of this writing period and kept me inspired and mentally tuned-in to the whole process against which this book is structured.

Amateur musical theatre requires fearless and hard-working producers and I'm lucky to have worked with some of the best. Blake Klein provided me with countless opportunities to hone my craft through Pint of Wine Productions, many of which have been my most fulfilling artistic achievements, never saying 'no' and problem-solving a way out of everything with zero fuss. Working with my friends Phoebe Gardner, Sarah Burrell and Becky East has kept me sane and I thank them for many of the ideas and experiments in this book, as well as the anecdotes that didn't quite make the final draft … More recently I've been inspired by the team of Ever After Productions, Charlotte and Matthew Gregory, Elise Betts and Emma Fraser who together have put me back on track and provided deeply fulfilling experiences.

Those who read early drafts and encouraged me include Kevin Sherwin and Adam Wachter. I'm grateful for those who provided their short 'perspectives' used throughout the book – I remain in awe of your work.

My parents facilitated not only my love of theatre but musical theatre, quickly indulging what was always going to be more than a hobby and allowing me to find my true self in the form and setting me on a path to work in this field. As a child I was borderline obsessed with writing books and scripts, which I would give to my Dad to take into his office on a weekly basis to have spiral bound, which in my childhood mind meant I had been 'published'. I'm so grateful to my Dad for indulging this practice and hope that seeing a real-life book in print some 30 years later makes you proud, despite it not being as commercially successful as the 'Woofa' stories would be. Lastly, my husband Ben to whom this book is dedicated for putting up with me always being at rehearsal and consistently supporting each project, however inconvenient it seemed.

Introduction

When you hear the words amateur theatre, the first things that spring to mind for many people are dusty church halls, creaky sets, wooden performances and over-inflated egos. But many people become involved in amateur theatre – perhaps through community centres and even school or university groups – because they recognize their ability to provide extra-curricular care to those who band together under the umbrella of 'theatre', a broad church that celebrates their interests and skills and brings communities together.

In the UK in 2023 on any given evening, potential audiences have their pick of hundreds of different live performances performed by amateur actors up and down the country. These range from premieres of hard-hitting contemporary drama through to new musicals, original writing and perennial favourites, performed in venues ranging from former swimming pools to converted gymnasiums and professional stages. At present, there are over 2,300 drama and musical theatre companies in England that are affiliated to amateur theatre organizations, and more than 3,000 smaller-scale youth and unaffiliated societies that together stage over 10,000 productions a year. The National Operatic & Dramatic Association (NODA), an organizational body for amateur theatre, estimates combined membership of over 100,000 people ranging in age from 8 to 80, with NODA-affiliated groups generating between £150m to £200m in ticket sales each year. While this is divided between plays, pantomimes and other forms of theatre, musical theatre is arguably the most popular form proving that amateur theatre is big business.

When the Covid-19 pandemic shut down live performance in all forms and forced a worldwide lockdown, thousands of amateur performers were days away from opening shows they had been working on for six months or more. Whole communities found themselves without their centre of gravity, friendship groups were broken up and companies disbanded. Many companies couldn't sustain the financial implications of closing shows so close to their opening, and with no concrete plan from the government for re-opening and seemingly no end in sight, found themselves having to shut shop for good. As producer Julian Marsh says to Peggy Sawyer towards the end of *42nd Street*: 'Think of the scenery that will never be seen, the costumes never worn, the orchestrations never heard … think of musical comedy, the most glorious words in the English language!' Sadly, no amount of show business 'chutzpah' could come to the rescue and amateur theatre, like everything else, was a victim of the global shutdowns and has had to find a new resilience in the post-Covid landscape.

Directing amateur theatre, and in particular musical theatre, is an art form in and of itself. Whilst many courses teach directing at both undergraduate and postgraduate level the focus is primarily on preparing the student for a lifetime of directing professional actors in professional shows. At this level the word 'amateur' is seen as a dirty word, thanks to outdated connotations and the idea that it can not be either financially or artistically fulfilling and therefore isn't worthy of specific study. Throughout this book I argue against this assumption, highlighting the importance of specifically working within the amateur sphere and how as a director your skills can be honed and refined to build performances out of untrained yet highly talented performers who come from all walks of life.

My own journey with amateur theatre began as most do as a young performer, migrating to the other side of the table at university to learn the craft of directing very much on the job. I believe directing is firmly an empirical skill that one learns by doing, observing and experiencing rather than being formally trained. Despite attending one of the world's top drama schools for postgraduate training in the field, most of my education has been in the rehearsal room itself learning from other directors and observing different ways of working with actors, staging productions and building rehearsals. No experience is wasted – every director despite their quirks and relative quality will give you something to take away, even if that's something that you make a note to *not* do in the future.

Given that so much of directing is learned by observing and absorbing, my number one tip above anything else is to see as much live theatre as you possibly can. I was lucky enough to be exposed to musical theatre at a young age and would keep notebooks where I would write down blocking, stage pictures and so on and even try to re-stage numbers with toys in my bedroom which all invariably led to my fascination with how theatre was made. Even a dreadful production will give you something to learn from. *Why* was it dreadful? *Why* didn't certain elements work? Keep a notebook of productions you have seen and make notes of the aspects that you liked and more importantly *why* you liked them and what was it that made them leave a lasting impression.

There's an assumption that the driving factor behind amateur theatre is its constant striving to be seen as professional in quality. This is a notion that I find inhibits and undermines the work being done by both cast and creative team, creating an air of self-consciousness that builds a metaphorical bar that everyone has to hurdle in order to succeed. Often you'll read reviews of amateur theatre that compare such shows to a professional production or use empty plaudits such as 'as good as anything on the West End'. Maybe your friends and family will see a production and say it seemed to be 'of a professional standard' as a natural reaction and impulse to please.

Judging an amateur production by comparing it to professional work is the wrong benchmark for success. Yes, you should be aspiring to a level of professionalism in your process and behaviours, but you need to embrace and unlock the virtues of the word 'amateur' or else that word will remain sullied forever. Amateur theatre by its very nature will never *be* professional theatre, and the assumption that that is the intended goal overlooks the inherent and many virtues the form itself contains. The virtues of amateur theatre are seemingly endless. It means community. It means friendship. It means making art for art's sake rather than money. It means exploration. It means collaboration. It means learning new skills. It means development. It means creating something new. Above all, it's a shared process with potentially like-minded individuals who collectively give their time and skills out of the sheer love of theatre, and that is a form of magic that can't be compared.

Despite also having worked professionally, I have never felt so engaged in a project as I have when directing amateur theatre. The feeling of people being in a room collaborating on a project because they want to be there, all rowing in the same direction is electric. Seeing people juggle busy lives and important jobs, forging life-long friendships, falling in love and going on personal journeys all for the thrill of putting on a production is unlike any other feeling you can have in theatre, and shouldn't be overlooked or ignored.

I want this book to inspire you in your journey with amateur theatre and to convince you as a director – or a potential director – that it's an area worthy of your time, skill and commitment. I feel we are at a crossroads for how we approach, engage with and produce amateur musical theatre in a contemporary context and I wrote this book partly to address the changes I want to see and be part of as we continue to inspire the next generation of theatre makers. Although no official statistics are kept on the make-up of NODA members with regard to race, gender, sexuality and ethnicity, amateur theatre is largely considered to be a white middle-class pastime. The reasons for this are deep-rooted but concern both the repertoire that is performed and stories perpetuated, as well as the gatekeeping nature of how societies are run, via a board of trustees or committee which in turn creates a hierarchical structure that encourages and can perpetuate malpractice.

Throughout this book I will highlight ways in which your practice can be as inclusive as possible, from selecting shows through to casting practices and working with a company of actors in the room. There is much work to be done on a larger level, specifically in regard to the shows that are being performed and the idea of repertoire, but I believe that interrogating your own practice and building affirmative change into your working methods by challenging assumptions, the notion of tradition and 'the way things have always been done' will help to dismantle and rebuild the industry in a fairer and more inclusive way.

How to Use this Book

If you're reading this book you no doubt have some experience with amateur musical theatre, or at the very least, some interest in it. Perhaps you're a member of a musical theatre company looking to learn about how to direct for the first time or an experienced director looking to refine your craft and discover new ways of approaching a show. As with any instructional book, it's important to state up front that there's no 'right' way to do it. This book is based on 15 years of personal experience and grounded in acting and directing training that was gained working with professional and amateur actors and organizations.

If you are a frequent and experienced director I encourage you to open your mind to new methods of working that'll keep your process alive as you approach your future productions. Challenging yourself will inherently mean you approach the whole process with fresh eyes and may just unlock different approaches that revive your passion and keep you working to the best of your ability. If you're new to directing I'm offering this book as an overview of the whole process with practical tips, exercises and work to do both inside and outside of the rehearsal room.

The structure of this book is designed to take you through all aspects of directing an amateur musical, from the initial conversations around selecting a show through to handling the performance run and effectively closing a show. The cycle and structure will be familiar to anyone who has been involved with putting on a show, beginning with a period of planning through to a slow build throughout rehearsal, climbing to an intense week or two of performances that hopefully ends on a high for everyone involved. The first section of this book **DIRECTING PREPARATION,** guides you through the pre-production process from selecting a show through to auditions and building a concept, in a mostly linear format that approaches the process in the order in which you'll likely work.

The second section, **DIRECTING PROCESS,** is very much the substance of this book and is designed to be your go-to section throughout rehearsals. Presented in a non-linear order, it explores how to stage a number, how to work with the ensemble and principal actors as well differentiate between different types of staging from book scenes to production numbers. I've envisioned this section to be dipped in and out of as appropriate throughout the rehearsal process and be frequently revisited when needed.

The final section, **CURTAIN UP, LIGHT THE LIGHTS**, offers practical observations on aspects of the production schedule that you will need to get to know and understand in order to guide the full company through to show week and beyond. This is complemented by an appendix that includes a glossary of key terms and words that you're likely to encounter throughout the directing process.

Many of the forms, charts and schedules included as examples in this book can be found on the accompanying companion website where blank examples can be downloaded and used for your own production.

This book is not designed to be read in isolation – I have listed a bibliography of the best books and resources that will complement this guide and assist you no matter what your level of skill and experience. Directing is a skills-based activity and one that relies on your building and maintaining a toolkit that should always be refreshed and challenged. Amateur theatre requires a specific skillset within that activity and one that will bring you joy, pain, sleepless nights and heartache time and time again but you'll always, I bet, find yourself going back for more.

ACT 1   Directing Preparation

Why Direct an Amateur Musical?

It is my belief that there is no 'right' person to direct an amateur musical. You may be someone coming to directing at any point in your life where you find yourself with more time, or a desire to be involved with a company but not wanting to be on the stage. Perhaps you're someone who has transitioned from appearing in shows to wanting to work on the other side of the table, or a stage manager or technical crew member looking for a more creative challenge. However you arrive at the desire, directing is an exciting and sometimes nerve-wracking job. There are many factors that may have delayed you volunteering or looking for work in the past, more often than not insecurities and an idea that someone else may be more suitable. Remember, all amateur directors have started somewhere. It may be a small cabaret or revue style performance, building up to a one-act musical with a couple of cast members. You may have even assisted another director on the job and are now looking to take on a whole show yourself. Surrounding yourself with a supportive team of people is the best piece of advice I can offer for even the most experienced directors.

One of the most important aspects of direction is preparation. It is common and advisable to admit that you will not always have the answer to the (many) problems that arise throughout the process, but preparation is key and will earn you instant respect amongst cast members, collaborators, committee members and colleagues.

A frequently cited problem with the role of the director in the professional sphere is that they are rarely compensated for the hours and level of preparation it takes outside of the rehearsal room. Equity rates tend to be flat-rate payments, unlike for many in the wider production team, and indeed cast, who are compensated for their time on an hourly or performance-based rate. For a director who is doing their job correctly, the pre-production, rehearsal and production process will occupy a part of your brain that refuses to shut itself off. It's common to lie awake at night wondering how a certain cast member will get from one quick change to another or thinking through a difficult scene transition. Be assured this is normal behaviour and something directors will frequently joke about as a show 'taking over their life'. On the one hand, this may sound intimidating but I have personally found the answer to many problems through the subconscious with solutions rising to the fore at many an inopportune moment. Succumbing to that feeling and embracing it is one of the exciting parts of directing. You'll benefit from keeping a notebook (or digital version) on hand at all times for when inspiration strikes and find it difficult to shake the show from your head.

Preparation covers every aspect of directing from your initial conversations about a show right through to the final dress and technical rehearsals. In this section, we will cover the preparation that goes into a show before the rehearsal process begins and look specifically at the work that can and must be done before you even step into a rehearsal room. You may find yourself attending numerous meetings in the early stages, from informal interviews with a committee who may want to hear about your background and approach to a show or even a formal pitch where you will be expected to come forward with a clear reason and vision behind your style, that in some circumstances may be competitive. No work is ever wasted – being asked to talk through your ideas for a show or even propose ideas for set design or concepts will help ground your work and give you experience in communicating these often abstract ideas that otherwise sit in your head, unexpressed.

Approaching a Production

What type of group are you working with? It might be a youth theatre, college or university group or a local organization in your town or city. In the UK there's a rich history of amateur theatre groups with many towns and cities having multiple groups that each have rich histories and different identities. Many contemporary musical theatre societies are born out of Operatic or Gilbert and Sullivan societies, formed in the twentieth century particularly in the post-war 'boom' period as a form of community activity. Others are attached to churches, village halls or other social groups that can even include specific unions or workplace groups. In the USA the term 'community theatre' is more common, but the remit is largely the same – to produce amateur productions of popular musicals to serve the community in which they exist. The history of amateur theatre is rich, vibrant and inspiring and I would encourage you to read one of the many books on the subject that explores how the practice developed and went on to form a bedrock and breeding group for many professional practitioners.

Different amateur theatre groups have different needs, aims and objectives and it's a good idea to familiarize yourself with these before you even begin to think about what musical they should produce. While the core elements will remain the same across the board, amateur theatre groups differ widely across the UK and can have quite varied remits. Most societies and groups will have a website where their goals and aims are usually clearly stated. If you're new to a group, I advise looking through their production history, images and archive if possible to get a feel for the type of group they are and the sort of shows that they are used to doing and have done in the past. Most NODA-affiliated groups will also have a copy of their constitution viewable for members to read. Whilst this may sound scarily formal, it can give a steer on the rules the society follows and can help guide your choices and decisions.

Important things to look for with a society or company:

- Do they state a number of shows a year?
- Do they have rules on who can be a member?
- Do they have guidelines on who can be considered for a principal role?
- Do they have a recent statement or commitment to diversity and inclusion?
- Do they hold open auditions?
- Does anyone who auditions get guaranteed a role in the ensemble?

Questions such as the above will help form your choices, particularly in relation to show selection. Knowing the boundaries over who can audition, who can be considered for a principal role and whether or not everyone who auditions is guaranteed a place in the ensemble will help you frame the show in your head and give a wider context of expectations at this early stage, avoiding any potential issues come the time of auditions. That's not to say you can't and shouldn't challenge the society's traditions or structures, but it's worth at least understanding what they stand for and what has worked for them in the past.

Working with a Society

Chances are if you are employed as an amateur theatre director you will have been hired by a specific society or group. Societies are usually structured with a committee of trustees who look after the day-to-day running of the group and handle the finances. Each society is structured slightly differently so I would encourage speaking to the Chair and Treasurer in the first instance to understand better how they operate. Make sure you ask questions up front about your role – there will likely be a lot of experience within the committee itself, so don't be afraid to ask about what has worked well in previous shows and what hasn't been as successful.

Contracts, Payments and Expenses

Most amateur theatre groups will pay their creative team for their time and skill. Some will have a standard set fee that is paid to each creative team member and others may rely on you to negotiate an appropriate fee. It's important to stress that this is unlikely to work out at a per-hour rate that effectively rewards you for your time. Directing as a skill is notoriously underpaid even in the professional world with fees that rarely take into account the work done in preparing for rehearsals and outside of the rehearsal room. Be open with the committee as to your expectations. In my experience, fees range from £1,000 to £2,000, depending on the scale of the show and the budget as a whole. Understand the room in which you have to negotiate – look up the minutes of their last AGM (usually published online) which will show you previous show budgets and will say how much previous directors have been paid. While you don't want to undersell yourself you equally have to be able to operate within a realistic budget for the production as a whole. Your fee will represent a significant expense for the show that all comes out of the money available to you for mounting the production. Consider suggesting a top-up model or base rate with profit share which protects the society in case the show loses money but rewards you further should it turn a profit.

Discuss your expenses up front – will the society pay for your petrol, train fare and so on, or will your fee be expected to cover all costs associated with your employment? Talking openly about this before you start work is vital as you don't want to find yourself in a difficult position further down the line. It's also worth talking with the treasurer about expenses directly related to the show such as costumes, props and rehearsal items that you may find yourself buying along the way. Make sure you understand how to claim back items and what is required in terms of receipts. Ask about any spending limits and how to get approvals and sign-offs for show-related expenses from the treasurer and understand the process for this at all stages.

In all instances, even if you find yourself directing for gratis, I would encourage you to draw up a simple contract of engagement that outlines the exact commitment required to the project. This may include dates, times of rehearsal and responsibilities over show week. This will protect both the society and yourself and underline the process with clear deliverables that can be confirmed and agreed before you start work.

Budgeting

My golden rule for directing is to make sure you are part of the budgeting process. I will refuse to work for a society where I'm not shown the full budget from the beginning of the process as it allows me to understand the remits within which I am working. Maintaining a budget should not be your responsibility – usually this is up to the treasurer and producer – but as a director you should have a working understanding of the budget everyone is working to, as it will dictate all aspects of your concept and vision for the show. Knowing you have a £300 vs a £15,000 set budget will help you understand the scale of the show you're expected to present and will feed into your initial plans as you start to envision your show. It's important to stress that a bigger budget doesn't necessarily equate to a better show – some of the best amateur theatre productions I have ever seen have been presented on a shoe-string budget as creativity and ingenuity have been born from necessity.

Knowing where the money is being spent and which departments have the most money will help in your approach as you build your concept. For example, knowing there's a very small costume budget will mean you don't factor in multiple costume changes or expensive period garments – instead you may favour a base costume with small suggestive embellishments which in turn dictate a style of show that isn't rooted in realism. Discuss this up-front with both the committee and the wider creative team. Your creativity and ability to turn any restriction into a positive will be paramount to the success of the show.

Figure 1.1 presents a sample budget of a larger-scale amateur musical, showing the various costs that need to be factored in. As you can see, the outgoings are varied and expansive, whereas the incomings are largely based around the expected ticket income, as well as any sponsorship or show fees that the cast will pay to be

FICTIONAL MUSICAL THEATRE COMPANY

Name of Production : Example Budget Palace Theatre

Production forecast

EXPENDITURE	Estimated			INCOME		Tickets + Non Tickets
Professional Fees			**Non Tickets**			
Director	1000.00		Programme / Merch Sales		300	
Music Director	1000.00		Show Fees		2500	
Choreographers	750.00		Sponsors		500	
Orchestra	4000.00		Advertising		500	
Audition Pianist	150.00		Audition Fees		650	
Stage technicians	300.00					
BSL Signed Performer	100.00		Total		4450	
	7300.00					
Publicity			**Tickets**			
General publicity	235.00	£	40,000.00	100% Capacity (Full House - 400 seats @ £20) x 5 Performances	£	44,450.00
Poster artwork	350.00	£	32,000.00	80% Capacity	£	36,450.00
Publicity Clothing Expenditure	100.00	£	30,000.00	75% Capacity	£	34,450.00
Merchandise Costs	100.00	£	24,000.00	60% Capacity	£	28,450.00
Posters and handbills	300.00	£	20,000.00	50% Capacity	£	24,450.00
Banners	100.00	£	18,000.00	45% Capacity	£	22,450.00
Printing programmes	385.00					
Photos	140.00					
	1710.00		**Profit v Loss**			
Other Expenditure						
Hire of Palace Theatre	5000.00			100% Capacity	£	11,240.00
Hire of rehearsal halls	1000.00			80% Capacity	£	3,240.00
Scenery	1000.00			75% Capacity	£	1,240.00
Transport of Scenery	200.00			60% Capacity	-£	4,760.00
Props	200.00			50% Capacity	-£	8,760.00
Costumes and wigs	750.00			45% Capacity	-£	10,760.00
Make-up	50.00					
Lighting and sound	5000.00					
Insurance	400.00					
Scores, libs and band parts	600.00					
Licence Fee	10000.00					
	24200.00					
Estimated Expenditure	£ 33,210.00					

Fig.1.1 Sample Budget.

part of the production. Again, as a director this shouldn't be your area of focus and a longer discussion on budgeting could form a different book entirely. You do, however, have a responsibility to understand how the budget works and how this relates to both the directing process and shapes your vision for the show itself.

Who's Who?

Collaboration throughout the process is key to relieving the pressure that a director can feel and sharing the load across all departments, as well as problem-solving and overcoming challenges that arise. One of the key things to learn is that as director you are not supposed to be infallible, or to have all of the answers. There's often a pressure felt by being the one 'in charge' of the production which can result in you not actively seeking help or trying to solve everything yourself. As in life, asking for help is a sign of strength and not weakness. If you find yourself creatively stuck on staging a number or scene, ask your cast for help. Solicit ideas, when appropriate, and don't be afraid of utilizing the minds you have in the room. Chances are your cast will be made up of performers with all manner of experience between them – instead of feeling you have to be in charge of every aspect, remember that theatre is instead an incredibly collaborative art form and one that thrives on working together.

Nowhere is this more important than with your creative team. Depending on the size of the show you are directing your team will vary in size but should usually be made up of the core creatives that hold it together. Generally these are made up of a producer or committee representative, director, musical director and choreographer. The wider team usually comprises a production manager, set designer, costume supervisor, lighting designer, stage manager and sound designer. It may then widen out further to roles such as make-up designer, wigs, children's manager, company manager and so on. Many of these roles will be dictated by the committee or company that you are working for and it's important to ascertain who is responsible for what at all times. Different companies will have their own sense of the roles required in order to succeed and tried and tested ways that have worked for them in the past. Figure 1.2 shows a sample organization chart that helps identify the different roles in a production team and a way that a show can be organized. Ultimately, as director it will not be your responsibility to create or maintain this wider structure – unless asked for input – but I include this to show a director's place within a wider production team in an effort to show you are not alone.

The number one thing to remember with your creative team colleagues is that they are also in creative roles. Many directors fail to understand that costume, set, sound and lighting designers bring their own creative expertise to a production, and you should work to ensure you are all on the same consistent page. Whilst you will ultimately bring a concept to them from which you'll all collectively work, they will also have their own ideas and thoughts on how the production should look, sound and feel. The key to this collaboration is establishing your concept early on and making sure this translates into all elements of the production. Just as you send your choreographer references, images and videos, do the same with these creatives to outline your vision in the simplest way possible.

Your producer should regularly hold production meetings that bring together the full team and allow you all to discuss any issues that have arisen. As a director, it is not your responsibility to drive these meetings, but you do need to be able to communicate across all different departments and keep everyone on the same page. With a good company or society you should be left to deliver on the artistic vision of the show rather than act as a director / producer, but depending on the size of the company and their set-up this may differ.

Musical Director

Your relationship with your musical director (MD) is probably the closest working relationship across the whole production. It is vital you work together throughout and present a united front at all times. You may find yourself working with someone brand new or an established member of the company, but in each case it is vital that you establish a core way of working that benefits the production as a whole. The boundaries between the two roles are pretty easily identified but there is space for some crossover in terms of interpretation and execution of songs and musical performances.

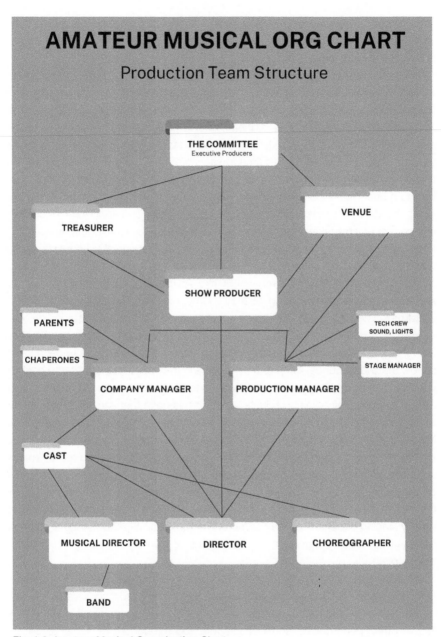

AMATEUR MUSICAL ORG CHART

Production Team Structure

THE COMMITTEE
Executive Producers

VENUE

TREASURER

SHOW PRODUCER

PARENTS

TECH CREW
SOUND, LIGHTS

CHAPERONES

STAGE MANAGER

COMPANY MANAGER

PRODUCTION MANAGER

CAST

MUSICAL DIRECTOR

DIRECTOR

CHOREOGRAPHER

BAND

Fig. 1.2 Amateur Musical Organization Chart.

The MD's job is largely to teach the full company the music and to maintain performances of it throughout. They will likely lead vocal call rehearsals that start with playing through the musical numbers (or "note-bashing", as we say), and the learning of rhythms well before you're able to stage a song or musical number. Depending on the complexities of the score this may take a number of sessions before songs are ready to be handed over for you to stage and direct. They will likely work through the score logically from start to finish, perhaps looking at more difficult numbers first in order to allow more time.

As director, given it's your job to manage the overall rehearsal schedule you'll need to work with the MD on a schedule that allows sufficient time to cover the music in the show. Be wary of under-estimating the time required for this to happen, even with songs that may sound simple or easy to learn. I have learnt from experience that it's often too ambitious to schedule a music and staging call of the same number in the same rehearsal. Actors need time to sit with the music, go away and commit it to memory or at least get it into their bodies before they're able to get it on its feet. Having a brief music call to recap the vocals ahead of staging is always advisable, giving the MD time to see how the song has taken shape and address any questions and correct any mistakes that may have crept in during the learning process.

I would sit down with the MD before you draw up a rehearsal schedule and work with them on a process that works from their perspective, asking them their opinion on how long certain musical numbers will take. As the schedule progresses you'll be able to find efficiency by utilizing different rooms, meaning you can work on scenes whilst music calls happen in a different space.

Your MD should lead their music calls, setting the pace and communicating their thoughts and ideas with the cast. I find it helpful to attend music calls to get a sense of how the show sounds, listen to the numbers in the voices of the cast and begin to visualize the show with your actors. I also like to be present when principal performers are learning their solos and duets, as it's at this point that you can begin to start to talk about the shape of the song from a musical point of view. I have worked with MDs who lean into the musical side of the job and those who are more like directors, and you'll need to judge the skills of the MD you're working with and ask them how you want to work together. Talk about the material before you rehearse so you're on the same page and can present a united front when talking to actors about the meanings and intentions of the song. It's also a good idea to give the MD a heads-up on any staging aspects that may compromise the musical performance as they will need to work with the actors on overcoming this or working through different performance methods.

It's important to remember that an MD's job does not end when the music has all been taught. Whilst they will likely be in the room for most rehearsals, they will continue to offer input to the cast from both technical and performance perspectives, shaping their performance and working with you throughout rehearsal to get the best vocal and musical performance out of the full ensemble. Always find space for them to give notes and continue to communicate with them throughout rehearsals so they know how the show is progressing. They should be your number one ally and confidant throughout the process – nothing should come as a surprise to them. It's also important to remember that they themselves will be performing during the show. They may be conducting the show whilst playing the keyboard part or conducting the band without playing. Either way, in show week they are the ones leading the show and performing as much as the cast. They will literally be in charge of the tempo of the show, the energy and the performance, leading from the front and providing a lifeline to the cast as you sit back and watch.

Choreographer

Aside from your MD, the choreographer should be your closest creative collaborator. Depending on the show you may find yourself doing double duty and choreographing the show yourself, in which case you'll find yourself devoid of another pair of eyes and creative mind, which can limit what you're able to achieve as well as pulling your focus during rehearsals. For larger-scale dance-heavy shows I would really recommend a separate choreographer. Not only will it broaden your creative team but it will allow you to focus on the production as a whole rather than find yourself pulled in multiple different directions at once. A choreographer's role differs largely from production to production and it's important to clarify with them what they are responsible for from the outset. Before the show is cast, divide up the numbers that they will be responsible for and any moments of dance and movement that you would like them to work on. You may find you want to give full numbers over to them to handle, or you may need to draw on them to take over movement within numbers that require a more stylized approach. Either way, I recommend outlining this division as early on as possible so both of you know which aspects you are responsible for. I'm lucky to have worked with excellent choreographers with whom I've enjoyed strong working relationships and this has been primarily because of honesty between us throughout the process as well as us sharing a creative vision.

Once the building blocks of your concept have been established, share this with them and discuss how to build movement into this overall idea. You both need to make sure you're working on the same show throughout. Discuss style and tone alongside more fundamental basics such as narrative and storytelling. There's no point in you establishing a sense of realism and your choreographer going for a brash and expressive style that rubs against the tone of what you have created in the scenes.

Producer

The production department will look after all elements of your show that are technical and help realize your vision in a practical sense. Different companies will have different set-ups, and it's important that you know who is in your team and their responsibilities before you start. A producer should be someone who heads the whole production team and drives the production forward. You should be in constant communication with them, and it's often their job to communicate your thoughts to the members of the team that need to know all of the relevant technical elements. Some companies may elect a 'committee representative' rather than a producer, someone whose job it is to be a bridge between the show and the wider committee. I would advise trying to push for a producer role to be created, as this centralizes the production process and allows one figurehead who is responsible for the show and its production schedule. The producer should also be in charge of the budget and making sure everyone sticks to their agreed costs at all times and does not overspend. As discussed in the section on budgeting above, this is vital for you as Director to be involved in. You cannot direct a show without knowing the overall budget and where the spend will be allocated.

Production Manager

A production manager should be a practical person and problem-solver who handles all aspects of the physical production. They are the bridge between you and the wider production and technical team, from working with you on a sensible get-in and tech schedule to sourcing props and booking technical crew to work on the show. You should have regular meetings with this person and ensure they remain up to date with any significant changes that occur in scenes, especially when they impact the technical aspects of the show. They may delegate roles from within their own line of work, for example finding someone to be in charge of props, but let them run their own department with as much or as little help as they need.

Stage Manager

A good stage manager in amateur theatre is like gold dust. If you find a good one, hang on to them for dear life. This is a difficult and often thankless role that's suited to a specific personality who has excellent theatrical know-how as well as being comfortable with the management side of the job. Once you are in the theatre you should hand over many of your responsibilities to them, as they take charge. Their job is to literally manage the stage and the people on it, calling and setting rehearsals, dictating the schedule and working across all teams as the leader during this period. If you're lucky, this person will have attended multiple rehearsals or at least some final runs to make notes and see the shape of the show. You should hand them a copy of 'the book' to allow them to make their own master version which includes all blocking, movement and set / technical moments that need to take place. They should understand all cues, from lighting to flies to scene transitions and become the 'go-to' for all and any issues that arise.

It's important that you encourage maximum respect for this role from the full cast. Stage managers are responsible for their safety as well as making sure they have everything they need for a successful run and in the theatre space their word is law. You should have regular meetings with your stage manager, updating them on changes and keeping them abreast of all stage activity. Make them your confidant and right-hand person and establish a firm working relationship that will lead to the success of the show.

Lighting Designer

A lighting designer will usually be the same person who operates the lights during the run of the show. Depending on the theatre and set-up, this may be a creative lighting designer who wants to attend production meetings early on and feed into the overall vision for the show or they may be more functional and come on board at the very end to deliver the show. The most helpful thing you can do for your lighting designer is to keep a copy of the book that itemizes and identifies different moments and beats where you require the lighting to change. Think about the mood of different scenes and which elements need to be in sharp focus as opposed to those moments that are less important but are used to create ambience and a wider setting. Assuming they will have read the script, they will have an idea of which plot elements are most important, but you shouldn't be afraid of describing which elements are most vital to the narrative and need to be highlighted. In a busy stage, lighting is your best tool to focus an audience's attention, usually done with spotlights and specials which have the ability

COMMUNICATING WITH A LIGHTING DESIGNER

Below are some key words to have in your vocabulary when communicating with your lighting team. Remember, if you don't understand a technical term – ask!

Naturalistic: lighting that reflects a natural state, e.g. a drawing room, a school cafeteria or office, using lighting that is natural to that environment.

Practicals: working lights on stage, e.g. a lamp, car headlights, a candle, etc.

Focus: the process of focusing a light on a specific actor, set piece or part of the stage.

Specials: can range from a tight overhead spot to something that is used to provide a 'special' stage moment such as a transformation or moment of magic.

Wash: a general cover of a stage area.

L.E.D: modern lighting equipment that uses LED's rather than bulbs. These can be programmed with a wide range of different colours, changing automatically without gels placed in front of the lamps.

Strobe: a quick flashing light effect usually used in chase sequences or moments of magic.

Movers: lighting equipment that can move between lighting cues after being programmed by a computer.

Spots: lights that can 'spot' parts of the stage, can also be follow spots, controlled from the front of the house manually by follow spot operators.

Gobos: metal cut-out patterns that are placed in front of lamps to act as a sort of projection. Often used for projecting windows and so on.

LX cue: the cue that indicates a lighting change.

to pin-point specific actors, properties and body parts that direct the audience exactly where to look. Depending on the limitations of your venue your lighting designer will have an array of different tools at their disposal and many options that can be created.

Once the lighting rig is up and running I would sit down with the lighting team and ask them to demonstrate the various 'states' that are pre-set and the options available. Knowing and understanding what is possible will allow you to save time during plotting and tech, so you don't waste time describing states that can't be made. Lighting designers will usually pre-save a number of different 'states' that can be reused, especially if scenes are repeated. These tend to offer general lighting washes across the whole stage or certain sections from which more lights can be built into.

Lighting design is an art, and one that in amateur theatre is rarely finished to perfection. Your job, along with the production manager, will be to keep the tech process moving and make sure your lighting designer plots enough of the show to be able to run. It's common for them to continue to make tweaks even after the first performance as they make corrections and add depth and detail into their design. Communicate the time available to the team and don't get hung up on perfection. The key thing to remember is that actors need to be seen. I see so many amateur shows where the actors aren't in their lights or their faces are in darkness. Above all, make sure the work you have done can be seen from the full house and everything else is a bonus.

Assistant Director

In professional theatre an assistant director is a role that is often used to allow you to maximize efficiency as well as giving you a second pair of eyes. The person may be a less experienced director, hoping to learn from you and the wider team before going on to direct shows on their own. The relationship between the two roles can be tricky, especially in amateur theatre where the professional boundaries aren't necessarily clear. I would encourage you to really think if this is a role you require, and if so, what you hope to get from them in the role. Committees may insist on you having an assistant, primarily as a form of training for a future director or to offer some guidance in their development. Work on giving them a meaningful experience – they are not your assistant in a traditional sense, there to sharpen your pencils and get you coffee – instead they can be a vital second pair of eyes and sounding board for ideas. Communication is key; set out expectations from the beginning and offer them a role description so they know what they're supposed to and what's expected of them.

Sometimes you'll be confronted with an assistant director who oversteps the mark and tries to assert themselves a bit too much into the creative elements of the show. They shouldn't change blocking or offer notes to actors. They are there to assist in your vision and help you communicate your ideas. They may well help you maintain performances and run scenes whilst you're busy working with other actors, but they shouldn't be interventionist or change things without your consent.

Show Selection

More often than not, the role of director is considered to be a very difficult and time-consuming one that isn't always for everyone. Many societies have a pool of people within the community that they draw on depending on availability and the demands of a show. The skills required for managing a large-scale ensemble-heavy show can be quite different to that of a smaller vocally challenging chamber musical, and knowing where you excel, and indeed which shows appeal to you, is often half the battle. Many societies in the UK have a fixed production team that go from one show to the next, a process that has its advantages as well as disadvantages. For a committee, the offer of a reliable, trusted team means there are fewer surprises along the way. However, it can also mean that the society can become 'stagnant', especially when it comes to casting. Members who audition time and time again will get very used to a certain way of working, that, if unchallenged, can be problematic and result in a stasis where the same people get the same roles. It's often difficult for members to feel that they are being seen with fresh eyes in every audition, and unconscious bias will begin to override the minds of even the most supposedly open creative teams.

To combat this, many societies seek pitches from potential creative teams. Often these take place in front of the committee and can range from an informal coffee to a Dragons' Den-style presentation where set diagrams, budgets and costume sketches are picked over and debated. Again, in both of these situations, preparation is key. As much as these meetings are about creative vision, remember that the most important thing is to assess the fit, which is something that should work both ways. Few amateur theatre directors find themselves in a position where they are desperate for the work, so it's important that these meetings feel right to you. Near the beginning of the chapter, I listed some common questions to ask up-front. The more you understand and establish the expectations from the start, the fewer problems that will arise later down the line. It's important you are up-front about all aspects, from your preferred working style to practical concerns such as availability and rehearsal times.

Sometimes a show will have already been chosen by the committee with rights secured and a venue booked. This is more commonplace, particularly post-Covid where budgets are committed and societies are being more careful in their season selection. Often shows are chosen 2–3 years in advance, as soon as rights are announced, due to the competition to be the first in a local area or to secure bookings at theatres with a specific show that carries a name. In these instances, creative teams may have previously been attached but have had to drop out, and so a new director is being sought. In these instances decisions are often easier, as you don't need to worry about the 'why' around a particular show. Instead you can focus on what you will bring to the role and how you would potentially direct it.

Choosing a Show

If you're in a position where you can select the show you want to direct you need to begin by asking yourself a number of fundamental questions. Sometimes you'll have a burning desire to direct a show and you'll attempt to force that on the situation, group and members you have available. However, this may be unwise – the show needs to suit the situation, the society and the actors you think you have available. I suggest asking yourself the following questions:

1. Who is this show for?

If the honest answer that comes to mind is 'you' then I encourage you to rethink. Many directors have a list of dream shows that they would like to work on, but this rarely aligns with the needs and wants of the company for whom they're directing. You need to think who is this show for: the cast, the company or the audience? In a perfect world the answer will be all three although that's not always the case. Sometimes a show suits the needs of the company in terms of contrasting with previous shows, showcasing specific talent or catering to the particular demographic of the membership. Other times the needs of the audience are put first, particularly if the society needs to build reserves and guarantee bums on seats. Different shows appeal to audiences in a different way and it's important to ask yourselves if you think you have the audience support behind that show, judging by the demographics of your usual audience base.

2. Why this show?

Draw up a list of five reasons as to why this show makes sense at this specific time. Perhaps the amateur rights have just been released or it's a show that hasn't been done in the local community for many years. Perhaps there's a major anniversary of the show or its composers that makes sense to attach this to. If you can't think of five clear reasons, you may need to go back to the drawing board.

3. What are you hoping to achieve from this show?

Is this a crowd pleaser? Will it bring in a new type of audience? Does it feature a more diverse set of roles that will hopefully attract new members to your group? As with any project, set yourself a list of desired outcomes that can be the deliverables against which you can measure success.

4. What practical considerations are there?

Think about what is required from the show, both in terms of physical production, cast, orchestra and crew. Does it require a specific set piece? Does it need a large orchestra or band? Are there children in the cast? List all of the considerations that spring to mind from reading the script and identify how difficult it may be to overcome each of these.

5. What does this show say in 2024 (and beyond)?

This is an important question that should be asked by you as a director, as well as anyone else involved with selecting the show. Consider the world in which we are living – does this premise / story / show deserve to be told in the current climate? What does the piece say about other cultures, communities, gender, race and so on? This isn't to say that *Kiss Me, Kate* or *Annie Get Your Gun* should be locked away forever; instead identify what they say about male-female relationships in the twenty-first century or their attitude towards 'otherness' and ask yourself if these are stories you want to be presenting and perpetuating amongst your company. Later in this book I'll speak more about creative ways in which you can make sense of some of these more problematic shows in the twenty-first century, but at this stage I urge you to think about the art you are putting out into the world in the current climate and our responsibility as theatre makers.

6. Am I the right person?

As a director, I believe it's your responsibility to ask yourself the most fundamental question of all: 'Am I the right director for this show?' This not only concerns the skills involved with bringing the piece to life, but also the wider context of the show and community in which it is being presented. On a practical level, be honest with yourself and your skillset. If you haven't had much experience with large casts and ensembles, perhaps first you should shadow another director who does have experience, before jumping into a large traditional show that will require lots of people-management. Perhaps it's a dance-heavy show like *On the Town* or *West Side Story* that may benefit from a choreography-driven director or someone with skills that will complement the demands each of these shows present. Addressing and identifying your skillset is a strength rather than a weakness; think about the type of show you're best at directing whilst thinking about ways to improve on those skills or areas in which you have less experience. Second, think about what lived experience you are bringing to the show and if the piece would be better served by a director from a different background. We all have a profile from which we can't escape, but acknowledging that and surrounding yourself with a diverse production team will only help the company and better serve the piece that you are presenting.

7. Finally, ask yourself if you *like* this show?

Most directors will say that it's not always necessary to be in love with the show you're working on, but it certainly does help. You will be required to live with the show in your head and on the page for many months, often as the biggest advocate and cheerleader for its merits. A company can easily detect when a director dislikes the show they are working on as it's often impossible to disguise. Your relationship and enthusiasm for the material will be apparent to the full company and you'll be expected to maintain the energy during difficult rehearsals, natural lulls and the many challenges that present themselves along the way.

Choosing 'Problematic' Shows

As I've touched on above, a key part of show selection is discussing how a musical fits within the contemporary landscape. The established canon of musical theatre works that are regularly performed on the amateur theatre circuit often go as far back as shows such as *Anything Goes* in 1934, and in some cases stretch back to the works of Gilbert and Sullivan and their contemporaries in the operetta world. To quote the opening lines from the aforementioned song, 'times have changed' and many works of musical theatre don't stand up in the world in which we now live for a variety of reasons.

Musicals are 'properties' and are looked after by an estate who sub-licenses the amateur performance rights to secondary companies who handle the administration on behalf of the authors or their estates. In many cases, this residual income can amount to hundreds of thousands of pounds worth of revenue each year from licensing amateur theatre productions around the world. For popular titles this can often mean that a show that was a flop on Broadway can continue to earn back its money years later through the secondary amateur market. Each estate therefore has a financial incentive to ensure their properties continue to be performed and in many cases work with first-class producing theatres to revise the property to kick-start a new lease of life and fix or address any sensitive issues with the material. In the case of *Anything Goes* for example the book was re-written ahead of the 1987 Broadway revival which then went on to be the version that would be licensed by Tams-Witmark, now Concord Theatricals. This was revised again in 2022 following the successful London revival which took a fresh look at the racist handling of two of the characters, creating a new sanctioned version of the book for amateur companies to now perform. This method of 'revisal' ensures that the property can live in the current climate and speak to a contemporary audience without finding itself stuck on the shelf and unapproached by amateur groups.

The same approach has been applied to shows such as *Annie Get Your Gun, Peter Pan, The Wizard of Oz* and even *Kiss Me, Kate* – favourites on the amateur theatre market but on shaky ground when it comes to gender politics and even comments on race and sexuality. Even contemporary musicals such as *Thoroughly Modern Millie* (2001) is, at the time of writing, unavailable for amateur licence whilst the authors work on an officially revised version of the book that updates its attitudes and language surrounding race. *Hairspray* authors Marc Shaiman and Scott Wittman withdrew a previous version of the show that was officially allowed to be performed without the correct racial make-up of actors needed to tell the story. Since the Black Lives Matter movement, this was rightfully corrected and the official wording from the licence holders now reads:

> MTI receives many inquiries about the casting requirements for Hairspray. At its core, Hairspray is a story about acceptance and inclusion (and rejection and exclusion) during the early days of the civil rights movement. The authors' artistic vision requires that, in order to clearly and appropriately tell that story, the cast members in the show accurately reflect the characters as written. As such, the Production Contract requires that the cast members in your production of Hairspray accurately reflect the character descriptions contained in the script. Note: The use of make-up to portray Black characters in your production (e.g., blackface) is not permitted under this Production Contract. By signing the Production Contract, you agree to inform the director of your production of the casting requirements and that such use of make-up is strictly prohibited.
>
> In the past, performance licenses for Hairspray did not include this provision. However, the authors have determined that expressly stating this requirement is an important component of ensuring that licensed productions of Hairspray accurately reflect the authors' intent.
>
> (Hairspray | MTI Europe (mtishows.co.uk))

Not all properties, however, are as upfront about the demands and challenges you will face as a director. Re-writing and officially re-publishing work is costly and in many cases legally impossible without the full cooperation of the original authors or estates. This does not, however, give you the right to start 'correcting' certain works and imposing your own vision on the book, lyrics or score, however problematic something may seem to you on paper. As I've mentioned above, when selecting the show in the first place, you should be fully aware of any potential issues and be sure this is the correct show for you to be directing in the first place. Rights holders are happy to hear from you surrounding any specific concerns you may have and questions that may occur throughout the process. In the past I have submitted requests via the licence holder which have been granted, usually when it is one or two tweaks or to change outdated and offensive language.

PERSPECTIVE: BUILDING A DIVERSE SEASON – ADRIAN HAU, CHAIR OF THE SEDOS MANAGEMENT COMMITTEE

The key to creating and sustaining a diverse am-dram society is finding and empowering members you have with a genuine drive and willingness to connect with and lift up people from underrepresented groups. You can create all the

Identifying and Building Your Cast List

Once you have decided on a show, you'll want to consider the cast who will bring it to life. The first thing to do is to identify the size of the principal roles and ensemble. Start by taking the information provided from the licence holder as well as from the front of the libretto. I always draw out a chart that helps me visualize the roles in the show and their relationship to each other. Under these I like to list any significant songs they are involved with and any specific skills that may be required as written in the script. This will help you build a visual identity for the production and get to know the characters away from being just a list of names.

As you can see in Figure 1.3, each of the roles are identified in relation to each other, their status and function in the show. This helps you visualize the cast you need and will help you craft your audition pack and casting breakdown. It's important to have a clear sense of what you are looking for in each of the roles, specifically in terms of the requirements. While I'd encourage going into auditions with a relatively open mind, it's important to have identified the specific requirements of the role in case you need to specifically recruit auditionees outside of the usual catchment of the society's base.

Go through the script using your visual map while noting any specific qualities that arise in relation to each character. Make a list of words used by the authors to describe each character, both in the stage directions and lyrics, using what is said about them by the other characters as well as themselves. The aim is to build a three-dimensional picture of each character in order to identify all the known facts about them in relation to the author's intentions. Often specific characters don't have much written evidence in the libretto and song lyrics, instead their roles were developed and crafted by the original performers and etched into the minds of the audience passed down in recordings and films. You may be surprised to see how little exists on paper to describe even the most iconic and familiar leading roles. The most interesting productions are those that cast roles with a fresh look at a character and find something new or different to say. In amateur theatre the idea of stock

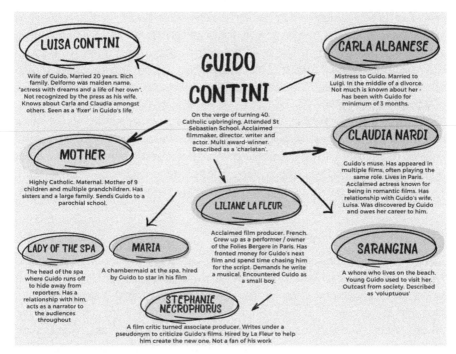

LUISA CONTINI

Wife of Guido. Married 20 years. Rich family. Delforno was maiden name. "actress with dreams and a life of her own". Not recognized by the press as his wife. Knows about Carla and Claudia amongst others. Seen as a 'fixer' in Guido's life.

GUIDO CONTINI

On the verge of turning 40. Catholic upbringing. Attended St Sebastian School. Acclaimed filmmaker, director, writer and actor. Multi award-winner. Described as a 'charlatan'.

CARLA ALBANESE

Mistress to Guido. Married to Luigi. In the middle of a divorce. Not much is known about her - has been with Guido for minimum of 3 months.

MOTHER

Highly Catholic. Maternal. Mother of 9 children and multiple grandchildren. Has sisters and a large family. Sends Guido to a parochial school.

CLAUDIA NARDI

Guido's muse. Has appeared in multiple films, often playing the same role. Lives in Paris. Acclaimed actress known for being in romantic films. Has relationship with Guido's wife, Luisa. Was discovered by Guido and owes her career to him.

LILIANE LA FLEUR

Acclaimed film producer. French. Grew up as a performer / owner of the Folies Bergere in Paris. Has fronted money for Guido's next film and spend time chasing him for the script. Demands he write a musical. Encountered Guido as a small boy.

LADY OF THE SPA

The head of the spa where Guido runs off to hide away from reporters. Has a relationship with him, acts as a narrator to the audiences throughout

MARIA

A chambermaid at the spa, hired by Guido to star in his film

SARANGINA

A whore who lives on the beach. Young Guido used to visit her. Outcast from society. Described as 'voluptuous'

STEPHANIE NECROPHORUS

A film critic turned associate producer. Writes under a pseudonym to criticize Guido's films. Hired by La Fleur to help him create the new one. Not a fan of his work

Fig. 1.3 *Nine* Cast List Diagram.

characters is very well established and many members find themselves cast time and again in the same type of role, despite being a different show. Resist this where you can and challenge your company to see themselves outside of the specific boxes they so frequently find themselves to be within.

That said, I urge caution casting deliberately against type for the sake of it, especially when it has the potential to be exposing for the actor in the role. Before you project or identify your own judgements on the role, complete the task above with the libretto and score, identifying the following elements of each principal role. Think about the core elements of the role, particularly any descriptions in the book or lyrics that define that role. There's a fine line between surprising an audience with a slightly different take on Madame Rose that potentially unlocks a different element of the character and casting a character so against type that they are instantly dismissed by an audience as being unsuitable.

Vocal Requirements

Work with your musical director on the specific vocal demands of each role. Think about vocal type and range but also stamina and the ability to perform the score in rehearsal and performance. Many licensing companies offer services to transpose certain songs to suit the keys of your performers but this can be costly and can have a knock-on effect on other performers and the ensemble. Equally, a good MD should be able to work with the cast on how to deliver certain notes within their own range, so don't be too beholden to the exact notes and vocal ranges given in the score. Often it's not just about the ability to hit / sustain the notes but also the vocal type and style the score demands. The roles of Mark Cohen in *RENT* may be similar on paper to Anthony Hope in *Sweeney Todd*, but their vocal styles couldn't be more different. One requires a tenor who can sustain a rock sound in an aggressive and narrative style, while the other requires a lyrical tenor who can sustain longer passages of romantic music over a large classical orchestra. Actors often get hung up on exact ranges, and stress and nerves can mean ranges are reduced in the audition room, but this doesn't mean they can't be worked on, and adapted, throughout rehearsals.

Dancing / Movement Requirements

Speak with your choreographer about the roles that require any specific dancing and the type of dancing they have in mind. Roles like Charity in *Sweet Charity* require a dancer who can deliver a string of dance-based numbers, so this skill moves from 'desirable' to 'necessary'. Some roles can be enhanced by having a confident dancer but may not be necessary to the story, or can be supported by others in the ensemble. Phyllis in *Follies* has been professionally cast with a more dance-based actor and other times with more of a singer, and both are acceptable ways of casting and playing the role. Again, go back to your chart and consider the core skills required and think about any workarounds that may be needed.

Doubling Roles

Often doublings are suggested by the authors and itemized in the libretto. Many times these are split out to offer more opportunities for actors, which I go into later on. If you're casting a smaller show or reducing a large musical down to a smaller ensemble of actors, consider how you can build a 'track' that takes in the different roles that need to be covered.

Age

Age is always a difficult factor in amateur theatre and is different to casting in the professional world where there's greater emphasis on actors being exactly age-appropriate. Each society or group will have a base of membership that draws from the local community and may be skewed one way or another in relation to age rather than offering an even spread. Knowing your membership again will mean you pick an age-appropriate show. *Spring Awakening*, *Carrie* and *Bring It On the Musical* require teenagers, or young adults acting as high-school age kids, to be able to pull it off effectively. Rather than fixating on exact ages and passing judgements on how people should look, try to think about the roles in relative age to each other. Again, use your character mapping above to identify the age ranges in relation to each other rather than fixating on exact numbers. This will offer you flexibility when considering different people for roles and open your mind to the possibilities within the overall casting.

Race and Ethnicity

This is one of the most important aspects to get right when considering casting and potentially one of the most difficult areas to consider. As mentioned previously, amateur theatre societies and groups don't tend to reflect the community within which they sit, meaning that the make-up of membership rarely maps onto the wider demographics of the area in which they are based. Speaking generally, very little work is done on outreach beyond a certain demographic and the racial and ethnic make-up of committees and the membership create a self-perpetuating cycle.

Within the casting world there is much debate over casting practice and what is ultimately the most equitable and inclusive method of casting a show. It's important to remember that professional theatre has tools at its disposal that you will not have – mainly the prospect of the role being a 'job' that can be effectively advertised and recruited for. Amateur theatre holds inherent bias in many ways, largely as it is asking people to give up their time, energy and skills for no financial remuneration. This immediately limits the pool of talent who is available to audition and ultimately cast from. Depending on the demographics of your community, only a slim margin of people will be available and willing to commit to a schedule, attend rehearsals and in many cases pay to be involved. This reduces the talent pool and disproportionately affects people from lower socio-economic backgrounds.

Your choice of show also feeds into the decision of who wishes to take part. Traditionally, shows that are seen to have all-white casts, either perpetuated through film versions, previous productions or the cast list itself, may have little appeal to performers from the Global Majority, who may not necessarily see themselves reflected in the lives of Ado Annie, Sarah Brown or Peggy Sawyer. An archaic assumption that these lead roles are by default 'white' will further isolate Global Majority actors and work must be done in casting notices and your audition pack to specify an open practice for casting. Amateur theatre is usually steps behind professional theatre in many ways, but as professional casting directors are finally demonstrating that casting diversely is a positive and necessary step forward, I hope this in time broadens the horizons of amateur theatre in turn. However, you mustn't wait for this to happen – you need to commit to casting diversely and affirmatively and work hard at all steps to do so.

The perception of amateur theatre as being far behind contemporary practice is perpetuated by memories of inappropriately cast productions of shows such as *West Side Story*, in which no Latina or Latinx creatives or cast members are involved in bringing the story to life. Whilst I understand that your local community may have a limited number of racially appropriate performers for such a show that is specifically about that community, serious questions need to be asked about the appropriateness of producing that show in the first place. Seeing that a UK-based amateur theatre society produced *The King and I* as recently as 2018 with not one south Asian performer in the cast again enforces this stereotype that amateur theatre gets a free pass when it comes to performing race and ethnicity outside of our own at the expense of performing the established repertoire.

Contemporary musicals, including those which are currently popular with amateur theatre groups such as *Ghost the Musical* and *Kinky Boots* were specifically written with roles for actors from the Global Majority. If these shows are unfamiliar to you, read the character descriptions in the libretto and pay close attention to the assigned race indicated by the authors. In these examples, the specified race is inherent to the role and the way in which the character has been written, and must not be altered. If in doubt, speak to your licensor who will be able to communicate the interests of the authors. Just because a role may not be 'about' race or have specific reference to the racial identity of the character this doesn't give you scope to go against the author's intentions, and the race will have been specified for a reason.

COLOUR BLIND CASTING

This is a casting practice where actors are cast regardless of race and ethnicity. The principle behind this is that the race of the actor does not come into play and isn't inherent to the character or narrative. Whilst this may result in all of Tevye's daughters being of a different racial background to each other, it does not, however, mean that the King of Siam could be cast as a white man, as the principle does not work two ways. Supporters of this form of casting believe that it encourages an openness from both cast and audiences, seeing it as an affirmative action to re-vision roles that have traditionally been seen (or assumed) as being 'white' roles.

Critics of this practice, however, claim that this can lead to tokenism which in turn can be unfair to the actor in question. The idea of casting blind disregards the fact that audiences in fact do read race, and in doing so make their own judgements that you cannot then control. In the example above, having Tevye's daughters be of different races is likely to lead audiences to make assumptions about his family history and relationships and can apply an additional level of reading onto the text that otherwise doesn't exist. A recent example of this in the professional world came from the 2017 Broadway revival of *Carousel*, where Joshua Henry, a Black actor, was cast as Billy Bigelow. While many people praised this casting (despite ethnicity not being noted in the libretto), others were nervous that it offered an additional layer of meaning between Billy, a Black man, domestically abusing Julie, a white woman (played by Jessie Mueller). Have these conversations with performers as part of the casting process and in rehearsals and understand that different actors will have different feelings to racial blindness. As the professional world continues to cast a Black Elle Woods, Ms Adelaide, Laurey, Ado Annie and Ariel, boundaries will continue to be broken and assumptions challenged.

COLOUR CONSCIOUS CASTING

Another casting practice concerns the opposite approach where race and ethnicity are consciously cast against type. *Hamilton* for example is perhaps the most high-profile example of a musical in which the white characters were purposefully written to be played by actors from the Global Majority, which in turn was used to shed light on the historical characters and show as a whole. More recently, Broadway revivals of *1776* have repeated this practice with both race and gender, asking audiences to deliberately read the race of the actor as being different to what is being performed.

ETHNIC STEREOTYPES – VOICES AND BEYOND

It's important to consider that in a musical it's not just the actor's body where race and ethnicity matter; voice also plays a large part in how a role is played and portrayed. You will hopefully never cast a white actor to play a role outside of their ethnicity, but it's important to also consider voice types, accents and dialect as much as physical performance.

Two of the most frequently cited examples in amateur musical theatre are the roles of Fagin in *Oliver!* and Tevye in *Fiddler on the Roof*. Routinely played by white non-Jewish actors, a heightened 'Yiddish' accent is often adopted to try and convey the character, which can quickly slip into stereotype and more often than not is borderline offensive. Be aware of your actors respecting the roles they are adopting and make sure you are clear on a line between an effective, realistic accent and a questionable pastiche.

Two contemporary examples can be drawn from roles that are attached to the voices originally portrayed in the film versions. The roles of Sebastian the crab in Disney's *The Little Mermaid* and Donkey in *Shrek the Musical* are examples where amateur performers face scrutiny and a grey area can sometimes emerge. Both roles are written as animals and memorably brought to life by voice actors from the Global Majority. In *Shrek* the role was voiced and brought to life by the Black actor Eddie Murphy, who, in turn, gave a specific reading of the role through his voice, dialect and accent, which was inherently Black. In adapting the film for the stage, the authors David Lindsay-Abaire and Jeanine Tesori maintained those elements Murphy brought to the role, creating a three-dimensional character to be played by a Black man. The libretto and score were written with this in mind, from a Barry White vocal pastiche number through to jokes, inflections and humour that stems from a Black dialect, rooted in Murphy's memorable performance. Similarly, Sebastian the Crab was created by Samuel E. Wright, performing signature songs in a Caribbean accent. In the amateur world however the characters are frequently played by white performers, but the performances given match that of the original performance, using the justification that these original voices are engrained in the audience's memories.

You then enter into a mode of performance where a white actor is adopting a voice, accent and mannerisms that are coded (and read to an audience) as a pastiche of a Black man. This cultural appropriation is inherently wrong and shouldn't occur. If it's not possible to cast the role within the named ethnicity of the role, I would remove the 'established' voice from the character itself and work with the actor cast to create a different voice that can land the comedy, but work within their own experience to bring the character to life, without changing the text. You shouldn't worry about defying audience expectations; it's more important that the voice is appropriate and not offensive. Think about the *function* of the voice before making decisions. Does the character need to present as 'different' vocally to those around them and if so, why? How can this be done within the remits of the actor portraying the role in a respectful way? Look to re-invent and re-interpret rather than recreate and treat voices in the same way you do body.

Remember, in these examples the blame cannot be laid at the feet of the actor; instead it is a director's responsibility to ensure that the actor finds the appropriate voice to bring the character to life in an effective and appropriate way. You shouldn't leave your actors vulnerable and open to criticism. Discuss the inherent issues early in the process and ensure they are comfortable, as well as the wider company. If you're not sure, ask beyond your circle and solicit a wider pool of diverse voices.

Gender

In reinventing and re-examining classic musicals, professional productions are frequently re-examining roles in terms of gender. The most high-profile example is Marianne Elliott's Tony Award-winning revival of *Company* which saw the character of Bobby reinvented as Bobbie. This was an officially sanctioned update made by Sondheim and Furth's estate that allowed Elliott to change significant parts of the book and lyrics to adapt to this gender reversal. It's important to stress yet again that you are bound by the rules of your licence and cannot switch the gender of characters to suit your needs. The actors playing the roles may indeed be of a different gender, for example in an all-girls school production of *Bugsy Malone*, but the characters they are playing have to remain the gender assigned to them in the script. Whilst many men would like to play Dolly Levi or Mrs Lovett, you cannot switch the genders without prior approval, which for amateur performances is highly unlikely to be granted.

Non-binary and gender-fluid performers should be encouraged to audition for a role that they identify with, without restriction. Again, the role itself won't be able to change gender to become non-binary without confirmation from the rights holders, but the performer should be free to perform as that role. Work with your musical director on transposing keys, where appropriate, to accommodate the performer and work with them on their specific needs when approaching the role.

Writing an Audition Pack

One of your first jobs as director will be to write and assemble an audition pack. This is likely the first time people will encounter your 'vision' of the show and understand what you and the production team hope to achieve. It's important to think about this as a selling opportunity that is public-facing – it will most likely exist online, shared on social media and emailed amongst members. Think carefully about the wording and make sure it is read by the committee for their agreement, particularly in relation to any guidelines and rules that exist within their constitution. Test the pack on friends and ask for their opinions on what questions remain unanswered or arise from what you have written and keep tweaking until you're happy with all aspects.

The most important things to consider are:

1. **Transparency**: be honest about what will be required by your cast. List all of the dates for the show, tech, dress, band call and when rehearsals will be. You may not have an exact schedule at this stage, but listing the frequency of rehearsals and where they will be taking place is vital. You want to make sure that everyone can make an informed decision when choosing to audition, saving you from potential issues further down the line. The same applies for any show fees or costs related to the production for cast members – whether they will have to provide any items of costumes, shoes, make-up, wigs, etc. Work with the committee and society to outline these expectations and ask about previous shows to see exactly what is required of everyone involved.

2. **Casting breakdowns**: this is probably the most important part of the audition pack and the section most people will focus on. Start by listing the roles available, usually found in the front of the libretto. As discussed above, identify any of your stipulations for the roles, giving an indication of the vocal style and range. Think about the requirements of the role you have already identified as well as any specific trigger warnings that should be present for people who may not be familiar with the show. Does the character have any specific difficult moments in the show or moments of intimacy? If so, these should be identified and prefaced in the audition notice and signposted to specific areas in the script.

3. **Audition style**: discuss how you plan to run the audition process and be crystal clear on what you require. Remember, you should be attracting people to audition so the more explicit you can be about the process the better. Will it be a workshop style? Will you require specific audition pieces (known as 'sides') and songs to be performed or can auditionees bring their own material? Be clear and specific in your instructions and what is expected, as well as identifying who will be on the audition panel and timescale for the process as a whole.

4. **Vision for the show**: briefly describe your vision for the show and how you anticipate approaching the production as a whole. This is your shop window for your concept, team and production so think about selling the merits of the show itself as well as your method of delivery. Provide visuals if possible and try to give the auditionee an understanding of how you see the production and why they should want to be a part of it.

Production Schedule

A large part of directing amateur theatre is based around project management and strong organization. In order to not become overwhelmed with the task in hand I always start by breaking down the show into manageable chunks with related timescales to keep on track. In professional theatre, the producer is usually the driving force of the production and will be responsible for creating a full production schedule, assembling a team and scheduling production meetings. In amateur theatre this balance can be different depending on the society or group you are working for and you may find yourself more firmly in the driving seat. Unlike professional theatre where everyone is being paid for their time, amateur theatre relies on a lot of goodwill with people fitting it in alongside their work and life schedules, which in turn means a greater level of organization may be necessary.

For productions where I've found myself in the driving seat, in this regard, I begin by creating a dynamic production schedule that details all of the necessary roles and responsibilities alongside a countdown to show week. This usually lives on a shared drive and is updated regularly as tasks are achieved or completed. Depending on the size of the show, this may involve multiple departments and be quite intricate in design or it may be a smaller list usually designed to prompt my own work and planning. Note that a **production schedule** is different to a **rehearsal schedule**, which you as a director will be in charge of creating and maintaining. These two schedules are designed to co-exist, with the rehearsal schedule featuring the cast and production team in the rehearsal room and the production schedule relating to the mechanics that surround the production as a whole.

Collaboration

Assembling a wider creative team is usually the job of the producer or committee. Often you may be asked for your opinion or thoughts on who you may like to work with; sometimes I have even presented myself to a committee alongside a specific choreographer and musical director. Further discussion on the wider production team, their roles and responsibilities and guidance on how to collaborate is included earlier in this book. Holding frequent production meetings, usually once every two weeks, are often the responsibility of the director. These should be scheduled in advance, either virtual meetings or in person depending on availability. Think about who should attend and circulate an agenda ahead of time, leaving space for each department to report back and provide any updates to the process. The production schedule should guide these meetings so everyone knows how far each person is along in the process and any outstanding issues that have arisen.

Auditions and Casting

One of the often spoken truths about directing is that good directing is 60 per cent casting. The exact percentage depends on who you are speaking to, but almost everyone agrees that good casting is one of the most important aspects of a director's role. Cast well and a mediocre production can be elevated to an excellent one, but cast badly and all of your work can be undermined and unravel in front of your eyes. Casting in amateur theatre is often the point at which a production process begins and can set the tone for the whole rehearsal period. Jealousies, egos and discontent with the process can extend way beyond the rehearsal room and into your personal life and the lives of others, and in extreme cases can end friendships. A process that's not transparent or mishandled can upset the tone for the entire production and rumble on throughout, creating a toxic environment for everyone involved.

Casting is ultimately gatekeeping and with any form of gatekeeping comes a power dynamic that people can choose to exploit and undermine. I have learned from experience that the best way around this is to create an open, inclusive and transparent casting process that is objectively as fair as possible. It's important to remember that there is no perfect way to cast a production – people will inevitably be disappointed and you can never please everyone all of the time. You need to keep a cool head and always act in the best interests of the show, making decisions as a team.

Golden Rules of Casting

1. **It's not personal**: in amateur theatre you are likely to be in a position where you are auditioning friends, family members and even spouses. You need to preface the audition process to people you know as being removed from you as a person and instead connected to you as a professional. You are being employed by the society to direct a production, of which casting forms a large part of that process. You need to compartmentalize your relationships outside of this process and operate on two levels. For people you are close to, I would remind them of the process and the fact you have to be objective, kindly asking them to consider the position that you are in. Often being frank and being open about the awkwardness of the situation is helpful to both sides. Set ground rules about when and what you will talk about to try to limit your personal relationship bleeding into the professional one and create boundaries for yourself reflecting what you will and won't talk about.

2. **Invite groups rather than individuals**: for all auditions the aim should be to get as many people auditioning as possible in order to widen the talent pool accordingly. Some shows may require specific performers outside of your usual networks in order to cast appropriately. I would advise you to focus on inviting groups rather than individuals. Messaging people and asking them to audition will set a dangerous precedent and heighten expectations. Try not to invite specific individuals to audition, even if you think they may be perfect for the role as you will never know the full extent of who will turn up on the day and you could find yourself in a compromising and potentially embarrassing position.

3. **Never pre-cast**: one of the biggest gripes in amateur auditioning is the sense, rightly or wrongly, that certain roles were pre-cast. The corollary to the above is to avoid telling people there's a 'perfect role' for them in an upcoming show or engaging in conversations about who would potentially be suitable for roles. However discreet you think you are, I guarantee these conversations will get out and can lead to a sense that the process hasn't been particularly open or fair.

4. **Treat everyone equally**: throughout all parts of the process ensure that everyone who auditions is treated the same. This goes from time allotted in the audition room to the way in which you communicate in front of others. Think about your own language and behaviours and the signals that you are putting out. Joking and reminiscing with some auditionees in front of others can lead to cries of favouritism. I like to play a game with myself where I imagine myself being watched by someone external trying to work out my connections with all of the people auditioning. This doesn't of course mean you have to appear cold or aloof, but instead judge your own behaviour and make sure it is consistent so that an outsider wouldn't be able to tell who you were related to, who was a best friend and who was someone you have just met.

5. **Offer constructive and timely feedback**: think about your communication directly following auditions, especially at a time when people may be feeling raw and disappointed. When people ask for feedback, it's usually done as a knee-jerk reaction to try and cover their emotions and place the onus back on the production team to explain their decision. Sometimes there will be constructive points you can make with regards to their skills and suitability for the roles. Other times feedback will be much harder, particularly as it so often depends on factors outside of their control, such as another person just being more suitable. Judge how far people are actually asking for feedback to learn vs how much it's just a reaction to disappointing news. Put yourself in their position and think about what you would like to hear. Equally, if they have asked for it you should write something, usually via email or – if it's a close friend – it may require a phone call. Remember, people will be raw and despite asking for feedback may not be ready to receive it, so judge how much you say and try not to be over-critical.

6. **Don't over-promise and do allow people time to sulk**: auditioning is a really raw experience where people are putting themselves up to be judged. Professional actors are used to this feeling and are often used to rejection, taking it as part and parcel of their day-to-day job. Amateur actors, however experienced, exist in a different sphere and so the act of auditioning is quite different mentally and emotionally. Remember, everyone is allowed time to sulk and be upset – these are natural emotions. People bounce back in a couple of days, but be aware that they may need space. Even your closest friends will require some distance directly following a casting decision – allow them that and make yourself available when they want to talk. It's natural to want to soften the blow and many directors find themselves over-promising additional duties, extra ensemble tracks and so on to try and offer an upside to not being cast in a principal role. Only do this if you are 100 per cent sure on what you can deliver as it's easy to get carried away and over-promise at this stage only for it not to work out later down the line.

7. **Never be rude**: as ever, maintain your dignity and treat others in the process how you wish to be treated yourself. Put yourself in their shoes and remember a time that you didn't get cast or you didn't get a job you interviewed for. Be

grateful for everyone who turned up to audition for you and be thankful for their time, even if on this occasion it hasn't worked out for them.

Pre-audition Workshops

These are often popular with amateur theatre groups who use them as a chance to showcase the show to their members, build excitement and allow auditionees to find out more about the show itself. They also act as a sort of rehearsal for the audition process that allows people to learn choreography for the dance audition and hear the music with the piano. Usually these are designed to note bash the music cuts, distribute scripts and scenes that will be used for the audition, talk about the process and the characters in the show. As a production team you should approach these workshops as openly as possible – this is a chance to capture as many potential cast members as possible, make them feel at ease with the production team and break down any barriers towards casting that many amateur actors erect themselves. Remember, auditionees will be using these workshops to decide if this is a show they want to be part of, so be as open and positive as possible. Treat everyone fairly and allow enough time to work through each piece of material, especially if there is any form of dance / movement audition, which can be the cause of much stress for auditionees.

Advertising Auditions and Open Casting

The policy of open casting is one that encourages anyone to audition for a role for which they would like to be considered. Some societies have specific rules about who is allowed to audition for a principal role – sometimes you have to be a member of the society first or have taken part in one of their shows in the ensemble. These guidelines are somewhat archaic and should be challenged where possible as they are barriers to inclusivity and can create bad feelings amongst members. Speak with the committee if you have any concerns and make sure you know any specific rules before you sign on to direct the project.

As detailed above, your audition pack should include all the relevant information that auditionees need to know about the production and be accessible to members and non-members alike, ideally available to download online. Regardless of the size of the group you are working with, you should advertise your open auditions as effectively as you can, utilizing social media in particular to draw in as many people as possible. It may be that you have to cap the number of people who physically can audition, in which case you need to be open about deadlines and it being 'first come first served'. Most societies will have a membership secretary or member of the committee who will manage the sign-ups and help act as a liaison between those auditioning and the production team. Make sure the information is consistent, accessible and clear and that communication between those wishing to audition and the group remains up to date.

Audition Formats

Depending on the nature of the show you may decide to run auditions a number of ways. The most traditional form of audition is via individual appointment, scheduling in 5-minute slots for each candidate to audition in front of an assembled panel. This is generally the fairest way to ensure that everyone gets equal time to deliver the prepared material, but can be overwhelming for the panel, especially if you have many people to see. Sometimes a group audition is preferred by directors and conducted in a workshop style. I have favoured this in the past as a way of seeing how audition-ees work together, respond to direction and work as a group. This may be helpful for productions such as *Godspell*, *Hair* and those that have a more devised feel to them. Either way, it's important to think about what the purpose of the audition is. Do you want to whittle down the list to find the best vocalists or are you more interested in seeing how people work together as an ensemble? Discuss with the production team what it is you want to gain from the process and plan accordingly.

An audition room should be as accessible and open as possible, designed to make the process as easy and stress-free for everyone involved. Be efficient both with your time and treatment of auditionees – remember this will set the tone for the whole production process. People will remember this part of the process above anything else, so make sure you are organized, welcoming and as enthusiastic as possible. Think about the physical space the auditions are being held in – a room should be big enough for a dance call, if applicable, with an appropriate 'green room' or holding room for people to wait and prepare. A smaller room for people to warm up would be welcome with plenty of signs to direct people where to go. Don't rely on the fact that people will be familiar with your set-up or surroundings – always envision everything from the point of view of a new person auditioning for the first time. The main space should have a piano or keyboard, be well lit and ideally have good acoustics to perform in. Engaging a 'runner' who can look after the auditionees outside of the room and keep the schedule running to time will be valuable in making sure the auditions don't over-run. Keep to time as best you can and make sure the whole process keeps moving.

DANCE AUDITION

Usually all forms of musical theatre auditions include a dance or movement call, led by the choreographer. This may begin with teaching a section of choreography in the room to see how quickly people pick up and follow a dance captain or choreog-rapher or it may simply be a performance of a pre-learned section of dance in front of the panel to judge performance style and preparation. Again, think about exactly what you want to learn about each of the auditionees – there's no point in making everyone learn a tap routine if they are auditioning for roles that don't require dance. Think about different levels of movement required in the show: perhaps you need a more experienced set of core dancers who will lead the more complex sections, in which case you can specify different levels within the dance audition. Communicate with auditionees about what you're looking for – are you looking for technical skill or performance? Is it more important to see how well people pick up moves at speed or how well they can bring their own personality to the movement? Let people know what you're looking for and it will help focus minds and calm the room.

SINGING AND ACTING AUDITIONS

While the dance audition is usually conducted as part of a group, the singing and acting auditions tend to be in private. Sometimes, I've used a workshop style to see different people read together or devise sections of movement, should it be a show that specifically requires it – although history has taught me this is not a favoured style of audition for most amateur performers. If you're holding individual calls, try to keep to time and be consistent with each auditionee. As they come into the room acknowledge them warmly, offer a quick pleasantry or piece of small talk to get them to settle down and then begin with hearing them sing their prepared vocal audition. Usually this will be a cut selection from the score of the show you are auditioning for. The advantage of this is that you'll get to compare apples with apples and hear the material in each of the auditionee's voices. It's easier for amateur performers who don't then have to worry about what to sing, how to make a specific 'cut' or worry that a pianist won't know the music, and it will be easier for your panel who won't be distracted by a new song and can begin to visualize people in each of the roles.

Audition Forms

The audition form is a vital part of the process designed as a point of communication between the auditionees and the panel. Keep these simple, but allow auditionees to express which roles they are interested in playing as well as to briefly list any relevant experience. Include a space for the auditionee's pronouns and how they wish to be referred to as well as their personal data including the best way of contacting them. I've generally found it's helpful to include all of the following in these forms:

NAs (Not available): ask each auditionee to list dates that they are unavailable, including for holidays, work commitments or other shows that they may be involved in. Ask them to be as honest as possible, on the understanding that availability may play a part in the wider casting decisions.

Method of communication: ask how they would like to be contacted following the audition. Some people would prefer a phone call to discuss a role; others will be happy with a simple email.

Access requirements: use this as a space to ask for any specific access requirements or needs surrounding the production. This could range from needing the script printed on blue paper or in large print for actors with different reading needs to concerns about the accessibility of the rehearsal or performance venue. Remember, not all disabilities are visible and allowing people space to discuss any specific needs will be welcomed.

Specific roles: asking auditionees about roles that they wish to be considered for is useful but can be limiting in terms of how people see themselves. Sometimes people will be reluctant to state certain roles that they have discounted in their heads as not being right for, when you and the audition panel may see them differently. Make sure you ask people if there are any specific roles they categorically do not want to play and respect their decision. This goes for the ensemble. Try not to be put off if people don't want to take a role in the ensemble – this could be for many reasons, quite often time. Try not to let this influence your ability to cast them in a principal role vs someone else who has said they wish to be in the ensemble as one person's decision shouldn't affect another.

Photo: I find it helpful to have a visual aid for when it comes to discussing the auditions. After a long day of seeing people back-to-back your mind will not easily be able to recall every woman with brown hair for example, and people you see early in the day may start to blend into each other. Ask each auditionee to submit or bring a photo with their audition form, or have a runner or committee member take a photo before each audition. Having this to refer back to will jog your memory and make sure no errors or miscommunication occur when discussing individual candidates.

Declaration: at the bottom or end of the form I would ask for a declaration that the auditionee has read and understood the full audition pack, including the essential dates and rehearsal schedule. This also extends to their understanding of the characters they are auditioning for, including the possibility of any sensitive material or trigger warnings that you have outlined. Your audition pack should include a detailed synopsis of the show, so if they haven't read the script in full they should at least declare that they understand the show they are auditioning for and any specific moments that you have made them aware of. Note that consent can shift and change throughout rehearsals and this form shouldn't be used against someone later down the line should they withdraw consent for any reason, but it allows those conversations to be had at this point in time rather than later, where things will feel more pressured.

How to Run an Audition Room

Place the panel in a line behind a desk to clearly mark out the space, with an area for the performers to stand that's not too close or distant from you all. Different groups may have different rules and guidelines as to who will be present in each audition so check with your group Chair ahead of time. At the minimum, the panel should be made up of the production team and audition pianist. Sometimes the Chair of the society or other trustee will be present to represent the interests of the society and act as another set of eyes. In many cases an impartial panel member will be invited, someone who isn't connected to the production team or society who can offer an independent lens on the proceedings and be impartial throughout. You may require a 'reader' to read opposite each of the auditionees, ideally someone who won't pull focus but is familiar enough with the material to allow each auditionee the space to perform.

I avoid making notes in real time and instead actively watch the full audition rather than sitting head-down holding a pencil. Make sure you're engaged and alert and be aware of your body languages and signals that you may be sending. Be encouraging if things go wrong and don't be afraid to start again, especially if nerves get the better of the performer. Auditionees may fixate on how much of the material you asked them to perform – try to be consistent, don't stop people mid-flow even if you've made a decision in your head. Allow everyone time to perform what they have prepared in full out of respect.

You may wish to offer some direction to each candidate to see how they respond and how adaptable they may be. Keep it clear and short and don't try anything silly like asking them to perform the song as an animal or other such horror stories one hears from audition rooms. Be purposeful – if someone has interpreted the role in a soft and subtle way, see if they can flip that on its head and offer a bigger performance that appears more obvious. This will test their ability to take your direction and give you a glimpse of how they might work in the room. Many times in an audition environment I find people freeze and repeat their performance without changing anything, in which case I would try a second time and try to make the gear shift more obvious. Remember, auditions are artificial environments where emotions are heightened and stress levels high so this may not offer an exact indication of how that performer will be to work with. However, you will certainly see who is responsive and who you will enjoy working alongside.

Sometimes you're hit with a brainwave mid-audition about someone's suitability for a different role to the one they are auditioning for. Try not to get too carried away in the moment and don't throw new material at them to read or sing at that time. Instead, ask them if they would be able to take 10–15 minutes to look at a different piece of material outside of the room and come back later to try it. Try to avoid cold readings and putting people on the spot as many people struggle with sight reading / singing, and this skill is unlikely to be one that you need for the performance.

Callbacks

Callbacks (or recalls) are a vital part of the process and allow you and the production team to see different sides of performers and, more importantly, how people may match and work together. Depending on how many people you have had audition, you will likely be faced with front runners and a shortlist for each of the roles. This is where the process becomes a jigsaw puzzle as you're faced with placing different potential couples and groups together to see who gels. These secondary auditions may also be a time to test a different type of skill – perhaps you now need to see specific vocal ranges or check a contrasting style of song to see if the performers are suited to the full demands the role entails.

Usually these auditions happen on a separate day. This gives you time to consider your decisions and have some distance from the audition room. Notify those you wish to call back as soon as you can and make sure you let them know what material you would like them to look at. Remember, people have lives and jobs and are unlikely to be able to learn whole new passages of text or songs, and it's not fair to expect them to do so. Encourage people to hold onto the sides and notes, and in some cases even hold a note-bashing session with the full group before you hear people individually. Some shows will have obvious casting for certain roles and others will have what I call a 'trickle down' effect, meaning that you may have three men in discussion for the role of Tony in *West Side Story* for example, and whichever doesn't get that role will likely get Riff and then the other one of the main Jets such as Action or A-Rab. Think carefully about who you call back and why – you don't want to waste people's time or get their hopes up unnecessarily. Think about what more you have to learn about someone and what can be gained from bringing them back.

It's important to remember that by coming for a callback, auditionees are inherently more invested in the process, so the stakes become even higher for them as they then start to visualize themselves in the role. They'll likely be able to see who else is in the running and this may mean everyone raises their game and tries that little bit harder to convince you that they have what it takes. Think about specific pairings – romantic leads should read together to judge natural chemistry for example, as well as tight friends and those who spend a lot of time playing opposite each other. Sometimes seeing one actor play against another will unlock a performance that wasn't present in the initial audition and so your ideas may shift. Keep an open mind and exhaust all of the opportunities that present themselves, and you may well be surprised at what you unlock.

One set of callbacks will likely be enough and you should really be able to make a decision from this new set of auditions. It's worth emailing the full audition list to let them know callbacks are happening, and for which roles. I always emphasize that the absence of a callback does not mean that someone hasn't been cast in the show – again be clear in your communication to avoid speculation and gossip that can get out of hand.

Making Decisions

After a round of callbacks you should be able to make a decision quite quickly as a full team. By all means sleep on your feelings and come back the next day with a fresh mind, but don't let things linger for too long as speculation will build and you'll start to lose respect from the auditionees. Discuss as a team the positives and drawbacks of each potential casting decision and work to ensure you are all as happy as possible with the outcome. Sometimes you may have to yield to your fellow production team and make compromises, so you should avoid being draconian and making decisions in isolation. Ideally you'll all be on the same page but often compromises are made in one casting decision to offset another. Avoid the notion that the director's say is final as this undermines the role of the choreographer and musical director. Listen to their concerns equally and try to weigh up the best options possible. It's always worth involving the society Chair and an independent arbiter in the final decisions for a degree of impartiality, as it is the Chair who will largely be responsible for any fallout and will have to justify the casting process to their fellow trustees and membership as a whole.

Problem-Solving

Sometimes you may have to be creative in your approach to casting. You may find that you didn't get that 'perfect' auditionee – or that a role requires a specific skill or has to be played by a specific type of actor, and they simply didn't come to audition. Avoid making rash decisions and compromising too early. As discussed above, roles written for actors of a specific race as identified in the libretto for example need to be respected, the same goes when gender is stipulated in text. You cannot change the gender of the character from what is written but you can be flexible with who performs that gender. Sometimes you may have to release a cast list with gaps, something that regularly happens in amateur theatre especially for male performers. Don't worry about holding further auditions for specific roles, often this allows focus and a chance for you to widen your pool of auditionees and advertise further afield. Think creatively about whether a role can be doubled by someone in the ensemble or if there's another way of presenting the role without changing the text or intention of the piece.

Announcing Cast and Handling Fallout

Before announcing your cast, look at the audition forms and see people's preferred methods of communication. With large roles I like to make phone calls to share the good news and to ask them to verbally accept it before releasing a full list. You want to avoid emailing a list that goes to everyone only for people to withdraw in disappointment, shifting the sands of your full cast list. I usually start at the top of the cast list and phone the principal performers first. This allows you to share the good news with them and answer any immediate questions they may have. There may be some additional context you wish to talk through certain performers with, especially if you have cast them in a different role than the one they initially saw themselves playing. You may find yourself having to sell a secondary principal role and be prepared that not everyone will accept on the spot – some may need some time to think it over. Be firm with a time frame and ask them to let you know either way by a designated time, so you can put the offer out to other auditionees if need be. For ensemble roles I usually include these in an email alongside the full cast, once you've had confirmations from the principals, but be aware some offered ensemble roles may be surprised and want to speak to you or the production team about this decision.

Rehearsal Schedule

Designing a Schedule and Sticking to It

PERSPECTIVE – FIRST-TIME DIRECTOR, FRANCISCUS PRINS

There is a bigger people management element to directing than I had realized before doing it myself. Your actors, of course, have many other commitments and responsibilities and these will inevitably bleed into rehearsals. Sometimes they may be late, or absent entirely at short notice, which could mean last-minute changes to your plans for a given rehearsal. When present, actors will bring baggage from their days with them; they may be tired, or feeling down, or a number of other ways. Your job is to work with them to channel whatever they are feeling into a productive rehearsal.

Surround yourself with a great team of people: it takes a village to put on a musical. You will want someone in charge of costume, props, set, lighting, and sound at least. The earlier you bring people on, the easier it will be to share your creative vision and ensure that you are all working towards a common goal. You will, of course, have opinions over props, set, lights, etc., but unless you're a theatre savant with unlimited time on your hands you will need help with these elements. Finally, make sure that you love the show you are directing. You will be spending a lot of time and energy on it. Further, remember that as amateurs we are all giving our free time up to do something we enjoy. This also applies to you as a director. Enjoy the process of creating a show and seeing your vision unfold.

One of the trickiest parts of the process is mapping out a rehearsal schedule that matches the needs of the show and production team alongside the availability of the cast members and the overall time you have to rehearse the production in. Juggling this is a specific skill and one that comes more naturally to some rather than others. In this section I'll guide you through the main considerations you'll have to make and share the best methods for planning an effective schedule that you can hopefully stick to.

As a general rule, tasks tend to take the time allotted to them, expanding and contracting as is necessary. I have rehearsed a full production in three days as part of a summer camp environment that has seen a full cast learn, block and stage a show ready to be performed in less than a week. There is no golden rule as to how long staging a musical will take – my preference is to balance an active schedule with one that allows for absences, holidays and other strains that are put on an amateur theatre schedule, but doesn't drag and go on too long. While you may think 6 months is an ideal time to rehearse a show, you actually may find that it offers too much time – momentum is lost, rehearsals are frequently missed and it's difficult to keep a cast focused over half a year as life demands get in the way.

The first thing to do is speak with the society you are working for and understand their requirements and expectations. Some companies have set schedules that work the same every year, balancing a summer show and a winter show, with a small gap in between. It's important to remember the process as well as the product – for many people rehearsals are their main social activity, and the rehearsal period is as much about coming together as a community as it is working towards a show and finished product.

Common Variables

Work out the dates of the show and plot these onto a spreadsheet or calendar. These dates are likely to be fixed with the theatre hire and offer a natural firm end to the process. Working backwards, make a note of any specific dates or periods where people are likely to be unavailable. This can include summer holidays, half-term dates, Christmas, Easter and so on. Mark these on the calendar as 'immovable'. Count backwards week by week and try to look at the overall scope of the time frame. Other immovables may include additional shows being performed by the society or group which may limit when rehearsal space or resources are available. Mark these down and you'll begin to see an ideal start point that takes all of these factors into account.

I have found that 3 months is usually the sweet spot for amateur musicals. This allows sufficient time for material to be learned and worked on and momentum to build without things going stale. Once you have decided on an overall time frame, lock certain dates in your calendar that are designated rehearsal dates. Most companies have set days they rehearse – usually this is two evenings a week and some weekends leading up to the show. Count these out, factoring in 2½ to 3 hours for each evening rehearsal and around 4 to 5 hours for a weekend.

I begin by drawing up a large schedule with each of these dates marked. An example of this can be found in Figure 1.4. Once a show has been cast I then create a secondary table that includes everyone's given availability at the time of audition. This marks their holidays, absences and classes, marked with a simple 'NA' (not available). I then work between the two spreadsheets, cross-referencing who is available and when, writing down the names of everyone available for each rehearsal based on their availability chart. At this point I also ask the production team for any rehearsals they can't attend, as this will play an important factor in what is possible to rehearse.

At this point, your spreadsheet will look something like Table 1.1.

From this, you'll be able to visualize exactly who you have available and be able to plan accordingly. Look for obvious groupings that mean you can rehearse certain scenes together. If Anna and Bill are playing the leading roles, target these scenes during these rehearsals where they are both available and consider how you could also utilize the other cast members who may be available. At some point you need to weigh up if it's worth calling a larger rehearsal if you only have a few cast members present – you will only have to repeat everything you have done when everyone else is back in the room.

	w/c 8 May	w/c 15 May	w/c 22 May	w/c29 May	w/c 5 June	w/c 12 June	w/c 19 June	w/c 26 June	w/c 3 July
Director									
MD					8,11				7
Producer			26,27,28	29			23,24,25	29,1,2	3,4
Eliza		16, 20, 21	22,23, 27, 28	29, 30, 1,2,3,4			19, 22, 23	26, 30, 1, 2,	3,4,5,6,7,8,9,10,
Higgins		17,18, 21 evening	26,27,28	29			23,24,25	29,1,2	3,4
Doolittle		15, 20		3,4	8,10	17,18	19,23,25		9
Mrs Higgins		15, 17, 18, 20, 21	24, 25, 26	31, 1, 4	5,7,8,11	12,14,15,16,18	19,21,23,25	26,27,28,29,30,1,2	
Freddy		16				9	22,23,24,25	26,27,28,29,30,1,2	3,4,5,6,7,8,9
Clara		11/17 NA	24 NA	31 / 1 NA		7			
Mrs Pearce		16-21 holiday			9,10,11			1	8,9

Fig. 1.4 Rehearsal Schedule.

Table 1.1 Availability Schedule

Mon 2 July	Thu 5 July	Mon 9 July	Thu 12 July	Mon 6 July
Anna, Bill, Emily, Ben,	Miranda, Kate, Philly, Ryan, Anna, Bill	All cast	Ryan, Kate, Anna, Bill, Emily	Anna, Bill, Emily, Ben, Miranda, Kate, Philly
NA: MD	NA: Choreo	NA: Choreo		
NA: Kate, Philly, Ryan, Miranda	NA: Ben, Emily	No NA's	NA: Miranda, Philly	NA: Ryan

First of all, I look for those rehearsals where I have 'all cast' or the majority available. I would ring-fence those rehearsals and mark in a different colour on the schedule to mark them as key. These would then be the rehearsals for which I would schedule the largest scenes or the trickiest numbers, knowing that I have the most people available together. Doing this in advance and categorizing these rehearsals as 'key' will help everyone to prioritize and hopefully protect that time in the context of the wider schedule. Decide with your production team what makes the most sense to cover in these rehearsals where you have the majority of cast available and mark this down on your master schedule.

From there I would look for smaller groupings of actors that can come together to rehearse smaller moments. Be aware that you should be ready to work on scenes that may not arrive in logical order based on the overall availability of the cast. Being prepared and ready to work on scenes out of order will allow you to maximize time according to who is available and when, rather than sticking to a rigid order of scenes and numbers as they arrive in the text.

This is where rehearsing amateur musical theatre differs largely from the professional world. In the professional realm it's customary to start at the beginning and work through logically, on the understanding that actors are called for all rehearsals and have no external competing commitments. Most professional shows begin at the start and work their way through the show systematically, sometimes starting work on a large number in Act 2 sooner rather than later if it's particularly taxing. In the amateur world you have to be more fleet of foot, and so having a full overview before you start will be vital in allotting rehearsal time at the right moments.

Usually your musical director will want the company to have a good grasp of the music before any staging or blocking can take place. I like to try and ensure at least 50 per cent of the music has been taught before any specific staging takes place, although, as explained above, that's not always necessary. It's important to inject variety into amateur musical theatre rehearsals to limit simply note-bashing and to try to introduce movement and staging earlier on to keep momentum in the process as a whole. Perhaps you start staging a few of the numbers alongside learning the vocals for another, balancing with table work (discussed later on) and scene work with the principals. Avoid staging a musical number in the same rehearsal where the vocal has just been learned – actors need time for the music to settle in their minds before being faced with movement, and often this happens outside of the rehearsal room.

Most directors prefer a sketched-out rehearsal schedule that can be dynamic as things shift. I like to have a firm schedule two weeks in advance, so people can plan their time accordingly, but I suggest you update this as you find your feet and begin to understand the demands of the show and how long certain sections will take. Be aware of overloading your cast – think about brain burnout and don't attempt to learn three dance numbers at once. Try and get one off the ground before introducing a second and third, and make sure you leave enough time to recap and revisit as you go along.

Write down a list of scenes and songs in your notebook and create a checklist to mark off each one as you rehearse it. You should aim to have three checks against each scene / song before you get to a stage where you can run – the first check is the first rehearsal on the scene or song, the second is a recap or revisit rehearsal and the third is a refinement. Keep tabs on what has been rehearsed and sections that may have been overlooked so you know where to focus your attention.

As discussed elsewhere in this book, think about efficient scheduling and split rehearsals utilizing the space at your disposal. A vocal call happening in one room alongside a larger dance rehearsal in another will help keep things moving and maximize your time. Sometimes this won't be possible due to space, but split your rehearsals accordingly to your advantage.

Communicate your schedule at the end of each week for the following two weeks ahead. I like to use a dynamic Google Drive or similar that the cast can access live and be alerted to any changes. Remember that this is likely to be dynamic due to the nature of amateur theatre and peoples' lives getting in the way. You will always be met with texts and emails just before a rehearsal explaining last-minute NA's. As annoying as this is, try not to take these personally and try to roll with the punches and be as adaptable as possible.

Props List

One of the first things you'll do with the production manager (PM) is assemble a props list that will be updated throughout rehearsals. It's important to identify props as early as possible so time can be on your side in terms of sourcing. You may be working with a company that has an extensive prop store, in which case this will be an easier task. Go through the script and mark down any essential props that you require for the whole show. Making a simple table such as the one in Table 1.2 will help keep this organized and trackable for all departments.

As you work your way through the script, make sure you mark down instances of repeated usage as well as notes that you have on how it should look and function. Are there any practical elements that need to be considered? Does the prop have

Table 1.2 Props List

Prop	Usage	Notes
Rolling Pin	Mrs Lovett, Act 1 Scene 2	This needs to be wooden and look distressed, not new. Has to withstand being battered regularly.
Pies	Mrs Lovett and Sweeney, Act 1 Scene 2 (also used by Toby and the wider customers in Act 2 Scene 1)	Have to be real pies that can be eaten by cast members and cut up as necessary.
Switch blade razor(s)	Introduced in Act 1 Scene 2 – Sweeney then holds onto them as a personal prop	Have to be blunt for safety. May be fitted with blood effects for the killings.

to be from a particular period? Don't assume your production manager will be able to read your mind – if needs be, include reference images and period specificities, as well indicate things like size that need to be taken into account.

Once you have assembled your full list, sit down with your PM and talk through the essentials and the 'nice-to-have' list. Depending on your budget you may well have access to everything you need, but working out with the team what is realistic within your budget is key. You will likely find yourself having to reduce your props list significantly, so itemizing the key items and those that are essential (e.g. Sweeney's razor) will help in your communications across the full team. Assume that your PM and tech team will be familiar with the show you're doing, but remember they will not have the intricate working knowledge of the show that you have at this stage, so don't shy away from over-explaining and being as obvious as you can be to avoid miscommunication.

Props are somewhat of an aesthetic choice – many successful productions avoid props altogether. This directly links with your vision for the show and the concept you have created. How stylized is the production? Do we need to see every single prop? Do they have to be realistic, suggestive or figurative? Some of the best musicals use no props and rely on imagination, but this is not going to work if you've created a hyper-realistic vision of the world on stage. Should characters be drinking, eating and so on in a realistic manner? Remember, consistency of approach is key, so if you have your characters drinking from real glasses in one scene they must continue to do so – you can't switch to mime halfway through the show.

Props vs Set

As you make your list I encourage you to mark down items that characters interact with, from stools to tables and chairs to surfboards and dumpsters. Once you have every element, you need to decide if it's a prop or if it falls under the remit of your set design. Some people will consider benches, stools, chairs and so on parts of the set whilst others will class them as props. Have those conversations early and make sure every department knows what they are responsible for.

Personal Props

Personal props are items that belong to the actor. They are usually things like money, glasses, cigarette cases, watches and so on – anything that can be about their 'person' during the show. These may not be specifically in the script but can significantly enhance the characterization. Encourage your actors to explore things like canes, walking sticks, monocles and cigarettes and use them in rehearsal to try to see how they work in practice. They would still fall under the remit of the production manager, but the actor would usually look after them themselves throughout the run of the show instead of collecting and returning to the props table.

Other props will be organized and arranged by the production manager and stage manager and kept on an organized props table at the side of the stage. Encourage your actors to get into the habit of collecting their props and returning them to the same spot, so nothing goes missing.

Rehearsal Props

The earlier you can rehearse with props the better. Anything that affects a performance (cigarettes, glasses, etc.) should be rehearsed into the show at each rehearsal. I would encourage you to work with as many 'rehearsal props' as possible to get your actors into the habit, as well as exploring different possibilities. For example, a feather boa used by one character may seem like an insignificant enough item, but allowing the actor to rehearse with it unleashes so many possibilities and options to explore how it can be used that can unlock a whole performance.

Costume

Once you have a budget in place, speak with your costume designer / wardrobe manager about what is possible with the money you have. For many shows, costumes will be hired as a set from a number of costumierers who specialize in the amateur theatre world. Have these conversations as early as possible as costume sets on popular shows get booked up early, so you want to know that any difficult or specific costumes will be taken care of. Disney shows and high-fantasy shows that include a degree of spectacle will usually need to be hired and sometimes this will even be specified in your performing licence. Costumes tend to cost a specific amount per character, so make sure this cost is taken into consideration and factored into the budget.

Your company may have a costume store or stock costumes that are continually used and sometimes hired out to local companies as an additional source of revenue. Period costumes that crop up time and time again, or dresses and suits from a particular decade, tend to be recycled between shows, so it's worth seeing what options are already available. It's very rare in amateur theatre to have a costume designer who builds a wardrobe from scratch, but I've been lucky enough to work with fantastic costume designers over the years who built each item within the overall vision of the show, so they do exist. When having these dialogues with your costume team, be specific in your vision and also assist them by being honest about the requirements of the role. Below are some questions to consider.

Practical Considerations

Do the characters have quick changes? Do they have to get dressed / undressed on stage? Do the costumes have to directly relate or match anyone else on stage? Do the characters have to dance or do any form of movement whilst in the costumes?

Artistic Considerations

What is the colour palette of the show? What is the aesthetic look of the show? What status do the characters have and how do these relate to each other across the company? What is the time period or periods that the show takes place in? What should an audience read from each of the characters?

You should come to your initial meeting with the costume department with answers to these questions as a minimum. Remember – you are the expert on the content of the show and should communicate any concerns or problems you foresee about how costumes are to be worn.

Sensitivities

A note on costumes and sensitivities. For many actors the costume call is a moment of peak anxiety as it's the first time they will see what they are wearing for the show. No matter how many conversations you'll have had, each actor will have a specific vision of how they will look on stage, which may or may not match with your design and the costume available. As many costumes are hired, they are rarely made exactly for the actor who will be wearing them, so there will be a good deal of fitting required. Actors ultimately want to feel comfortable and look good; remember everyone has some element of insecurity of how they look and their bodies. Forcing people to wear costumes they hate will never end well and can ruin the show for an actor. You have to respect the actor's sensitivities whilst maintaining the overall look for the show with the material you have available. Be flexible where you can but don't pander and change costumes at the first hint of a 'diva fit'. You need to equally remember that the costumes have been made / altered / sourced by another human with feelings and their own sensitivities, so encourage your cast to remember this at all times and be considered in their feedback. Work WITH your cast to ultimately make sure they feel good about what they are wearing and that it's in keeping with the character they have developed. This includes everything from shoes to hats and jewellery. No detail too small.

Concepts and Understanding a Show

A director's vision is what propels a production forward. A musical can be thought of like a steam train – a huge unwieldy piece of machinery travelling from one destination to the other with dozens of people on board. Within this metaphor, think of yourself as the motor driving the production forward; the engine, providing the energy and forward momentum; the driver, navigating the course of direction; and the station master, responsible for the safe delivery of the cargo and the passengers.

One of the first and potentially most important aspects of the role is how to understand the show you're expected to deliver. It's obviously not possible to do this fully until you have your cast in place and so now is the time to really get to grips with your material.

How to Research a Show

There are differing schools of thought about approaching a show and how much preparation should and can be done. I am of the opinion that we learn from history and it's foolish to imagine any production in a bubble. Some directors, particularly those inexperienced in musicals will maintain that watching the film adaptation or listening to numerous cast albums clouds their vision. I personally find this pretentious and counterproductive. Unless you're directing a new musical, each musical you direct will have most likely been handled by creatives with much more experience than yourself, and hiding from their experience is both futile and arrogant. This is not to say that you can't and won't have your own answers, but to ignore what has gone before, both the successes and failures, does not lead to you succeeding.

READ CONTEMPORARY REVIEWS
For most major musicals you can read reviews of their original productions (and revivals) for free online. Websites like DidTheyLikeIt.com aggregate the reviews in one place; older shows may require some extended research, but nothing that doesn't take a bit of light research on Google. I like to compile the reviews in a digital document, to refer back to in the future and continue to read alongside the rehearsal process. What exactly are you looking for? You can use these as objective assessments of the piece as a whole, searching for common threads in criticism. Think of it like looking at a road map where someone who has trodden this route before has put red circles around the tricky bends, icy patches and sharp inclines. In most cases, reviews offer professional assessments of the pitfalls and problems you're likely to

come across in your own journey with a show. Highlight and group common criticisms, in both the material and the delivery. Whilst reading that a song in the second act 'dragged' repeated times doesn't mean you'll be allowed to cut said song to speed along to the conclusion, but it does give you advanced warning that the show as written can encounter that problem. You can then be armed as you stage that song and think ahead about how best to address this. Maybe criticisms focus on the stage being overly busy at certain points, the plot difficult to follow or the resolution not clear. These offer practical criticisms, which you can watch out for and attempt to overcome. What is less easy to resolve are comments that pass judgement on the music, the structure or the intricacies (or lack thereof) within the book. You mustn't get hung up on these perspectives, and instead consider what you CAN control, and think about ways in which you can solve these specific problems in your own production.

LISTEN TO CAST ALBUMS

In line with my notes above you'll often hear musical directors tell casts to not listen to the cast album of the show they are rehearsing, often because it threatens to overshadow the work done in the rehearsal room. I find this practically impossible – I don't think I've ever done a show where a cast or creative team have maintained this – and would actively encourage the opposite. As a director, you should think of yourself as an explorer, piecing together elements of a show into a giant puzzle. Listening to the cast album(s) is a significant part of this process. Not only does it bring a show to life and off the page, but it can inform artistic and practical choices, while once again learning from the work that has gone before.

REVIVALS AND REVISALS

For many shows numerous cast albums exist and are readily available on streaming services as well as in physical formats. It's important to remember that your licence to produce a musical is often the right to produce it in its original form. Sometimes different versions exist – *Anything Goes* and *The Wizard of Oz* are two popular examples where a specific version is licensed via the publishing company. In all cases, it's important to familiarize yourself with the correct recording from the outset. I made the mistake of falling in love with the 1994 recording of *Damn Yankees* before understanding the musical differences between the revival and the original and remaining disappointed right up until the final night that the only licensable version was the original. It can be frustrating, especially when the revivals often feature more exciting vocal arrangements, different keys and sometimes sanctioned fixes to issues in the book.

The most important thing to do is make sure the musical director and choreographer are using the same reference recording throughout. I have been involved with too many shows where the choreographer has worked from the 1998 recording of *Oklahoma!* for example, which uses new orchestrations particularly in the 'Dream Ballet' and dance sections, only to find out at the 'sitzprobe' that the orchestra will in fact be playing something entirely different. Remember too that many recordings are cut and truncated to fit onto one CD disc, so it's worth asking your MD to go through and mark up your score, if you can't do this yourself. Knowing where extra bars, cuts and dance breaks are will save you so much time in rehearsal, and mean things like the sitzprobe and tech go as smoothly as possible.

Contemporary shows such as *Big the Musical, Shrek the Musical* and *The Addams Family* changed significantly before they were licensed to amateur groups. In these cases, the licensing house will often have a reference recording that matches the score you are performing. This often happens when a show has made significant changes to the material following a Broadway run, and the capturing of the original Broadway cast recording. For older classic musicals, I find Jay Records and their collection of 'complete recordings' indispensable as they provide every beat, scene change and piece of incidental music, as well as cut songs and extended dance breaks. The more familiar you can be with this material, the better. Use them in the same way as you use the script or vocal score – as a blueprint for your own vision and artistic ideas. What makes musical directors bristle is an over-familiarity with the material that brings about replications of original productions. It's not uncommon to be able to hear at an audition which version an actor has grown accustomed to, as they breathe in the same place as that performer, copy vocal runs and even subconsciously start to replicate their tone. I find it useful to offer the cast at the first rehearsal a specific cast album as reference but always encourage them to find their own way through the score.

On a practical level, cast recordings are invaluable for learning the material, be it in the shower, on the school run or on an exercise bike. However, remember that sometimes mistakes are difficult to correct, so you should be aware and flag changes and mistakes in the score to stop them creeping into a performance. Again, letting the show enter your subconscious by repeated listens pays dividends. The beauty of directing a musical vs a play is that you have the music as a tool to listen to on the move. I personally find my best ideas for staging come whilst listening to a number on the commute or at the gym or at a time when my brain isn't forced to sit down and think on demand. I also find it helps to absorb yourself in the musical world of that composer. Directing *Funny Girl*? Listen to *Gypsy* and *Gentleman Prefer Blondes*. Directing *Into the Woods*? Listen to *Assassins* and *Passion*. By understanding and succumbing to a composer / lyricist's wider work you deepen your understanding of the material you are delivering. Think of it as reading around the text, and I promise you'll find enjoyment in discovering and cross-referencing similar moments between the shows that will help inform your decisions in the rehearsal room and will ultimately enrich the production.

READING THE SOURCE MATERIAL

As well as understanding the show in the form you are going to be directing it, I find it sometimes is incredibly useful to have a working knowledge of the source material that has inspired it. Over the past 20 or so years musicals have frequently been adapted from contemporary source materials such as films from the 1980s and 1990s, but producers have a long history of purchasing the underlying rights to a successful property, be it a book, a play, a film or documentary, and putting together a creative team to turn it into a new form – a piece of musical theatre.

The much-talked-about 'original musical' is a rare and tricky being. In recent seasons, shows such as *The Prom* and *A Strange Loop* have won accolades on Broadway, but have proved to be trickier to sell in a highly globalized and competitive market where name and brand recognition is a key factor in driving audiences. The same can be said for amateur theatre. As discussed above, companies are likely to choose shows that have brand recognition, and you are more likely than not destined to direct a show based on a pre-existing property. This may be a contemporary musical such as *Made in Dagenham*, *Shrek* or *Sister Act the Musical*, or indeed an older show such as *Oklahoma!*, *Oliver!* or *Carousel*. In each case, there will be source material for you to engage with, that will present new challenges and questions in your preparation process.

As a director you should be familiar with the adaptation and aware of the work that has gone into transporting it from one medium to the other. Even if you aren't necessarily familiar with the source at first glance, the musical is more than likely adapted from something, the details of which you'll find in the title page of the libretto. The answers to your questions are likely to be contained within the libretto. Under no circumstance should you attempt to fix the adaptation by adding new sections of dialogue or changing the structure. This also extends to adding 'cut' songs that may exist for the show, preserved in recordings and different productions.

Watch / read / engage with the source material and write down the answer to these questions early on in your director's journal:

1. What are the major *structural changes* to the source material and why?

2. What are the major *plot changes* from the source material and why?

3. Which *characters* have been added / removed for the musical version and why?

4. What has been *gained* by adapting this source material into a musical form and why? (No need to focus on what has been LOST through adaptation as this will not provide an answer that you will find helpful in directing this version.)

Feel free to turn back to these answers throughout the rehearsal process. Sometimes during a tricky rehearsal, you may find help in the answers you have given yourself. Maybe you'll need this at tech, following a final rehearsal room run or in a moment of crisis following the dress rehearsal. Remember *what* this show is about and *why* it exists and you'll find clarity in your decisions.

You may find that many cast members will choose not to engage on this level of detail, and that is of course fine. Some may be interested in researching the role of Dolly Levi as written by Thornton Wilder in *The Matchmaker*, but you should frequently remind them that they are playing the role as written by Michael Stewart in *Hello, Dolly!* Of course one informs the other but for amateur actors it can confuse interpretation and slow down a rehearsal process, especially if everyone in the room is not operating with the same established knowledge base.

Understanding Context and Social History

Aside from the material itself, understanding the context and social history is one of the key factors in preparing to direct a show, and something that should never be overlooked. Reading biographies and memoirs of famous directors, you will frequently learn about their long research trips to far-flung corners of the world to immerse themselves in cultures and settings related to the show or film they were about to begin working on. Whilst this is obviously cost-prohibitive and largely not practical for most people in the real world, there are certain elements that you can absolutely recreate.

Perhaps you're directing RENT, Jonathan Larson's bohemian rock opera set in 1990s New York. The show itself is extremely specific to the time and place in which it is set, and a deep immersion into this world will allow you to imagine the production from costume and set through to the types of performances you'll want to encourage your actors to create. While most amateur directors won't have first-hand, or even second-hand knowledge of Greenwich Village in the 1990s, there are endless documentaries, podcasts and YouTube videos that will help you immerse yourself into that world. Very little of this will require any specialist research access, unless your interest extends to this, but the internet will really be invaluable.

Go through the script on a second or third reading and begin to underline words, phrases and locations that crop up. These may be words that the characters say, locations they reference or specific places in which the scenes are set. The language of Grease for example features many 1950s terms and slang used by young people at the time. West Side Story features very specific locations and wordplay that is now seen as archaic. Set up a digital file-sharing platform such as Google Drive where you can begin to collate your research and be prepared to share this as you go. Coming to production meetings with visual reference points will be invaluable for all members of the production team and make conversations with the designer, lighting team and wardrobe so much easier so you're working from a collective shared space. Later down the line you may wish to share this with your cast to encourage total immersion into the world of the show and make sure everyone has shared reference points that can be utilized throughout the whole rehearsal period.

CREATE A GLOSSARY

After a close read of the text as in the underlining exercise above, pull out each of the words and phrases that you believe need glossing. The chances are that if you have had to look up any words (either spoken as text or in stage directions) then your cast will have to do the same. Keep a running glossary in your director's journal and don't be afraid to refer back to them.

Certain shows may include lots of technical language or jargon specific to the world and context of the show itself. It's worth remembering that just as you and the cast may struggle to recognize these, your audience will also, and unlike you, won't have the convenience of hearing them multiple times and seeing them written down on a page. Once you have created your list, rank the words by order of importance to the narrative and telling the story. Some words may be throwaway, idioms used by certain characters that resist explanation or at the very least won't require discussion. Highlight those words and phrases that are specific to the plot. These are the words that audiences will need to know in order to remain engaged throughout. For example, *RENT* includes frequent references to the drug 'AZT', which at the time was an experimental treatment for HIV. Within the libretto the characters themselves never spell out what this is, as in their world, this is assumed knowledge amongst themselves. A lot of audiences watching the show in 2024 (and even in the 1990s) won't necessarily recognize this reference and it is your job to ensure that it is clear who is taking it and the implications this has on the character. Making a note of these moments early will ensure they remain flagged when it comes to staging, and remind you to invite discussion with the cast at the appropriate time.

For shows with incredibly specific language references, consider reproducing your glossary in the programme or free-sheet to the audience for them to familiarize themselves with before the show. I remember the 1993 London revival of *Grease* had a fun glossary included in the programme relating to 1950s America. Whilst few of the words were consequential to the understanding of the plot, it made for a fun addition. In all cases your cast should understand every word they are saying at all times and should be encouraged to speak out or ask questions if they are unsure.

The exercise above should also help you identify anything you don't know, including words and phrases. As a director, actors will ask you often publicly, what a word or phrase means. Being prepared with an answer will help build confidence and show that you have put the time in preparing for a rehearsal. Whilst it's always okay to say you don't know the answer to a question, there's no real excuse in the digital age for not having looked something up before a rehearsal and having an answer ready.

Two examples I can think of deal with musicals from the 1950s and 1960s. In *How to Succeed in Business Without Really Trying* the character Smitty references Metrecal – a diet drink that was used in the 1960s as a precursor to the more familiar Slim Fast we would know today. Without Googling, myself or the actor (or anyone in the room for that matter) had never heard of it and so the gag never worked. Knowing what this was before a rehearsal will help you think about ways of staging the joke so that it carries some form, or is thrown away, knowing that an audience in the 2020s won't have a clue and it's not really worth the effort to signpost. Another example comes at the end of *Sweet Charity* where a 'good fairy' enters to speak to Charity and makes a joke about the audience watching 'The Good Fairy' on CBS. This will always fall flat however you stage it, but knowing the context will save time and allow you to stage the (unnecessary) moment in the most efficient way possible to get through to the end as Charity lives 'hopefully' ever after.

CREATE A WORLD MAP

No matter what show you're directing, it will have a setting. In many cases this will be extremely specific. It may be grounded in real life with iconic locations that audiences will recognize (e.g. the New York City of *West Side Story*, *Annie* and *Hello, Dolly!*); fantasy locations with a very specific internal geography (*Into the Woods*, *The Wizard of Oz*) or more open, transient spaces where time and place are more liminal (*Godspell*, *Cats* and *Pippin*). In each case, it's helpful to create a map of that world and ensure that everyone involved with the production understands this at all times. This will be done on a much more granular level as we begin to look at blocking scenes, but at this point in the process the overall world map is more important.

You don't have to be an expert cartographer or artist to be able to make a solid and usable map – the main thing to do is be as specific as possible. Again, comb through the script for locations – those where scenes are set and those that are referenced directly and indirectly throughout the show. Prioritize those locations that are key and where the bulk of the material takes place. This is not intended to be a set design, although it may form the basis for conversations with a designer. Think of it more as a visual aid for you building up the world in which the show operates, be it realistic or fantasy.

In this example from *Into the Woods* (Figure 1.5), the map shows the key locations mentioned throughout the show. The topography is drawn from my own imagination. The script doesn't specify how far the locations are from one another. Does it

Fig. 1.5 World Map.

matter how far the Baker's house is from Cinderella's stepmother's house or Jack and his mother? Probably not. The distance doesn't relate to any action within the story, instead all of the characters are drawn into the woods, wherein Granny has a cottage and Rapunzel has a tower. In this example, you are free to create your own world and, more importantly, your own internal logic. The key thing is to STICK TO IT throughout. Having this visual map will help you as you begin to stage the show. The audience may not know that Cinderella's house is a 'quarter or a league hence' from the tree where she visits her mother, but the actor will and this will inform their choices (which side of the stage do they look towards when they wistfully mention 'home' and so on) and help create an internal logic that the whole company can stick to.

A show such as *My Fair Lady* has a geographically specific map that is worthy of some study. From the key locations of Covent Garden where the show begins through to Henry Higgings's house on Wimpole Street through to Ascot and The Embassy, there is a precise world in which the show operates. Drawing this out and understanding the differences between the spaces is helpful in knowing the journeys in between. Knowing how far Eliza or her father have travelled by taxi helps to inform certain acting decisions. Knowing the distance in real terms that Dolly travels from Vandergelder's Hay and Feed store in Yonkers to the 14th Street Parade in *Hello, Dolly!* will guide acting decisions and choices – from how an actor enters the stage to the energy levels they begin a scene with, and so on.

Real places and locations have *energies* that can be researched and understood before being reconstructed onstage. Understanding the buzz of Covent Garden market at opera kicking-out time will inform your staging of the opening scene of *My Fair Lady*. Knowing how the East Village sounds, smells and feels will help in your staging of 'La Vie Boheme' in *RENT*. In these examples, specificity is key. The more research you can do and the more this can bleed into the world you create on stage, the more authentic the production will feel. It is up to you to inspire this sense of specificity to your cast and engage them in the process of doing their own research.

Shows that are not as geographically bound by location mean that you can be freer to create a map that suits your needs. *Cats* and *Godspell* are two shows that spring to mind that are traditionally set in a sort of 'everyplace' that's often open to interpretation. Whereas *Cats* gives you the location of a rubbish dump, and is usually a single unit set, this doesn't mean it can't have its own world map. In fact, it's sometimes more important that shows such as this DO have a clear map as otherwise actors can feel that they are wandering around in infinite space and time which lacks grounding. In this example, I would ask where is this rubbish dump and what does it contain? This extends beyond the set design of the physical space and should come early in your discussions with a designer to ensure everyone is working from the same sense of place.

CREATE A VISUAL MOOD BOARD

Once you've created a map of the physical world of the show and the linguistic world of the show, the next step is to create a wider visual mood board. One of the easiest ways to do this is via social media – I often use sites like Pinterest and Instagram to gather images, videos and links that I will want to refer back to. If you happen to rehearse in an environment where you can leave materials or use a pinboard / wall, I would encourage creating a physical mood board that can grow throughout the rehearsal process. This is common practice in a professional rehearsal room where you may rehearse a cast daily for three to four weeks at a time. Engaging the cast in this task early helps bring them on board and maintain a collective effort from the start. Think of it as a mood board that can build and build, right up until the final dress. The stronger the central reference points are, the stronger the sense of pull the company will feel in the same creative direction.

Perhaps you're rehearsing the show *Hair*, the tribal rock musical rooted in the hippy culture of the 1960s. You could set up a joint Pinterest Board or Google Drive where images and videos could be shared, outside of rehearsal and discussed when all together or virtually through your various social media groups. Many of these contexts are far removed from the everyday life of amateur theatre performers. Imagine a cast member playing Berger coming to rehearsal fresh from a shift as a nurse in a hospital. The communes of 1960s America and resistance to war in Vietnam will feel worlds away from their day job, but having this visual entry to dive into before, during and after rehearsal will help everyone in the room re-align to the world of the show you're creating.

Costume, set and lighting designers may indeed have their own versions of such mood boards and it's important to let them know that yours aren't intended to direct them or step on their toes. Instead, the aim is to create one overall aesthetic that can be drawn on by both the cast and creative team.

CREATE A TIMELINE

Lastly, it's worth creating an accurate *timeline* for the show. More often than not these can be simple and linear: a show begins at the start and continues in a linear structure with a middle and end. It's important to understand the structure that the musical is written in, and for this to be consistently conveyed to your cast and creative team throughout rehearsals. One of the main considerations is *knowledge*: at what point in the narrative do characters learn certain facts or feel certain emotions. Knowing this order will help you direct realistic performances.

Musicals set backwards: *Merrily We Roll Along*; *The Last Five Years*

Musicals set in 'real time': *The 25th Annual Putnam County Spelling Bee*; *Hedwig and the Angry Inch*

Musicals set in liminal time: *Songs for a New World*; *Assassins*

Memory / flashback musicals: *Funny Girl*; *Evita*

EXERCISE

Once you've identified the structure of the musical you're working on, try now to divide it into two timelines. The first could be called **'Show Time'**, and would reflect the order of events as they are presented on stage. Usually this can be drawn from the scene / song structure which often includes specific dates if they are indeed relevant. Once you have drawn these out as they are below, you could then make a new list called **'Real Time'**. Here you can re-order any of the events strictly chronologically, as outlined below for the musical *Evita*.

SHOW TIME

26 July 1952: Eva Peron is announced as being dead

July–August 1952: Eva Peron's funeral

1934: We meet Eva Peron aged 15 in Junin

1934: Eva moves to Buenos Aires

1943: Right-wing coup benefits Juan Peron

22 January 1944: Eva and Peron meet at a charity event in Luna Park stadium

1945: Eva and Peron marry, Peron is arrested

1946: Peron is elected President of Argentina

1947: Eva begins her 'Rainbow Tour'

1951: Eva announces her run for Vice President

Flashback: Eva recounts moments of her life in flashback

1952: Eva Peron dies

REAL TIME

1934: We meet Eva Peron aged 15 in Junin

1934: Eva moves to Buenos Aires

1943: Right-wing coup benefits Juan Peron

22 January 1944: Eva and Peron meet at a charity event in Luna Park stadium

1945: Eva and Peron marry, Peron is arrested

1946: Peron is elected President of Argentina

1947: Eva begins her 'Rainbow Tour'

1951: Eva announces her run for Vice President

26 July 1952: Eva Peron is announced as being dead

July–August 1952: Eva Peron's funeral

For shows that aren't explicitly historic, you are unlikely to have exact times and dates, but the same exercise can be done. A show such as *West Side Story* for example doesn't offer specific dates, but does offer an incredibly tight timeframe in which the scenes take place:

West Side Story – List of Scenes
Act One
Prologue – the months before
5.00 pm: The Street
5.30 pm: A Back Yard
6.00 pm: A Bridal Shop
10.00 pm: The Gym
11.00 pm: A Back Alley
Midnight: The Drugstore

The Next Day

5.30 pm: The Bridal Shop
6.00–9.00 pm: The Neighbourhood
9.00 pm: Under the Highway

Act Two
9.35 pm: A Bedroom
10.00 pm: Another Alley
11.30 pm: The Bedroom
11.40 pm: The Drugstore

The reason this matters concerns the energy and impetus from scene to scene and act to act. It is your job to manage the time between scenes and the pacing of the show as a whole. Understanding the short gaps in time between events is key, as it dictates the actions and energy of each character. Knowing that Tony meets Maria the same day he has sung 'Something's Coming' and that both 'Maria' and 'The Balcony Scene' occur almost in real time following the 'Dance at the Gym' drives the action forward. The whole action of the show spans just one day and one evening, making the forward motion feel urgent. Not only does this help instruct practical decisions, such as costume, hair and make-up, but it also dictates the energy of the piece as a whole and the state the characters are in.

For a show such as *Gypsy* which spans roughly a decade from start to finish, the same task can be done but instead emphasis should be focused on how time is used and how quickly. Many musicals use montage scenes to show the passage of time ('I Know It's Today' from *Shrek*; 'Twelve Days to Christmas' from *She Loves Me*), and in turn this increases the pace of a show. In these instances, your timeline can reflect the time spent in each year or moment, to give you a visual indication of the show's overall structure.

EXERCISE

- Draw a single straight line on a landscape page and start to plot the main points using the song titles.

- Instead of placing them out evenly across the line, consider the time in real terms spent between each number. How much distance should be between them? What has happened in that time between scenes? What have the characters learned in that time?

- From this you'll be able to visually see the pacing of a show in relation to the time span of the show, which in turn will show you faster and slower moving beats and scenes.

A further exercise may be extending this exercise to the cast and asking them to each make a *character* timeline that runs alongside this *global* timeline. Within the musical itself different characters may learn pieces of information at different times, and visually seeing this written down is invaluable for each actor to understand their character arc and journey through the world of the show.

Cultural Specificities

Shows that have a specific cultural setting or themes that require deeper engagement can provide excellent options for amateur theatre groups, and can be an exciting way to engage with a local community or widen out the remit of each group. Many of these conversations will have already been had during the show selection stage (see earlier sections), but if you're a director for hire you may not have been privy to these conversations early on.

Popular am-dram musicals with specific cultures and contexts include:

- *Fiddler on the Roof*: The Jewish pogroms in nineteenth-century Ukraine
- *Hairspray*: Race relations in 1960s Baltimore, USA
- *The King and I*: The transition of power in Siam (modern-day Thailand) in the late nineteenth century
- *Once on This Island*: two communities in the French Antilles archipelago in the Caribbean Sea

These are musicals that are frequently performed in the UK, yet deal with communities and cultures external to where the shows are being performed. These shows have a long history of being performed on Broadway, the West End and beyond at various times during the past 50 years that has shaped the context of each revival. As a director, your job is to present a sensitive and nuanced production that not only plays the text and score as written, but engages with the world and story the show is trying to tell.

I don't necessarily subscribe to the idea that one cannot direct, or indeed perform, outside of their lived experience. However, for each of the shows mentioned above (and of course many more), there are elements that are inherent within them that require sensitive understanding and detailed research. Whilst a Broadway revival of *Fiddler on the Roof* without a Jewish creative team or cast would seem unheard of, it's a show that is frequently performed by amateurs at a mix of levels and popular with audiences and performers.

If I were asked to direct *Fiddler*, as a non-Jewish person, I would first attempt to surround myself with a Jewish creative team, be that an MD, choreographer, assistant director or even cultural consultant. If this wasn't possible, I would perhaps offer an alternative show suggestion. Speak to your committee about what may be possible. Perhaps this could involve outside voices, workshops and talks from different community organizations where a full-time production team member may not be possible, but you should be prepared to do the work to ensure sensitivity and authenticity. *Fiddler on the Roof* is a show that on many levels transcends cultures. During its Japanese premiere in 1967 the creative team worried the piece wouldn't translate in terms of culture and understanding of the basic premise of the story. Instead they found themselves shocked to hear the audience and critical reaction who instead commented that the show felt 'so Japanese'.

Whilst the perspective and direct plot points of a show may feel unrelatable on paper, what you can do is consider how your own lived experience tracks to elements within the show itself.

DIRECTING A CULTURALLY SENSITIVE SHOW

Start by making a list of the core story and actions within the show. In the case of *Fiddler*, the direct actions include the persecution of the community by the Russian soldiers, most specifically in the Pogrom scene at the wedding. Make notes of actions within the narrative that map onto historical context and events, gathering as many facts as possible to share with the full company.

History and Facts

Immerse yourself in the historical events and facts surrounding the context and world of the show. An understanding of the main events leading up to the French revolution will of course only enhance your understanding when directing *Les Miserables*. Knowing the specific events leading up to Pearl Harbor would help you in directing *From Here to Eternity*, just as an understanding of the USA's position in the South Pacific during the Second World War would help ground your knowledge of the time period of that specific show. Again, remember few musicals deal with historical fact as history. It is wise to understand the differences in 'real' life events and map them against the events happening within the timeframe and world of the show. Understanding the key differences will help as you begin to address the perspective from which the story is being told. Consider also who is telling you these facts and from which perception they are being presented. Look for inherent bias and research multiple sources. The war in Vietnam for example is seen incredibly differently depending on which side it is being viewed from.

Words and Music

There may well be cultural specificities within the score of the musical you are directing. An understanding of the klezmer sound achieved by Jerry Bock in *Fiddler on the Roof*, particularly in sections such as 'The Bottle Dance' for example, will enhance your delivery of this particular moment in the show. Presenting these moments authentically is important, from thinking about relevant accents and dialects that the lyrics may be written in through to the specificities of the instrumentation used at particular moments. Your job is to research these moments and communicate these to your cast and creative team to ensure they are handled sensitively and effectively within the wider context of the show.

Stage Directions and Settings

Similar to above you may find yourself in the position where you're directing a specific scene that falls outside of your lived experience. 'The Sabbath Prayer' in *Fiddler on the Roof* for example is a key moment in the show that requires knowledge of this ceremony and tradition. You can't rely on the stage directions to instruct you in all cases – research must be done ahead of time as to how this works in practice. Why not bring a consultant on board with lived experience of this specific moment who can instruct you in how it should be done properly and carefully? Maybe ask them to attend the rehearsal where you stage the moment, or speak to them outside of the rehearsal room on the best way to approach it. Either way, it is your job to convey your workings out to your cast so they gain confidence in your approach. Remember, actors themselves may be acting outside of their own lived experience and will be looking for you for reassurance and guidance on the specificities within their character and the show. You should never leave them in a vulnerable position to figure it out themselves. Instead invite the conversation from the beginning and learn together to build confidence and ensure it is handled sensitively and effectively for both cast and audience.

ENGAGE WITH THE PERIOD AND STYLE

For less specific moments in the show I find immersing yourself in the wider context is extremely useful during your pre-show preparation. One of the best ways of doing this is through galleries and museums that bear relevance to the world you are looking to create. Directing *Oliver!* may seem simple given our general assumptions on the Dickensian period, but spending half a day at a gallery to take in the artwork of the time and the contemporary world of the show will help you visualize the world you're trying to create. Directing *Made in Dagenham the Musical* will be enhanced by an understanding of Britain in the 1960s. It doesn't always have to be directly relevant

– seeing furniture, sculpture, artwork, advertising, artefacts and so on will all act as creative stimuli. Take pictures of what you can and take your notebook to write down your reaction to pieces on the spot. You never know when inspiration will strike. I found inspiration for a concept for a production of *Into the Woods* in the National Gallery, viewing paintings from the nineteenth century that suggested a certain colour palette that became the tone for the whole show and informed scenic and costume design. Take in as much as you can and record everything that inspires you.

I want to stress that this work should take place throughout your whole journey as a director and doesn't all have to be foregrounded. Equally, your study doesn't end the day rehearsals begin; you'll find yourself frequently going back to these notes and creating new ones as the rehearsal process develops.

What Is the Show About?

This may feel like a fundamental question, but it is one you should write at the top of each page in your journey or notebook. Ask yourself at the start of each scene as you begin to rehearse: **what is the story we are trying to tell?** Even the most obtuse of musicals that refuse to fit the narrative mould or traditional structure are about *something*. I always think of Sondheim's much-quoted opinion of *Oklahoma!* vs *Carousel* in which he famously stated in his appreciation of the latter, '*Oklahoma!* is about a picnic, whereas *Carousel* is about life and death'. Whilst this withering assessment may sound glib, you should ask yourself, and ask your cast what the show is about in every rehearsal. Not everyone in the room has to agree on every detail but asking that question of a scene, a moment, a song, a short moment, will keep you connected to the text and moving in a forward motion.

You may find answers differ between scenes, acts and even within songs. Try and reduce yourself to key words. Kander and Ebb's *Chicago* front-loads this question in the very first moments of the show, before the overture starts:

> Ladies and Gentlemen. You're about to see a story of murder, greed, corruption, violence, exploitation, adultery and treachery. All those things we hold near and dear to our hearts.

While this may feel like a basic reduction, those key words literally tell the audience what it is they're about to see. More often than not this is handled in a much subtler way through the set-up of the opening song or scene. Audiences are at ease when they understand what they're seeing. There's a well-touted maxim that says an audience can handle anything you put in front of them as long as it is successfully developed in the first 10 minutes. A well-written musical will do the work for you and make it clear what the show is about.

Knowing this will inform your concept of the show itself, and what you are bringing to the foreground in your interpretation. While it's unlikely that you will suddenly unlock new meanings in shows such as *Gypsy*, *Heathers* or *Cabaret*, what you CAN do is foreground certain aspects and themes that you feel speak to you, all within the remit of what the show is about.

Ask yourself: what is the key principle that interests you in this show? Consider *Cabaret* by Kander and Ebb. Directors the world over have presented the show in various forms, from commercial West End and Broadway revivals through to community productions and even those at schools and colleges. As a director you need to present your vision as clearly as possible, and often this is described as a 'concept'. Don't be put off or scared of this loaded word – it can mean as much or as little as you want it to.

When we read a novel each person who reads it will have a different visual picture of everything from the characters to the setting right through to the smells and tastes it evokes. Even if the author is particularly descriptive, no two people will create the exact same images or come away with the same interpretation of the book as a whole. Ask five friends to describe the same novel and you'll get five different answers. The same can be said of a musical. In many cases your interpretation is clouded or haunted by the ghosts of previous versions. To use the above example, there will be few directors who don't have a strong vision of Liza Minnelli and Joel Grey from Bob Fosse's Oscar-winning film. Even those who haven't seen the film will be familiar with the poster, the iconography or clips that enter their subconscious. Your job is to try to come to the material with the freshest eye you possibly can and take away from it an honest reaction that speaks to you.

Directors can choose to build their concept through their own lens and the way they perceive the show. Just as the five friends would offer five different interpretations of the same novel, the same could be said of five directors approaching *Cabaret*, as this potted history shows:

Hal Prince, Original Broadway production: a contemporary allegory that uses a giant onstage mirror to reflect the audience back at itself, letting them see themselves as part of the catastrophic events.

Bob Fosse, film adaptation: realism of the German nightclub scene with only diegetic songs surviving, emphasizing the entertainment and dark underbelly of the period.

Sam Mendes, 1998 Donmar and West End: semi-immersive, expressionist and overly sexual portrayal that distances the audience emotionally from the politics

Rufus Norris, 2006 West End: places the Holocaust as a central metaphor ending with a final image of the cast and Emcee naked in a gas chamber

Rebecca Frecknell, 2021 West End: immersive experience that places the audiences at the heart of the show suggesting they are implicit in the destruction of democracy as the cast slowly 'conform' before our eyes, showing the slip into fascism that can happen without resistance.

In all cases, the directors are working with the same source material, but each highlights different aspects of the show that in turn creates different effects for the audience. In each case creative decisions have been made that are connected through direction, performance and scenic design, highlighting the overall concept for the show itself.

Creating a concept in a professional setting is often born from the reason behind staging the show or reviving it in the first place. Why this show, now? Is there a new political relevance to the piece? Have current events shifted how audiences can portray the show? Does the current climate call for something light-hearted and non-taxing for audiences? Has the show been tweaked or re-written to suit modern day sensibilities? In most commercial cases these questions will be answered by producers first with a concept coming second.

In drawing together your concept, ask yourself this question: What is the show's key function?

- To educate?
- To entertain?
- To explain or enlighten?
- Catharsis?

Shows such as *Guys and Dolls* are generally produced with a primary goal to entertain. *The Scottsboro Boys* or *Parade* on the other hand offer audiences an education in a specific event or period of history they may not already be familiar with. *Follies* may offer middle-age and older audiences some elements of catharsis. Of course, these are not mutually exclusive terms and it's highly probable that your show can function in different ways. Figure 1.6 offers a simple Venn diagram that details how shows

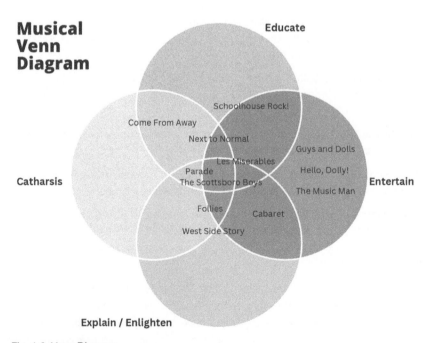

Fig. 1.6 Venn Diagram.

can have multiple functions. Obviously on a base level all musicals are designed to entertain, as we're asking audiences to spend their hard-earned money and give up an evening to watch and the last thing they're expecting is a lecture void of entertainment. What this diagram shows is how musicals can have a primary and secondary function, above that of just a simple piece of entertainment. It's important to identify the primary function when establishing your concept, as this will act as your guiding principle as you begin to piece together your ideas.

Establishing a Concept and Seeing It Through

The word 'concept' is not a dirty or scary word. Don't be afraid to use it around cast and creative teams, but at the same time it is your job to demystify it from the start. Some may panic, mistaking it as 'high concept' theatre that could see you present *Anything Goes* on a spaceship rather than an ocean liner. In short, think of it as your own perspective on the material and your vision of how the show will be presented. Establishing a concept and seeing it through are two entirely different challenges, and something that requires space to unpack during the preparation stage and before rehearsals begin. From experience, concepts need to be effectively communicated at all stages and successfully carried through in order to work, and they rely on the full creative team, and indeed cast, being all-in. Below are key aspects to consider when making your proposed concept a reality.

BUDGET

As discussed above, the budget for a show dictates most aspects of its delivery. At this point you'll hopefully have had a meeting with the committee or treasurer and have a solid enough idea of the money you have on hand to produce the show. As discussed elsewhere, budgets in amateur theatre can be particularly tight. Knowing your break-even point is key. In an ideal world you would work alongside a producer or treasurer who would keep control of the budget from the start, and alongside a production manager and other members of the creative team who would be tasked with ensuring the show sticks within that framework. Your job as a director is to work within this budget to see your concept through. Having a low or small budget should not necessarily curtail your ambition and in fact, in many cases, it presents you with much more room for innovation and interpretation.

I've worked with societies where the question of money is kept from the director and from experience this is counterproductive. You should know the scale within which you are expected to deliver the show – at the very least, you should know the money that is available for sets, props and costumes. An understanding of what lighting and sound equipment is available in the venue is also key, as well as any technical restraints or 'rules' that you have to follow within the venue.

With the help of the world map and timeline you have created, go through the script and make note of any elements of staging that might require investment – what is required as an absolute basic idea and what can be presented in a more creative way. Sweeney Todd's barber's chair is richly described in the libretto, along with the mechanism used to kill each of his victims, falling down a chute and into the cellar ready for Mrs Lovett to make them into pies. On the most basic level, this description suggests a two-tiered set and the ability for Todd's victims to be disposed of quickly and efficiently. Requirements such as these should be flagged and itemized and discussed early in your planning with the society and committee. Every show tends to have at least one non-negotiable element, be it *Miss Saigon*'s infamous helicopter through to *Phantom*'s falling chandelier. Identifying this early on is often a good way to start to build a concept within the restraints and resources you have available.

For example, if your costume budget for a cast of twenty is £500, the chances are period dress and frequent costume changes will be out of the question. Instead, think about how this money could be used. Instead of staging *Jesus Christ Superstar* in expensive period dress, this may help guide you to creating a concept set in 2024, where cast members can provide and share their own pieces of costume, or costume can be sourced relatively cheaply. This will no doubt have been a consideration before the show was selected. A show like *Top Hat* or *42nd Street* for example generally calls for many costume changes and expensive items such as cocktail dresses and tails that soon add up. Even *A Chorus Line*, which can have a shoe-string costume budget, dictates a change by all cast members for the final song, where precision is a key factor and everyone must look identical, whether you choose to go for the iconic gold top hat and tails or something altogether different.

A modern-day or plain / neutrally dressed production of *Carousel* or *Oklahoma!* for example may evoke a contemporary edge to the shows that could heighten their message and social relevance without changing a word of dialogue. Perhaps your costumes for *Guys and Dolls* will be all black with each character having just a different style of hat for identification. *West Side Story* could be entirely told in two separate colour palettes to represent the distinction between the Sharks and the Jets. Don't let a budget deter you – instead, let it be your guiding principle throughout. Have those difficult conversations as early as you can and press the committee for firm answers. It will help you build your concept effectively and guide your creativity in discovering the show as a whole. If your budget gives you lemons, make the sweetest lemonade you can.

The same can be said for set and technical requirements. Using your preparation exercises above, look at both your timeline and your world map for the show you have already created. Within this, identify specific elements that are 'non-negotiable' as discussed above with Sweeney Todd's chair. Once you have these listed, you'll easily be able to pin-point the elements that may prove problematic to the wider production team. At this point don't be afraid to bring in your set designers or production managers, as they will also be helpful in contributing ideas. Once you have listed the 'practicals' ('working' elements within a show'), you can begin to think creatively about how to realize them.

CASE STUDY

I directed one of the first amateur productions of Sunset Boulevard *to be licensed. The show is remembered for the giant set, realistic practical car, descending staircase and sumptuous orchestra. Rather than direct the piece in a traditional proscenium arch, it was to be performed in a 150-seat off-West End venue that is a converted Victorian swimming pool. Rather than panic at the challenge, the restraints of the venue and size of the space became an asset in telling a much paired-down version of the story and one that would be ultimately very different to the original London and Broadway productions.*

My starting point for this production was one of the biggest challenges, that of Norma Desmond's car and the car chase earlier in Act One that brings Joe Gillis to the house on Sunset. With no feasible way to use a car, as many amateur productions had hired and replicated on larger stages, instead I used that restraint to unpack the wider concept for the show. Knowing it would have to be represented rather than realistically portrayed I considered how car chases and car scenes were filmed in the period of silent movies. I found footage of car facades and headlights placed in front of a rolling screen, where the moving backdrop would be projected. The effect was created on screen by a wind machine, sound effects and so on that gave the illusion of what the camera would then film. This led to the wider idea of the whole show taking place on a Hollywood sound stage, complete with flats, visible props and 'illusions' that showed the artifice of the film industry and the people who worked within it. The overarching concept then became the company of industry professionals literally creating the film in front of the audience. This allowed a distancing that placed the musical Sunset Boulevard *within the frame of a show being filmed and created.*

There was a duality within the production of the ensemble as filmmakers and as actors within the piece that suited the nature of the show that is split very finely between a small set of principals and a medium-sized ensemble. It had the double advantage of involving more cast throughout the show as a whole as they were visible throughout in the process of the filming, meaning it allowed more opportunities for a larger society than the show would usually offer. Superficial restrictions and restraints that you face should be treated as creative problems to solve, rather than setbacks to overcome.

I directed a production of How to Succeed in Business Without Really Trying *in the same small ex-swimming pool described above. One of the elements of the script is an elevator. Given huge budgetary restraints, a working elevator is rarely possible. I came up with the idea of sliding door screens that could come together to form an elevator door and be rotated by the cast and opened up to simulate the idea of an enclosed space, and the opening and closing of the doors that was specifically written into the script. Again, by addressing this problematic practical moment first, I then extrapolated and built on the idea to create a wider concept of moveable doors and screens that then became the whole design of the show. Easily moved on casters by the cast, the playing space was effortlessly manipulated and the screens quickly and seamlessly became everything from external walls to urinals to a bank of mirrors.*

VENUE

Aside from the budget, the venue you will be performing in is the most important aspect when putting together your concept for the show. As early on as you can in the proceedings, you should ask for a site visit and you should schedule these regularly throughout your production process. In many cases amateur theatre companies perform in the same venue for many years and get used to the intricacies and challenges each one has. If you are new, or find yourself directing in a venue you don't know, speak to as many people as you can about their experience and grill them on their past issues and snags that they have encountered.

One of the first things I will do in this situation is go and watch something in the venue where you'll be directing. It could be anything – if there is another show before yours by the same or different society, go and see it armed with your notebook. You need to experience a performance from the audience's perspective and be aware of any challenges that it throws up as early as you can. At this point, or at a site visit, consider these questions below:

1. What are the sightlines? Are there any blindspots or restricted areas? Note areas that will be tricky for some members of the audience. Work out how many seats and which ones can't see certain elements of the stage so you can avoid staging important moments in these sections.

2. How high is the stage? Will the actors be above the heads of the audience? Can you have additional staging or levels on the playing space, or does it risk getting too high?

3. Who is raked? Are the audience looking down at the stage or looking up? This is an important consideration for many reasons as it affects the energy of the space and shifts the balance between audience and cast. If it is the auditorium seats that are raked, the floor becomes a key visual playing space and should be treated as such.

4. What is the size and shape of the playing space? This is a fundamental question and one you should know from the very beginning. This will dictate all of your staging decisions going forward.

5. Where are the entrances and exits? Mark these and commit to them, ensuring your cast know them at all times.

6. Where are the runarounds and crossovers? How can the cast journey backstage? Note the pressure points of backstage traffic.

7. What is the fly space and wing space? As above, think about backstage traffic and storage of sets, props, costumes and cast members.

8. Is there a curtain and orchestra pit? A traditional pit signifies a particular type of show for an audience. Consider not just sound design but also the physical distance and relationship you want the cast to have to the audience. A traditional pit is designed as a buffer between performers and audiences, which is a key reason why many modern musicals place the band onstage, incorporate them into the onstage design or have them perform remotely.

Once you have got to grips with your venue, drawn out your basic stage diagrams and considered the potential drawbacks, the next thing to do is to draw up a list of the **top five features** your venue has that you think connect to the show you are directing. Make them short and concise and focus on the feature of the space that you want to embrace when building your concept. For example:

FEATURES

1. Large size of stage
2. Flexible seating
3. Four entrances / exits
4. High ceiling and lighting rig
5. Built-in balcony.

Now you have these five features, think about the **benefits** that these features have and add those next to your list, as in Table 1.3. Taking this into account, you can start to see the building blocks of your concept and how these practical elements can be the cornerstones and starting point of your ultimate vision for the production.

Using this example, let's consider how this could be applied to a production of *Sweeney Todd* (see Table 1.4).

Table 1.3 Features and Benefits of the Venue

Feature	Benefit
Large size of stage	Will allow large cast of 25+ all onstage together
Flexible seating	Audience can be positioned around the stage, not necessarily end-on
Four entrances and exits	Easy access to the stage, can move lots of people / props / set pieces on quickly allowing a slickness
High ceiling and lighting rig	Height can be used in design and staging
Built-in balcony	Can be used to create two separate playing spaces, differentiating between spaces and status

Table 1.4 Features and Benefits of the Venue for *Sweeney Todd*

Feature	Benefit	Concept
Size of the stage	Large stage will allow large cast of 25+ all onstage together	Large-scale production, big choral sound, no role doubling required, large ensemble representing the full extent of Victorian society
Flexible seating	Audience can be positioned around the stage, not necessarily end-on	Immersive element, audience in thrust formation to feel part of the action. Interact with the audience
Four entrances and exits	Easy access to the stage, can move lots of people / props / set pieces on quickly allowing a slickness	Minimal set elements, props ensemble can be used to build various sets and locations with tables, chairs and benches
High ceiling and lighting rig	Height can be used in design and staging	Step ladders can be used on castors to represent different elements of society and hierarchy amongst the ensemble with the Victorian feudal system
Built-in balcony	Can be used to create two separate playing spaces, differentiating between spaces and status	Used for Sweeney's salon above the pie shop to differentiate the locations on stage

You can see how itemizing these practical elements can lead to you beginning to creatively respond and think about how the show can look and feel. It's much easier to start your exploration from the ground up, rather than taking a concept-down approach which can see you forcing a circle into a square and potentially creating more issues later down the line.

ATMOSPHERE

Another element that's connected to the venue is the atmosphere. Each venue brings with it its own unique atmosphere that is something you should identify and lean into within your overall concept. For example, a converted lecture hall may prove difficult to adapt to the dark, seedy environment you want to achieve for your immersive production of *Cabaret*. A brick venue under a railway arch may give you a perfect industrial palette for creating a grungy production of *Godspell*, but would be less suited to a production of *Shrek* or *Seussical*. There are only a limited number of things you can control in the wider atmosphere of a venue and each type of theatre space brings with it its own audience expectations.

SCALE

The overall scale of the production is the final key element to consider when building your concept. Scale is dictated mainly by budget, as discussed above, but one element that feeds into this is audience expectation. Usually this is set by the cost of the ticket. Purchasing a ticket is a form of contract between audience and producer that provides the former with an experience as described and provided by the latter. Amateur theatre audiences have a wide range of reasons for attending a production, the predominant one being support of family, friends and colleagues. Prices are generally set by the break-even point, but it's important to remember that with that price comes certain expectations. An audience paying £20 to £25 per ticket may be surprised to be greeted by a show that has no set, ordinary costumes and limited orchestra or band, no matter how good the cast and production are. Certain musicals (*Shrek*, *Beauty and the Beast*, etc.) set their expectations by way of familiarity with the source. Audiences are probably not likely to be expecting an 'auteur' take on a Disney classic to see a plain-clothed, bare-feet production. In certain circumstances the rights holders control this by only providing a licence if the appropriate costumes and design elements are used, particularly if the show is associated with a brand such as Disney or another popular intellectual property.

Communicating this through your marketing is your best way to set audience expectations. If you're directing a familiar title, using artwork that they will recognize will set the expectation of familiarity. I always treat the marketing and artwork used to sell the show as an extension of the concept. You need to be clear about what it is you are selling to an audience. Think about the colour scheme, palette and fonts that are used on your flyers. Is this a show aimed at children? Is it aimed at families? Is it going to replicate the professional production that many will be familiar with? If you are offering a darker take on a classic, your marketing imagery needs to reflect and pre-empt that for audiences. You are in charge of managing the expectations of your audience.

PERSPECTIVE FROM A THEATRE DESIGNER, JOHN WINTERS

Less is more. For a play, you can usually strip it back to the bare minimum and let the acting shine through, but musicals are meant to be fabulous! Don't imagine the original production but smaller, read the text, come up with a vision (doesn't need to be original) and write it down. Then go with your designer and have a lot of fun. Then the pain begins, you've got to strip it back, and be brutal – less is more. It's far better to do less to a higher quality than lots that looks flimsy or unfinished. Which probably means getting a high finish on your costumes is more important than building a city-scape upstage. The annoying scene that appears only once but requires an entirely different room, can probably just be set dressing. If that means your vision needs tweaking, tweak it, rip it up, and then use your new lens to assess the design, strip out what you don't need, but that vision needs to tie everything together.

A good designer will help you do this, as a director you need to articulate why it is important, keep the vision alive, but not overrule other people's expertise. And if that means you're creating spaces with moveable furniture, decide how it's getting on and off and rehearse it with your cast from the beginning – musicals suck mirror balls if they have a scene change more than a few seconds. That all sounds quite clinical, so my last bit of advice is counter to the above – make sure there is something to be in awe of, it doesn't need to be scenic even, just something that gets your company and audience excited.

SUMMARY

By this point you'll be in a position to seriously consider envisioning your concept and ready to put it into action. Your notebook should be full of research – images, photographs, drawings and notes made from your preparation that will in turn feed into your overall idea. Having considered the practical points above, you'll be in a position to summarize your ideas and start to present them as building blocks.

The chart in Figure 1.7 is an example of how you can use these building blocks to literally build your concept from the ground up. I have reduced the exercise for brevity, but feel free to expand on each of these building blocks as necessary.

Concept = Communication + Consistency

COMMUNICATING A CONCEPT

Once you have built your concept and become more confident in its delivery, the next stage is growing secure in communicating this to both cast and creative teams. It's key to have your concept available in multiple forms, as you will be asked repeatedly for how you see the show, whether that's for the company's website or promotional material or even programme notes.

ELEVATOR SUMMARY

This will be a 1–2 sentence description of how you plan to create the show. Think about reading this afresh and how this would work as promotional material. It should be a short summary that communicates your core idea and vision for the show.

LONGER DESCRIPTION

This will be a paragraph-length description of your concept that can be communicated on things like the audition notice, so auditionees can see your 'vision' for the show and see how you plan to present it and what is potentially different about this version.

SCENE-BY-SCENE BREAKDOWN

This will be useful throughout the whole rehearsal process to communicate to your cast how your concept carries through from scene to scene. There may well be

Research Summary

FLEET STREET - THE WORLD OF THE 'PENNY DREADFULS'. SWEENEY TODD FIRST APPEARS IN A 'PENNY DREADFUL' THE STRING OF PEARLS 1846. PURPOSE OF THEM? SERIALISE AND ENTERTAIN THE WORKING CLASSES. CHEAP, THROWAWAY PAPERBACKS. HOW WERE THEY CREATED? PRINTING PRESSES. LED TO A BOOM OF PRINTING AND PUBLISHING. GOTHIC STORIES, FOCUSED ON CRIME. UPPER CLASSES BELIEVED THEY LED TO BAD BEHAVIOUR AND IMMORAL ACTIVITY. EARLY DAYS OF THE PRINTING PRESS, HOW WERE BOOKS AND NEWSPRINT PRODUCED? VICTORIAN 'BEEHIVE' STRUCTURE, AS PER ORIGINAL BROADWAY PRODUCTION.

Application to the Show

PURPOSE OF THE MUSICAL: TO ENTERTAIN AND PROVIDE CATHARSIS. MELODRAMA, GOTHIC, LARGER THAN LIFE CHARACTERS AND IDEAS. QUASI OPERATIC. IDEA OF SWEENEY AND MRS LOVETT BEING A PART OF THIS STRUCTURE. PRINTING PRESS AND MANUFACTURING WITHIN THE VICTORIAN WORKING SYSTEM. IDEA THAT STORIES AND IMMORAL TALES CAN IMPACT PUBLIC BEHAVIOUR. FAKE NEWS AND MISINFORMATION. RULING CLASSES OF THE JUDGE / BEADLE. LOWER CLASSES OF ENSEMBLE AS WORKERS WITHIN THE PRINTING PRESS SYSTEM, CREATING PENNY DREADFULS. MRS LOVETT'S PIES BECOME THE NEWS/PAPER THAT WE CONSUME - WE ARE BEING 'FED' IDEAS BY THE SYSTEM.

Budget

LARGE BUDGET: FULL ENSEMBLE CAST, FULL ORCHESTRA, BESPOKE SET, BESPOKE COSTUMES TO FIT THE PERIOD / IDEA.

Venue and Atmosphere

CONVERTED LECTURE HALL, LACK OF NATURAL THEATRICAL ATMOSPHERE.
HEAVILY RAKED SEATING, PRESENTATIONAL VENUE WITH AUDIENCE LOOKING
DOWN AT THE STAGE, MOST SEATS HIGHER THAN THE STAGE. PLAYING SPACE
VERY SMALL, VERY HIGH STAGE. ONLY ONE CENTRAL ENTRANCE AT THE BACK.
HAVE TO USE THE HEIGHT OF THE VENUE. NO WING SPACE, NO FLY SPACE, NO
PIT.

Practical Elements

MULTIPLE DEATHS. SWEENEY'S 'DEATH CHAIR'. NEED FOR SCENES TO PLAY ON
TOP OF EACH OTHER, FORM DIFFERENT LOCATIONS THROUGHOUT THE SHOW.

Concept Summary

FULL STAGE BECOMES A VICTORIAN PRINTING PRESS. LARGE CENTRAL
PRINTING WHEEL COMPLETE WITH SPOOLS, ROPES, PULLEYS AND A
WORKING PRESS MECHANISM. ORCHESTRA ARE ONSTAGE BEHIND THE
PRINTING PRESS AND ARE VISIBLE THROUGHOUT. SPLIT LEVEL SET WHERE
FULL ENSEMBLE CAN OPERATE THE MACHINERY THROUGHOUT. COSTUMES
ARE ALL MADE OF NEWSPRINT, ALL PROPS INCLUDING PIES ARE PAPER-
BASED, THE WHOLE WORLD IS MADE OF PAPER. WE ARE 'CONSUMING' THE
PAPER AND THE PENNY DREADFULS AS IF THEY WERE PIES, BEING CREATED.
EACH NEW DEATH FEEDS INTO THE MACHINE AND THE POPULOUS BECOMES
HUNGRY FOR MORE GRUESOME STORIES AND WORSE DEATHS. SWEENEY
AND MRS LOVETT ARE OPERATING WITHIN THIS MEANS OF PRODUCTION.

Fig. 1.7 Concept Summary.

bumps in the road as you map your concept onto the show itself. Expect some friction within the script, lyrics and even songs, but the fun of directing is working out these problems alongside your cast. Make sure your cast are on the same page at all times, and reinforce before each rehearsal how this particular event or moment maps onto the overall show you're attempting to create. You should attempt to write a full breakdown ahead of a rehearsal, but be aware this may shift and change. Bring your actors into the process and allow them to find nuances and ways that their characters or intentions can draw out elements of your concept you may not have thought about.

COMMUNICATING TO PRODUCTION TEAM

One of the most relevant stories concerns the original production of *Carrie the Musical*. Director Terry Hands of the RSC was in charge of mounting the original production of the show in Stratford-upon-Avon. His communication to the design and production team was to 'make it like *Grease*', referencing the well-known musical that's also set in a high school and shares similar settings with the Stephen King story of Carrie White. Somewhere this was lost in translation and *Grease* became Greece. The design and costumes then became white tunics, more at home in the ancient Greek world of a Sophoclean tragedy, the complete opposite of what was originally intended. This anecdote proves the point that effective communication in your conceptual ideas to the full production team and cast is needed to follow through effectively. The best way to do this is to share your work and bring everyone along with you from the start. Whether this is through presentations, images, videos or frequent check-ins, make sure that everyone understands and you're all on the same page.

CONSISTENCY

Your concept should be air-tight by the time the show is ready to be performed, but part of the joy of the rehearsal process is exploring ways in which the concept can be played with. Maintaining consistency is one of the best ways of making the application successful. Ask your actors if they feel everything is making sense and anything that stands out to them. Even the most least aware audience member will be able to spot holes in your approach and begin to lose patience with a concept that is maybe only ever 75 per cent effective in its delivery. This is true of even the most basic concepts – for example a show that doesn't use props and relies on mime. Many successful productions use mime to convey everyday items that characters may engage with and audiences generally buy into that almost immediately. What becomes confusing, however, is when a character then picks up and uses a pen or pair of scissors after all the previous props have been imaginary and mimed. Why this prop? Is there a reason? What is the significance of this prop? These are all questions audiences will immediately ask, and if there is no clear reason to offer, the concept begins to unravel.

Another frequent conceptual mistake relating to consistency is to do with space. You may be using a non-naturalistic set with just a door frame to signify an entry point. One character may 'knock' at the imaginary door, another may walk straight through it and another may mime opening a physical door on a hinge. An audience will be confused if there's a lack of consistency within the concept and you'll immediately lose them. Think through the internal logic and establish key rules within your concept that work and remain consistent throughout.

ACT 2   Directing Process

Welcome to the Rehearsal Room

This next section is focused on the director's process and will take you through the act of staging and directing the show itself. From working with actors to running the full show, this section should be your go-to for understanding the core elements of your role within the rehearsal room and the active role of direction. As the rehearsal process is underway, I'm beginning with a simple list of Top 10 tips for directing amateur actors. If you do nothing else, commit these to memory, read them before each rehearsal and be free to add your own. I've included simple summaries under each one, but each of these tips will be unpacked in more detail throughout the coming sections.

Top 10 Rehearsal Tips (in no particular order)

1. Be prepared and on time

As we've discussed elsewhere, preparation is the key to directing. Never turn up to a rehearsal not knowing what you're doing. At the absolute least, read the scene on your way to rehearsal, re-read it, jot down thoughts and know what you want to achieve. The second your actors sniff out that you are unprepared you have lost them and it will be an uphill battle to win them back. The same with being on time and STARTING on time. Establish discipline from day one and remain consistent.

2. Don't touch actors

Under no circumstance should you touch your actors without their consent. Dragging them across the stage and moving them into position is never welcome. It shows a breakdown and laziness in your ability to communicate. During a dance number or staging rehearsal it may be necessary to try and move actors into position, but should only be done if vital. If you must, ask consent.

3. Don't give line readings

Similar to the above, reading a line to an actor to demonstrate how you would like it to be said shows a breakdown in your ability to communicate. It's lazy and the second it is done takes away authority from the actor and breaks the relationship between you. It may be easy to read a line as you'd like it said, and many will do this subconsciously. It never helps. I'll discuss ways of getting around this in later sections.

4. Begin each rehearsal with a warm-up

Amateur actors are coming from all walks of life often at 8 pm on a Thursday evening after a day of work / childcare / home and life stress. Don't just dry launch into a scene or number – devote 5 to 10 minutes before you start to bring the room together, set the tone and mentally get your cast in the same collective space. I promise this will make the world of difference in how your rehearsal then unfolds.

5. Don't lose sight of your vision and concept

If you've done your homework and your vision and concept is strong, this should be easy. While rehearsals will pull you in different directions and many times challenge your concept, see this as friction to be overcome. A solid concept will overcome any rehearsal room challenges, and if you're lucky the challenges you meet will only strengthen it.

6. Amateur actors are amateur actors

Even if you have experience of working with professional actors, you have to remind yourself constantly that amateur actors, however experienced, are amateur actors. You may find yourself directing ex-pro, 'resting' actors or those who have trained. If so – fantastic. But in this relationship, they are amateurs. This means they are not being paid to be in the rehearsal room (usually the opposite – they are often paying to be there), which shifts the dynamic. This is not their job; in most cases this will be taking place alongside their job. They have lives that may interfere with your rehearsal schedule. They may be late, they may have childcare issues, they may get sick. Whilst you can certainly treat amateur actors in the most professional way possible, you have to remember that in most cases this is a hobby and an extra to their lives, albeit a very enriching one.

7. Write everything down and make active notes

There's nothing worse than a director who changes their blocking and staging week to week. Again, actors will forgive this once or twice, but the second this becomes a recurring feature of your style you will lose the faith of the whole company. Encourage actors to write down their blocking once agreed and make active notes at the end of each rehearsal. Remember what you have set, what you have said and what you have promised. Create 'rehearsal reports' (more on these later).

8. Encourage collaboration

That said, being overly prepared and prescriptive in your blocking can feel restraining for an actor. Try to enter each rehearsal with an open mind and let your actors bring ideas to you. Rather than start a scene by telling everyone strict blocking, encourage discussion about the scene, the actions and the events at each moment. Directing a scene should be a conversation with actors, never a one-way lecture on where to stand and when to raise your eyebrow.

9. Measure out your stage

If you remember anything from this book please let it be this. It's a simple and easy task at the start of each rehearsal that establishes the playing space and is perhaps the most helpful thing you can do for your actors. Even if you can't have a stage manager on hand to tape out the set at each rehearsal, the very least you can do is measure the width of the playing space and mark it with chairs. It will make your life 100x easier and your actors will thank you for it.

10. Say 'Thank You'

This may sound like a rather obvious tip and something you should be doing without thinking, but you'd be surprised how many people ignore this simple appreciation of thanks. Growing up at various drama, dance and music schools we were instructed to never leave a rehearsal room without thanking the director, the pianist, the choreographer or anyone else involved with the rehearsal. This should extend to you. Thank the cast, the rehearsal pianist, your fellow production team, the person who turns up to open the door of the church hall. Remember – everyone involved in amateur theatre is doing this for nothing. Your thanks means everything.

Beginning a Rehearsal

How you set the tone for a rehearsal will differ from personality to personality. One of the best pieces of advice I can give is to maintain consistency. Amateur actors bring with them a whole world of experience, anxieties and hang-ups into the rehearsal room, most of which will not involve you, so providing a consistent, and supportive environment will help put actors at ease.

The First Rehearsal – Setting the Tone

Think of actors as being within your care throughout the process. Remember, amateur theatre is as much about the **process** as it is the **product.** No one will care how good a production was, how much money it made or how many NODA awards it won if the process to get to that point wasn't enjoyable at best or traumatic at worst. Don't be that director who is so focused on the final product that they forget about the process.

The first rehearsal is your opportunity to say this to the cast and present your idea for not just the show but the process as a whole. Remember, people are choosing (and often paying) to be part of this process, giving up 3 to 6 months of their lives and working around work shifts, childcare, travel and so much more. This is your opportunity to thank people for their commitment to the casting process, repair any bruised egos or missteps along the way and present yourself as the calm flight attendant and also captain that they'll look to as you work together to bring the show to life. Never be fearful of reinventing yourself. You may have directed countless shows, with this company or others, or worked with the majority of the cast before. This doesn't mean that your approach and style can't change. Be honest, open and, above all, democratic in your approach to establish a company that will hopefully embrace your style and vision and work with you to achieve the shared goal.

I would call a first rehearsal as close to the casting announcement as possible. This will help build on the momentum from auditions and allow you to introduce the whole process to the company with the show still fresh in their minds. The post-casting period is often the trickiest part of the whole production process as you and your team will be managing disappointments, fielding questions about ensemble tracks and even reassuring those who find themselves in principal roles that the show will be a success. For some in the ensemble, this may be a raw rehearsal as they come face to face with those who maybe got parts they wanted to get, inviting judgement and potentially more questions related to the intricacies of casting. It will likely be the first time the company is seeing each other together and it will suddenly all feel very real.

Your primary role is to provide a hard-reset for the company, which may include yourself. This is a fresh experience and one that everyone is entering into on the same footing, and it's important to bear that in mind. You may have done the same show before with two or three of the cast for example. Save those stories for the pub after rehearsal. This moment is not about history, it is about the **present** and you need to work hard to make that be felt by the whole room in this important rehearsal.

As well as resetting interrelationships within the company you should also attempt to do this yourself with the cast, rebalancing any issues that may have arisen during the casting process. Use this rehearsal to re-establish yourself in this role and present positively your vision for the show. Thanking everyone for their acceptance, briefly explain the casting process and that your production team are delighted with the assembled cast. Avoid going into individual cases or making sweeping statements about the process, usually things like, 'we could have cast this show three times over', 'any one of you could have been a principal role', 'we had to turn away so many talented people for the ensemble' and so on. Instinctively you may feel that statements like this will bolster a cast and make them feel genuinely lucky to have made the final cut, but rather than sound positive, statements such as these can come across as shallow and oddly patronizing. A simple thank-you for their participation in the process is all it takes and avoids your words getting twisted, fed-back to unsuccessful auditionees and even being used against you in situations further down the line. Since it's important to remember too that there may be some actors who, after this rehearsal, decide in fact the show isn't right for them or that the role offered just isn't worth the time they are being asked to devote to it. In many ways this first rehearsal is as important as your pre-show meeting or pitch to the society, at this point people are still weighing up the cost / benefits of the experience and impact it will have on their lives, most of which you can't control. At the end of the day people will make their own decisions and I encourage you to be gracious and accepting of these. This first rehearsal is your final sales pitch and hopefully the start of a productive and creative working relationship.

Establish Your Values

I would ask yourself at this point to sum up what your *key values* are and commit these to paper – ideally the notebook you bring to rehearsal so you are faced with them every time you start work. It is up to you whether you share these with your cast. You may find they are personal and the process of sharing them is potentially exposing. I would encourage you to share them if you can – ideally at this first rehearsal. These values will guide your behaviour and approach to directing a show. There will most likely be crossover between these core values and the ones you commit to in wider life, but their application in terms of the task in hand will be telling.

For example, mine are the following:

1. **Professionalism**: not to be confused with the distinction between amateur and professional, this extends in practice to time management, organization, efficiency and how you communicate and speak to the company.

2. **Process as well as Product**: ensuring that the process remains as enjoyable as the final result and remembering the shared goals of why everyone is in the room together.

3. **Creativity**: remembering we are creative humans who can harness this skill for problem-solving

PERSPECTIVE – AMATEUR THEATRE DIRECTOR, CHRIS ADAMS

The tips I wish I'd been given when I started directing are: firstly, don't cast too many people! You may be blown away by the talent you see at auditions and be tempted to add a huge ensemble, but be realistic. Having 35 people crammed onto the stage will be distracting for your audience, and your time and focus will be spread thinner in rehearsals. Secondly, encourage your cast to discard any pre-conceptions of the story and their character. Many of them will be familiar with cast recordings and YouTube videos and they may be tempted to recreate those performances. The joy of amateur theatre is that you are often forced to think outside the box and be creative! Finally, keep things social. Your company will bond more effectively if they know and trust each other. Everyone is there to have fun, so make sure you balance the hard work with some social activities too. Your production will benefit if everyone looks like they're having a good time!

Schedule

Take some time to think about how your first rehearsal should run in order to give a solid introduction as well as generate excitement for the upcoming process.

Table 2.1 shows a suggested schedule for the first rehearsal. I would always start with a full company call that involves as many people as possible, ideally with as few NAs ('not available') as you can achieve. The first hour will be a time to expand on all of the above, as well as introductions to the full creative team. This may be a time to give practical information about rehearsals, where to park, access, and so on. Be aware of overloading at this point, or if you do, make sure you follow up with important information in an email.

Having the time to talk through the show in moderate detail will help the cast understand your process and ideas as well as sell them on your overall concept. I find visual aids very helpful – you can share your notes, research and mood boards that you have created to demonstrate your commitment to the process and to establish your general principles for the show itself. Make sure everyone on the team gets to speak and introduce themselves, even those who may not be at rehearsal full time or around until the end of the process. Getting the cast to see the number of people involved with the production will add to the 'it takes a village' mentality that drives successful amateur theatre so each person understands that there are many people devoting their time and energy to the project as a whole.

After some icebreakers and introduction games, you may want to take an informal break. Sometimes refreshments are provided, other times people are encouraged to

Table 2.1 Schedule for the First Rehearsal

Time	Required	Location
7.00 pm	Full company: Meet and greet with full cast and creative team. To include set model, production concept and general introductions	Main Hall
8.00 pm	Icebreakers	Main Hall
9.00–10.00 pm	Full company with MD, vocal warm-up and learning opening song / final song / company song	Main Hall

bring and share their own snacks. I would make sure the final part of the rehearsal is productive in terms of learning something. More often than not, this will be a large company vocal number, usually an opening song, closing song or finale. This will help your MD get a sense of the room and how quickly people pick things up and also how people will work together. Something joyful (if possible) that breaks the back of the number and sets the tone for the rehearsal process and helps everyone end the first rehearsal with a sense of achievement.

Rehearsal Room Charter

I find that establishing a simple set of rehearsal room guidelines early on will help you in building trust as well as showcasing the style in which you want to work. While you don't want it to appear too constricted, setting expectations will calm nerves for the whole company and probably answer a lot of lingering questions that the cast will have but may feel uncomfortable asking. Remember, a lot of cast members will want to know: will this project be worth their time, will they have fun in a safe environment and will the end product help showcase them in a way that they are proud of? I like to frame these guidelines as a form of mutual expectation. If the cast follow their side of the bargain what they can expect from you is:

1. Organization and preparation so their time won't be wasted
2. Not being called when not needed or for just small amounts of time
3. A fun experience in which everyone works together towards the same creative goal

For this to be achieved, you will ask the following of them at rehearsal:

1. **To turn up on time and be ready to start at the scheduled time.** Understanding that sometimes life gets in the way, agreeing on a system of alerting the production team of any issue in a timely manner that will allow things to be rescheduled if needs be, or moved on the spot if people are simply running late.

2. **To enter the space ready to work and use the time effectively to get the most out of the rehearsal.** Understanding that rehearsals have significant costs attached to them and every extra hour can chip away at a budget in terms of room hire or rehearsal pianists. Being ready to work and socializing in breaks and either side of the rehearsal is key to getting the show up and on its feet.

3. **Phones and electronic items to be placed on silent.** It is perhaps too much to ask in 2024 for phones to be turned off and put away, but at the very least their use should be minimized so as not to create distraction. Many people record their vocal tracks on their notes apps and so on, and so phones do have their use in the rehearsal room, but you shouldn't be aware of people having conversations and scrolling through TikTok.

4. **Appropriate footwear and clothing should be worn according to the rehearsal schedule.** Mainly for safety – dance numbers and so on should command a certain rehearsal uniform that allows actors to move uninhibited.

5. **Respect other actors.** A rehearsal room is a place to make mistakes and rehearse, not to expect perfection. Mutual respect between the whole cast is incredibly important and understanding that each actor is on their own journey is key.

6. **Closed / open rehearsals.** You should mark on the schedule if any rehearsals are closed rehearsals as otherwise people can assume they are all open. Usually I invite actors to attend any rehearsals they wish – that may mean turning up early or staying late to watch a scene. This can be an important part of the learning process and sometimes it can be helpful to have others (silently) in the room, so long as they don't provide any distractions. However, this is not always fair on the cast members rehearsing, so I would keep an active dialogue as to which rehearsals will be closed. Sensitive scenes or difficult scene work may fall into this category. Use your judgement and communicate with your actors as to their needs and schedule open / closed rehearsals as necessary.

Handling Conflict

For the most part the rehearsal room will be a happy and productive place where you collectively enjoy working towards the same shared goal. There can be times, however, when tensions fray and conflicts happen. The most important thing to do is remember that this is amateur theatre – you are not saving lives. There is very little that can't be solved calmly, diplomatically and with a positive outcome for all parties. If you've set out your rehearsal room charter and your personal ethics, you should be able to bring the full company with you, but that doesn't always guarantee it will always be smooth sailing. Managing a rehearsal room and company is similar to a school teacher working with mixed ability students and keeping everyone focused and moving forward together whilst dealing with issues that arise, factions and insecurities.

INSECURITIES

Tension usually arises in rehearsal rooms as a manifestation of insecurities. Actors will have different levels of insecurity and apprehension during rehearsal, which you may find heightens the closer you get to the production. Lashing out, snapping and trying to correct you are all examples of misdirected insecurity. Whilst a lot of the time this may not be your fault, it's within your collective interest to identify and resolve these issues the best you can. It could be that the actor is frustrated at not knowing their lines as well as they thought, which puts them on edge and means they're unintentionally sharp with you or other actors, or they may be feeling insecure in their blocking, anxious about their costume or trying to maintain their vocal health. Try not to take things personally – you will likely be the focus of their misdirection but stay calm and don't rise to their level. If necessary, break the rehearsal immediately and allow everyone some time out to cool off. If the tension has occurred from a scene, break and try something different. Attempt a different song, repeat a different scene. Don't linger on that moment, instead diffuse and come back to it.

GOLDEN RULES

Do not shout. Do not belittle. Do not show off or flex your ego. Do not highlight errors or dwell on mistakes. Take a beat, take a breath and don't react until you have assessed the full situation. Don't rise to anything in the moment. Don't talk about cast members to other cast members and avoid being dragged into conversations that you wouldn't be comfortable with everyone hearing.

The most effective thing to do is establish a clear procedure early on for any issues that may arise throughout the rehearsing of the show. This may be a committee member or company manager who can act as a neutral body to resolve any issues, meaning the integrity of your directing work and the process don't get caught up in other issues. Outline this from the start and be open with the company on how they can communicate issues. I would also encourage regular check-ins to take the temperature of the company and allow a space for concerns to be aired and discussed. This can be done in an adult and controlled way that encourages feedback. It could be something as simple as a group pause at the end of rehearsal and asking if anyone has any questions or concerns and if everyone is happy with the work you have done that rehearsal. Much like not going to bed on a fight or with unresolved tension, I try not to end a rehearsal on a sour note. Resolve what you can and identify anything that you need to return to, but allow the cast space to share their concerns and assure them you will come back to them on anything that requires it.

Remember to also look after yourself. You will need time and space to let off steam – perhaps to other members of the production team or maybe to friends and family not connected to the show. Try not to hold things in – if you have concerns or problems, identify the best person to hear these and find a resolution.

Rehearsal Technique

The primary goal of each rehearsal is clear – you're working towards a shared vision and deadline – that of putting on a show. The timeline is therefore set and it is your responsibility to guide everyone to that finish line as successfully as possible. Start each rehearsal by reinforcing that shared mission, recapping where you are within the schedule and focus minds on the task in hand.

Warm-Up

Establish a warm-up routine that works for you, the MD and the choreographer. I know that being pushed for time and the practical stresses of a rehearsal schedule can sometimes force you into ignoring a warm-up, but I guarantee that beginning with a simple, short one will pay dividends and allow a collective focus. Depending on what the rehearsal is covering, a longer physical warm-up may be required by the choreographer or vocal warm-up from the MD, so it's worth agreeing this in advance and factoring into your plan. Amateur actors will each have a different view on warm-ups – some will hate them and find themselves turning up late on purpose and others will refuse to sing full-out unless they have a vocal warm-up. It obviously depends on the roles people are playing and the demands of the rehearsal itself, but don't be afraid to put your foot down and establish a routine.

The main reason for insisting on a warm-up is to bring a collective energy to the room and focus minds on the next few hours. Use it as an opportunity to set expectations for that session, explaining to everyone what you hope to achieve by the time rehearsal ends. This helps actors know where they are going, so no surprises turn up and they know their time won't be wasted. You can even use it for a minute of 'parish news', any important updates from the production team and things the cast may need to know.

Amateur actors are coming to rehearsal often after a day of work, commuting to the rehearsal venue, handing childcare, cooking dinner, balancing life-work stress and so on. Rehearsals will no doubt be in the evenings after probably a very long day and you're expecting actors to focus, learn new things and sometimes leave themselves emotionally raw and vulnerable during scene work. Professional actors rehearse during the day when our minds are more focused and ready to take in something 'new'. With an amateur rehearsal schedule you're battling against natural instincts and it can be hard to get everyone on the same collective page.

Examples of Rehearsal Warm-Up Exercises

EXERCISE 1: PREPARATION

Ask your company to stand in a circle, filling the space. Join the circle yourself and encourage your production team to also be a part of the collective session. Begin with a simple relaxation exercise, inviting the actors to 'shake off the day' and release themselves from the stresses they may have brought in with them.

- Close your eyes and breathe in for 10 beats and out for 5. Repeat 3 times.
- Roll shoulders up to your ears and exhale, sending them down sharply. Repeat 3 times.
- Roll shoulders and neck to the side, being careful with speed.
- Roll arms overhead in circles getting larger and faster. Start forwards and then go backwards.

- Shake out the stresses of the day – begin by shaking feet and move up through the body getting more and more aggressive until the whole body is moving.

Extend this exercise as you see fit. This can be developed through isolated body warm-ups, stretches and even extended into a vocal warm-up depending on the intended outcomes of the rehearsal. Even completing the most basic version above, in just five minutes, will help bring everyone into the same collective space and be ready to work, having relaxed their body and unpacking the stress of the day.

EXERCISE 2: MENTAL EXERCISE

Following the short physical exercise, extend into a moment of reflection.

Remain in the circle with eyes closed. Ask the company to mentally pack up their 'baggage'. This may be anything from work stress, emails that hadn't been sent, family conflict – anything that distracts from the moment. Encourage them to visualize this 'baggage' and any stresses of the day and lock them away for the next 2 to 3 hours.

Ask them to strongly visualize the reason why they are there in the room, what is their reason for being in the show? Ask them to place this thought at the centre of their mind and force it to overcome anything else currently clouding their mind. When they open their eyes, in their own time, they are in the room with that thought at the centre of their mind and are ready to begin rehearsal.

Having prepared everyone mentally and physically for the rehearsal it's a good idea to explain the structure of that coming rehearsal and establish what you hope to be achieved by the end. Ask the cast if they have any questions, any reflections since you last met or anything that could potentially get in the way of this new rehearsal succeeding. Keep it short and positive, but address any concerns people may have at that moment.

EXERCISE 3: FOCUSING ON CHARACTER

With the cast assembled in 'warm-up' mode I often use this as an occasion to extend it slightly into an exercise that allows them to build and develop their charac-ter or characters. It's important to stress that finding a character is something that is cumulative over the full rehearsal process and may not offer immediate access to the actor. Repeating an exercise such as this as a warm-up before a rehearsal will encourage actors to play and experiment before getting into the weeds of the libretto and songs. It also allows a creative connection between principal perform-ers and ensemble, democratizing the space and dismantling the hierarchy that's naturally in-built to the show's structure.

Building your character

This exercise can be done for any show, be it a realistic musical with well-defined characters, a show where actors are expected to 'create' their characters or those with more fantastical and well-known characters. It gives the element of choice to the actor and puts them in control, using it as a workshop that can then be brought into more formal scene work.

- Have the actors walk around the room at their natural pace, in their own world, avoiding others. As they walk, ask them to visualize their character in front of them, specifically thinking about the way that they **walk.** Ask them to make a choice about the walking style and gait. Is it heavy? Is it laden? What part of the body leads them? What's their natural posture and speed?

- When you clap your hands they have to become that character whilst still walking, thinking about elements of their characters that they know that may affect their choices. As well as walking, think about how they hold themselves. Which part of their body is dominant?

- Explain that they can experiment and make choices to find something that feels right for them and their character. Tell them that they are currently operating at a 5 on a scale of 1 to 10; 1 being the closest to their natural self and 10 being the most exaggerated version of the character they can achieve.

- Experiment by moving up and down the scale, getting them to exaggerate and minimize these character traits. Encourage play and fun, starting within their own world and then extending it out to incorporate others in the room and their relationships between them.

Doing this exercise repeatedly allows actors the chance to 'play' with their characters and discover them outside of blocking or scene work. Get them comfortable with the idea of 'accessing' their character as quickly and efficiently as possible. Sometimes having a simple action, the twitch of a nose, a posture, a style of walking that helps connect them into the character with ease will allow them to effectively go between their real selves and their character during rehearsals. Have them identify, write down and solidify these traits and 'access points' as to commit them to memory.

EXERCISE 4: STATUS WARM-UP

Should time allow, another company warm-up exercise concerns status within the world of the show. Relative status should be something that you discuss regularly, being aware that it will no doubt shift and change at different moments of the show.

- Shuffle a deck of cards and give everyone in the room a card. Explain that Aces are high and feel free to include Jokers, but place them at the bottom of the status tree.

- Once everyone has seen their card, ask them to silently arrange themselves in the room in a straight line, from highest status to the lowest. Obviously people will only know their own status, so it's up to everyone to act and behave in relative terms to the status to establish within the room who is 'high' and who is 'low' and who is in between (and where).

- Set a time frame of a few minutes and countdown to ensure they make decisions and stand on the line.

- Once settled, ask them to each show their card to the room and see if they managed to stand in the right order. You can discuss the behaviours of each card in the deck relative to each other, and how this translates to showing this on stage.

- Next, repeat the exercise but without the cards. Ask the company to think about their characters (if they have multiple, their 'key' character) and do the exercise again, forming a line from high to low. Ask them to do this in silence first, then open it up to discussion. It will be interesting to hear their thoughts, especially as they may well all have quite different ideas about their character in relation to others.

- Depending on the show, you may be able to repeat this exercise at different stages of the show, Act 1 or Act 2, which will allow you a chance to discuss the differences and changes as the show progresses.

The two exercises above are examples of warm-up exercises that you can do at different points in the rehearsal period. Beginning a rehearsal with one of these will help focus the minds into the world of the show and allow you to break out into the rehearsal that's upcoming.

PERSPECTIVE: A MUSICAL DIRECTOR'S TOP TIP, SARAH BURRELL

The most important aspect of the director-MD relationship is communication. Whether it's about when scene change music starts (half way through a sentence, after the last word, on the last syllable, when a scenery or set piece has moved – the possibilities are endless!), what the narrative drive of a song is, or even what the rehearsal schedule is, it's impossible to achieve anything if you don't have open lines of communication.

Structuring a Rehearsal

Unlike professional rehearsals, amateur theatre rehearsals tend to be much shorter, multiple times a week. However the schedule is carved up, time will inevitably feel tight. As well as factoring in time to cover all of the music, staging and choreography, you'll also need to contend with multiple absences and plenty of recapping in order to retain information and build momentum.

The time you take to structure each rehearsal therefore becomes incredibly important. As mentioned above, I prefer beginning each rehearsal with some form of warm-up activity before launching in, so I favour the 'funnel out' approach rather than 'funnel in'. This means beginning a rehearsal with the largest group of people you need and reducing further as the rehearsal goes on depending on what you're looking at, rather than the opposite. The 'funnel in' method I find works better on a weekend, where you can build a rehearsal, usually with principals, leading up to a full company section. This gives people some added flexibility around a weekend, fitting it around their life and work.

Golden Rules of Structuring a Rehearsal

1. **Only call those who are needed**. This seems simple, but this is a common complaint amongst amateur actors. Don't waste people's time by having them sitting around doing nothing. Think ahead and plan. Don't make up the schedule in real time depending on who happens to be in the room.

2. **Be mindful of time and effort ratio**. I always find time to work out where the cast are coming from and how convenient the rehearsal location is for each person. This will help you make decisions in planning. Knowing that someone drives an hour to rehearsal or has to get three buses will help you factor in their life outside of the rehearsal room and not call people for unnecessarily small amounts of time. If someone has one line in a scene or enters near the end and you know you won't get to that bit, don't call them. Add them in later. I use the one-hour minimum rule; you don't want to ruin someone's evening by calling them for anything less than an hour of work.

3. **Make a plan and stick to it**. People plan their lives around your rehearsal schedule and it's important you don't stray from the path. Actors don't like to be surprised – if you say you will rehearse one scene or song don't change that at the last minute. Actors will have prepared, both mentally and physically, for that rehearsal by looking over their lines and blocking. Throwing them off is never a good idea and can lead to a chaotic rehearsal structure that's difficult to walk back from.

Table 2.2 is an example of how I might structure a singular rehearsal wherein the whole cast are called for a production of *Follies* on an evening rehearsal.

As you see, this starts with a full company and 'funnels out' to less of the cast being required. A weekend rehearsal may look slightly different (see Table 2.3).

This weekend rehearsal flips the structure and 'funnels in', meaning you start the day with principals and grow to include the full company. This allows you to end the rehearsal together and summarize what has probably been a week of hard rehearsal, bringing everyone together with a sense of unity. One of the biggest complaints you may hear from the company is that they never get a sense of the

Table 2.2 Schedule for a 'Funnel out' Rehearsal

Time	People Required	Covering	Location
7.00 pm	Full company	Warm-up	Main Hall
7.15–8.15 pm	Full Company Young Buddy, Young Ben, Young Sally, Young Phyllis	Prologue / Overture into Beautiful Girls Loveland Quartet	Main Hall with Director and Choreographer Breakout Room with MD
8.15 pm	Break		
8.25–9 pm	Full Company	Putting the Young Quartet into Opening	Main Hall
9.00–10.00 pm	Sally and Ben (Young Sally and Young Ben)	Too Many Mornings (staging and music)	Main Hall

Table 2.3 Schedule for a Weekend Rehearsal

Time	People Required	Covering	Location
11.00 am	Phyllis Ben	'Could I Leave You?' Vocals 'The Right Girl' staging	Breakout Room with MD Main Hall with Director and Choreographer
12.00 noon	Phyllis, Ben, Sally, Buddy		
12.30 pm	As above plus young counterparts Dancers	'Waiting For the Girls Upstairs' (recap) 'Mirror, Mirror' (recap)	Main Hall with full team Breakout Room with Dance Captain
1.00 pm	Lunch		
1.30 pm	Full Company	Warm-Up	Main Hall
1.45 pm	Full Company	Running pages 1–19	Main Hall
3.00 pm	End		

work being done in rehearsals that they are not in. Some shows are written as such that the ensemble never shares scenes with some of the principal performers. This division can lead to a lack of coherence within the company, so I would encourage and schedule in regular show-and-tell type moments where everyone is invited to see what others have been working on. This helps forge a sense of community and breaks down any potential 'us vs them' sentiment that can crop up in companies.

Making Use of Space and People

With any luck, your rehearsal location will have a number of rooms available to you. Usually they are structured around a bigger hall and a number of smaller 'breakout' rooms. It's important to know what you have available and what you are allowed to use. Ask those questions early and plan with your production team for maximum efficiency. Breakout rehearsals are often the most efficient way of working, coming together to showcase or slot scenes together so everyone can see what has been worked on before the end of the session.

It's important to schedule a formal break. Remember, this is a social activity for many amateur actors, so even a 10-minute tea and gossip break goes a long way. I find scheduling this will help avoid questions and keep focused.

PERSPECTIVE FROM AN ACTOR-DIRECTOR, ELISE BETTS

'If I was the director, what would I do?' That's the question I've found myself asking during many rehearsals of shows I've been lucky enough to be cast in. I've never actually considered it a transition from actor to director, but rather a very natural progression. I don't usually consider myself one or the other, I'm very much still an actor but I'm also a director, and each one complements the other. The idea of directing was always intriguing to me, but it seemed to be this overwhelming job that I'd only seen executed by people I considered to be creative masterminds. I found that the answer was to jump in and do it confidently (also … spreadsheets). I was lucky that I learnt things that have shaped my craft from many different directors that I have been fortunate to work with (the author of this very book being one!) I also pride myself on my organizational skills and trust that my ideas are good.

I realized that, in my experience as an actor, I knew a lot of the questions that would be asked of me as a director, so I was able to tackle them before they were asked! Ultimately, it's the people that shape you. I've learnt so much from colleagues, friends and casts that have helped mould me. I am always learning – and I always will be. I will always be grateful for and open to new ideas, new paths and honing my craft with like-minded individuals.

Creating and Establishing Trust

Trust is your ultimate aim, is earned over time and must be maintained across the whole company. From simple acts such as always starting on time, always being prepared and effective scheduling through to how you manage a rehearsal room, actors want to feel like the show is in solid hands from the outset. Building this trust early will keep actors on your side and maintaining it will ensure you're all working towards the same goal.

Establishing a power dynamic but remaining collaborative should be your ultimate aim. More often than not, actors will know you outside of the rehearsal room. You may find yourself in the position of directing and working with friends or even people you don't necessarily get on with socially. In amateur directing it's important to level the playing field so the whole room feels equal. Someone external coming in to watch a rehearsal shouldn't be able to tell your individual relationship with members of the company. This goes from being blood relatives through to being married to the leading actor. You have a responsibility to remain neutral at all times and adopt a rehearsal persona if needs be.

TOP TIPS FOR ESTABLISHING AND BUILDING TRUST

1. **Start on time**: I've said this before and I'll no doubt say it again. I always hold onto Oprah Winfrey's quote 'you teach people how to treat you'. This is incredibly important. If you present as efficient, start on time, remain disciplined and punctual, your cast will naturally adopt this habit and quickly. You set the tone and teach people how to behave through your own behaviour.

2. **Call actors by their name**: this comes down to mutual respect. Aim to learn people's names as soon as you can and make an absolute effort to do so. If you've done a thorough audition process then you'll probably find yourself halfway there before the first rehearsal begins. Learn the names of the full ensemble and not just the principals. Play name games at the start of the first few rehearsals if you need a refresher. Nothing loses trust and respect faster than a person in authority not bothering to know your name. This continues into the rehearsal process – no one wants to be called 'Cinderella' or 'Calamity' for weeks on end. When addressing actors, address them by their names.

3. **Allow time for notes to sink in**: I'll speak more about giving effective notes later, but for now the point is to give your actors space to 'sit' on a note. A lot of people need to work on their role outside of the rehearsal room and count on addressing a note in their own time. Don't push people before they're ready or expect something to transform perfectly in front of your eyes. If a note crops up multiple times, address it in private rather than in front of the company.

4. **Remain calm**: this is sometimes harder to do than you'd think and I'm certainly guilty of not always remembering this rule. Imagine yourself as a flight attendant during turbulence. You have a whole plane of people looking to you for reassurance that things are going to be OK. A director is the same for a company of actors. No matter what problems occur, whether it be at the final dress, a messy tech or a rehearsal issue, you are the one to whom others will look for reassurance until the turbulence has subsided. Keep your cool and don't be afraid to step away and out of the room should you need a moment to gather yourself. The second a cast sees you lose your cool, their trust is dented.

5. **Don't be afraid to say you don't know**: you will be asked a million questions throughout the rehearsal process. Some may be sensible, others less so. I was once asked during a dress rehearsal by a cast member what they should do if they needed the toilet during the show. In your position of authority it will be expected that you'll know the answer to everything people ask you. This will never be true. Don't be afraid to simply say, 'I don't know but I'll get back to you'. Sometimes this is the most powerful way of building trust – a cast will see you as honest rather than someone clutching at straws for an answer on the spot. As long as you answer the question once you DO know, you'll build trust and respect.

6. **Equality**: as I touched on above, establishing an equal rehearsal room is incredibly important. As a director it's your role to level the playing field at every opportunity, from casting and the hangover of those decisions through to deciding who in the ensemble should stand front and centre. Your every decision will be judged and second-guessed and you shouldn't leave yourself open to criticism of favouritism for whatever reason. This extends into the hierarchy within the company, from the leading players through to the ensemble. You should divide your time between everyone as evenly as you can, within the remit of the needs of the show. Don't neglect the ensemble in favour of the principals and vice versa.

HOW TO SPEAK TO ACTORS

The relationship between actor and director should have a degree of formality but not feel overly or explicitly one-way. You need to find a voice and style of speech that remains authoritative but doesn't patronize or sound overly aggressive. You will naturally mix instruction with explanation and questions as you discuss a stage in a scene – be mindful of mixing those three ways of working, trying not to lean too heavily on any one of them. If your tone is too instructive you end up telling and thereby limiting an actor; too much explanation can overwhelm and sap creativity; and too many questions can undermine your authority and waste time. Find a balance and remain wary of how you are presenting yourself at all times. Try not to raise your voice, lose your temper or appear sarcastic – your tone will be monitored at all times as actors look to you for guidance. Be aware of when your tone may be off or misunderstood and correct it in the moment. A simple apology will suffice without dwelling on an issue, moving past it creatively without lingering.

Directing the Ensemble

The history of the Broadway ensemble is fascinating and well worth your time investigating and tracking alongside the timeline of musical theatre's development. In doing so, you'll quickly identify the different 'types' of ensemble and understand why certain shows are written the way that they are, and in turn are more suited to the needs of your society than others. In brief, the potted history of musical theatre divides the ensemble into the following sections:

A BRIEF HISTORY OF THE ENSEMBLE

Pre Golden Age (1933–1942)

Developed from operetta, these shows tended to have a distinct singing and dancing ensemble. In the days of the pre-integrated musical, shows were less narrative
in structure and producers and authors relied on different 'troupes' serving different
functions on stage. It was rare for a singing ensemble to have to dance and vice
versa. Skills were isolated and ensembles were large, similar to an opera chorus
who were less integrated into the plot and had little interaction with principal
performers.

Examples: *Porgy and Bess*, *Show Boat*, *On Your Toes*, *Lady in the Dark*.

The Golden Age (1943–1959)

Throughout this period musicals largely featured integrated books and scores,
meaning the scope for ensembles continued to grow and grow. Most did away
with the idea of dividing the singing and dancing chorus and instead wrote ensembles who had to do both, and in doing so became more integral to both the plot
and the world of the show.

Examples: *Oklahoma!*, *Brigadoon*, *Wonderful Town*, *My Fair Lady*, *West Side
Story*.

Change and Reinvention (1960–1970)

As society shifted away from Broadway as a central pillar of popular culture, so
did the shows. On the surface, ensembles remained similar to before but were
more established and in many ways more integral to the narrative and visuals.
The musical as a form began to wrestle with this change as pop and rock were
heard on Broadway for the first time, from *Bye Bye Birdie* through to shows such
as *Hair*, which dragged counterculture onto the stage, and *Promises, Promises*,
which used a different type of 'sound' in the score and pushed the role of the
ensemble further.

Examples: *Hair*, *Hello, Dolly!*, *Fiddler on the Roof*.

Concept Arrivals (1970–1980)

As Sondheim and Furth's *Company* lands on Broadway the role of the ensemble
shifts again to becoming almost non-existent. Throughout this period writers experiment and push the boundaries further as shows lean darker and more introverted,
shifting the form to invite introspection. *A Chorus Line* dominates the decade and
presents a firm appreciation for the ensemble by placing their story centre stage.

Examples: *A Chorus Line*, *Company*, *Grease*, *Follies*.

Mega Musicals and Sung-through (1980–2000)

As 'the British invasion' lands on Broadway, the role of the ensemble shifts again
to compete with the scale of productions such as *Cats, Miss Saigon* and *Les*

Miserables, as audience expectation shifts to seeing 'more' on stage. Ensembles arguably grow larger again as audiences tend to favour spectacle over substance. Resistance builds in more intimate musicals as a backlash against this commercialism leading to a divide between 'mass market' shows and those targeting audiences with different tastes.

Examples: *Dreamgirls, Cats, Phantom of the Opera, Crazy for You, RENT, Beauty and the Beast.*

Economy (2000+)

As costs grow and the economy shifts, new musicals begin to employ fewer and fewer people. There's a general sense of ensembles shrinking and more labour being included on each ensemble track. In the 1967–1969 season a total of 259 ensemble performers appeared on Broadway, compared with 165 in the 2018–2019 season. Whilst the scale of some shows remained large, roles were covered by a smaller number of people, as a sense of economy became vital to the lifespan of a successful show.

Examples: *Next to Normal, Dear Evan Hansen, Kinky Boots, Shrek the Musical.*

You will have no doubt discussed the ensemble requirements with a committee when choosing a show. More often than not amateur theatre relies on shows that have a larger ensemble, mainly for economic rather than artistic reasons. More 'roles' and bodies onstage translates into greater opportunity for members as well as driving larger ticket sales through friends and family coming to see the show. Whilst there are many excellent 3–5 person-musicals, it is shows with larger ensembles that sell better and provide a greater chance of breaking even or turning a profit.

Non-Audition / Audition Ensembles

One of the first things to establish is whether the company you're working with has an open casting policy when it comes to ensembles. Many societies like to use the ensemble to offer roles and opportunities to the whole membership, meaning that anyone who wants to can be in the show rather than audition for a competitive 'place'. This determines not only the strength of the ensemble but establishes a sense of worth amongst the players that you can harness. In general, human beings tend to work harder at something when they feel they have 'earned' it, and so knowing that you were chosen to be in an ensemble gives a different sense of pride and achievement for being there. That's not to say that a non-auditioned ensemble is less grateful, you may find the dynamic is slightly different.

I've yet to find a society who doesn't struggle to cast men in ensemble roles. Male roles in musicals tend to dominate in a world where fewer men are engaged with amateur theatre, so the balance is always in the men's favour. Whilst many auditions can be cut-throat for female performers, the bar is often lowered for men which can create a differing dynamic.

Types of Ensemble

LARGE 'EXPANDABLE' ENSEMBLE

This is the most common form of ensemble for amateur musical theatre as it's the most inclusive form of performance. From 'Golden Age' shows such as *Oklahoma!* through to modern musicals such as *Shrek* and *Side Show*, they provide ample opportunity for additional players to be added into the show. Not only are they written with large ensembles in the libretto but the world of the show allows you to 'expand' almost indefinitely to suit the needs of your company. Fairy tale creatures, freaks, farm hands and villagers can expand in each scene, hopefully within the limits of the size of the stage, and you'll find this form of ensemble usually is the most diverse in terms of skillset.

FEATURED ENSEMBLE

Many book shows in the Golden Age onwards offered featured moments for ensembles. You may cast an actor in a main ensemble track but be able to 'pull out' specific characters within the show that they cover. *How to Succeed …* and *Guys and Dolls* are great examples of shows where actors can begin in one part of an ensemble (Salvation Army Band) then 'break out' to cover speaking roles within a different set (a gangster or Hot Box Girl). This allows you to utilize different skills within your company and spread the wealth in terms of opportunity, rather than cast someone in one singular small role.

DANCING ENSEMBLE

Certain shows lean heavily on a type of dance that can be separated out from the general ensemble. Shows such as *West Side Story, 42nd Street* and *Sweet Charity* each have 'expandable' ensembles, but at the same time offer scope for specialist dancing ensemble who can be featured in some of the larger moments. This is where you can separate skills and utilize those in the company who can cover these moments, be it an extended tap break, a larger dance or even a specialist fight sequence. Remember – not everyone has to do everything, you can divide and conquer to make best use of everyone's different skillsets.

INTEGRATED ENSEMBLE

Shows such as *RENT*, *A Little Night Music* and *The Bridges of Madison County* offer quite difficult, smaller ensembles than shows from the Golden Age. These tend to be quite vocally specific and place greater significance on individual skills required. Generally they tend to be prescriptive in terms of size and can't be expanded as those above. Their roles are often more integral to the plot and more importantly the vocal tracks – often offering solo lines, close harmony and other elements – mean that they can appear quite demanding, but are ultimately very fulfilling.

Creating an Ensemble 'Track'

As a director you may find yourself constantly extolling the virtues of a role in the ensemble in order to get a disappointed auditionee to take on the role they didn't originally see themselves playing. For many people a leading role is their ultimate aim, and a great deal of disappointment can be tied up with not getting their dream role. Often it takes time to convince actors to take a role in the ensemble, and you should balance yourself between convincing and not begging. If you have worded your audition forms correctly you should already know if someone is willing to take an ensemble role, yet be prepared that in the cold light of day an actor may indeed decide the ensemble is not for them and decline to accept. In this case it's wise to thank people for their time and move on graciously. Don't fall into the trap of over-promising in order to get someone to accept an ensemble role – it rarely ends well.

What you can do, however, is be as prepared as possible when you offer an ensemble role to a performer so that they know at the point of offering exactly what they are signing up for. Refrain from sweeping statements about how many numbers they will be in, how many dance solos and 'featured moments' they will get. You can't promise this to everyone and the chances are you will forget and the actor will remember. When those solos and moments don't materialize, you'll have over-promised and under-delivered in their eyes, which will leave a bad taste all round.

The best way to negate this is to draw up a clear ensemble 'track' from the beginning. A track is the full range of roles that each individual performer will have, that will likely differ from actor to actor. Once you know what and who you are working with, it will pay dividends to spend that time in the early stages drawing up these tracks so you can be specific with those in the ensemble at the point of offer. They'll be more likely to take you and the show seriously if they can visualize exactly what's on the table. You may be able to negotiate a reduced rehearsal period and periods of absence because of this, which will help in your quest to build the best ensemble you can find.

While tracks can't always be fully finalized at this early stage and are often subject to change, drawing them up, however, will help you visualize the ensemble in full and let you see where any gaps are. You can utilize skills seen at the audition and offer actors the opportunity to see exactly how they will be used throughout. Rather than offering a blanket one-size-fits-all ensemble track, talking people through their role in the show will lead to an overwhelmingly greater acceptance response. Not only will this be useful in casting, it'll also be used by everyone from Wardrobe to Sound and Stage Management, so is worth your time creating and updating whenever anything changes.

Table 2.4 is an extract of the female ensemble track I created for a production of *Side Show*. As you can see it's broken down by scene and by individual performer.

Table 2.4 Example of a Female Ensemble Track

Ensemble Member	Scene 1 to 4.1	Scene 4.2 (Flashback) to 5	Scene 6	Scene 7	Scene 8
Sarah Smith	Three Legged Man	Doctor	Three Legged Man		Reporter
Katie Morris	Bearded Lady	Auntie	Bearded Lady		Reporter
Alice Grimes	Half Man Half Woman	Doctor	Half Man Half Woman		Reporter
Regina Falange	Tattoo Girl	Doctor	Tattoo Girl	Dancer	Reporter
Ceri Simmonds	Venus	Doctor	Venus	Dancer	Reporter
TBC Female	Fortune Teller		Fortune Teller		Reporter

In creating the track it's worth bearing in mind the skills of each performer and also spreading the wealth of the performers you have to hand. Go through the show scene by scene and make notes of which roles are included at each section and what exactly is required, both in terms of staging and vocally. Once you have this drawn up you'll be able to visualize who and what is needed throughout.

Tracking out the Show

Using Table 2.5 as an example, I suggest tracking out the entire show in a similar fashion, dividing between the lead characters and the ensemble characters. Lead characters should be defined as those where one actor will play them *continuously* throughout the show and not play anyone else. Ensemble characters may range from unnamed roles in scenes (man, woman) that can be split and allocated amongst the ensemble through to those roles with greater identity that may be featured in one scene or another. Use the list of characters at the beginning of the script to cross reference with your table and start to build a picture of how your ensemble will look.

Once you've done this for the whole show, you'll be able to plot this against the actors you have at your disposal. Take note of costume changes and people being needed in scenes that follow each other, and various logistical questions that may arise.

Doubling

Doubling means where one actor plays a number of different parts, usually featured roles from within the ensemble. Depending on your requirements you may need to double roles or at the other extreme, separate roles that are frequently written to be

Table 2.5 Track for an Entire Show

Scene	Lead Characters Required	Ensemble Characters Required
Act 1 Scene 7 (Tevye's Bedroom)	Tevye, Golde, Grandma Tzeitel	Chorus, Solo Voices, Fruma-Sarah
Act 1 Scene 8 (The Village Street)	Motel, Chava, Fyedka	Man, Woman, Villagers, Mordcha, Avram, Shandel, Yussel, Sasha, Russian
Act 1 Scene 9 (Part of Tevye's yard)	Tzeitel, Tevye, Golde, Hodel, Bielke, Chava, Shprintze, Motel	Motel's parents, Relations, Guests, Four Men, Rabbi

doubled in order to share the wealth amongst the cast. As musicals became more susceptible to tighter budgets, authors began writing doubled roles primarily out of economy rather than any specific artistic reason. Producers are never happy with paying people to sit backstage and appear in just one scene, so the act of doubling became common to maximize someone's stage time. There are some examples of thematic doubling, where a role is written to be played by the same actor for both efficiency and narrative links. Cinderella's Prince and The Wolf in *Into the Woods* spring to mind as the best example of this, as The Wolf appears in just one scene. Rather than have that actor sit backstage for the rest of the show, they reappear as Cinderella's Prince. Thematically it tracks that this predatory 'womanizer' fits both of these roles and there's much joy for audiences when they discover the same actor is covering both roles and what this means within the structure of fairy tales and the stories that the characters appear in. Obviously the role can be played by two separate actors without anything really being lost – it gives more people a chance of a featured role and can accommodate a performer who for whatever reason can only attend a handful of rehearsals to enjoy an isolated scene.

In the example shown in Table 2.5, the role of Grandma Tzeitel is often doubled with that of Yente the Matchmaker in *Fiddler on the Roof*, usually out of economy and convenience as the actors are often of similar ages. Again, the parts can be separated out if needs be to offer a wider spread amongst a cast with nothing being lost. Use doubling to your advantage to plug gaps in the ensemble tracks, and if required, secondary roles. It shouldn't be over-used unless it is a conceptual choice. For example the Tooting Pie Shop's celebrated revival of *Sweeney Todd* used a small 11-person cast covering all of the roles, including a doubling of The Beggar Woman and Pirelli, that on paper reads as extremely unconventional. Remember, you do not have creative licence to change any part of the musical you are presenting and must be careful in doubling that you do not breach the terms specified in your contract with the rights holders. If in doubt, check with the licensor to avoid problems occurring later down the line.

Size of Ensemble

Once you've been through the show and tracked the ensemble roles, you'll be in a better position to decide on the size of the ensemble needed. As mentioned above, this may depend in part on whether you're auditioning for the ensemble or having an open-door policy. If it's the latter, you will have to work out the possibility of having everyone on stage all at once and any practical issues that may come from having a large group. It may help to divide the ensemble into different groups outside of the individual tracks. For example, *Shrek The Musical* has a large expandable ensemble that can suit a wide range of performers. As well as the above exercise tracking any named roles or those with lines, making a similar table with regards to the core ensemble roles will be helpful in further assigning parts throughout the production and ensuring you have coverage in every scene.

Core Ensemble Tracks in *Shrek the Musical*

Once again, go through the script and make a table of where every ensemble 'group' appears. In each of the above groups you can have as many ensemble members as your budget and space will allow. This does not mean everyone will be able to be everything. If your aim is to spread out the roles throughout the whole show and allow as many people to be involved as possible you can separate these groups in various ways. However, for reasons of economy you can equally design a core ensemble track that incorporates a mix of these roles. Seeing everything laid out in a table will allow you to create logical tracks that not only provide sufficient coverage throughout the show but will also give a meaningful track to an ensemble member that keeps them busy throughout.

In the example in Table 2.6, the * indicates featured dancing moments where you will want to utilize those in your ensemble with additional dancing skills. Looking

Table 2.6 Track for the Core Ensemble Roles

Ensemble Track	Scenes
Villagers	Act 1 Scene 1
Fairy Tale Creatures	Act 1 Scene 2, Act 2 Scene 7, Scene 9
Captain and Guards	Act 1 Scene 3, 4, Act 2 Scene 2
Knights	Act 1 Scene 8
Skeleton Dancers*	Act 1 Scene 8
Duloc Dancers*	Act 1 Scene 5
Duloc Citizens	Act 1 Scene 5
Rats (tap dancers)*	Act 2 Scene 1
Wedding Choir	Act 2 Scene 9

through the list, consider which groups require strong vocals and potentially a mix of soprano, alto, tenor, bass (SATB) harmony. This will help you start to identify the different ways of breaking down the full ensemble. Based on the above, you could create three tracks that look something like the below:

Track 1 – (Character Featured): Fairy Tale Creature; Knight; Duloc Dancer; Rat

Track 2 – (Vocal Featured): Villager; Captain and Guard; Duloc Citizen; Wedding Choir

Track 3 – (Dancing Featured): Fairy Tale Creature; Skeleton; Duloc Dancer; Rat Dancer

Having these identified as soon as you can after the auditions will not only help you present cast members with an honest and realistic vision of what they can expect in the show but will also help you as you begin to schedule rehearsals. When drawing this up, look at the availability chart to track large gaps of notified absence which may help your decision when assigning tracks and groups.

Older shows, such as those from the Golden Age, may have much simpler ensemble tracks and won't require as much breaking down from the start. However, I would advise you to do a similar task so you can see exactly what the shape of the ensemble will be.

Core Ensemble Tracks in *Oklahoma!*

As you can see from Table 2.7, in a show such as *Oklahoma!* the ensemble is much less defined and, instead of multiple groups moves as two groups – male and female. This is standard in many musicals of the period and even many contemporary musicals. Rather than change multiple characters throughout the show, the ensemble tends to stick to one character, appearing and reappearing in different scenes throughout the narrative. They tend to move as a pack and are expandable as per

Table 2.7 Core Ensemble Tracks in *Oklahoma*!

Ensemble Track	Scene / Song
Male / Female ensemble at the railway station Possible featured dancers	Act 1 Scene 2 – 'Kansas City'
Male / Female ensemble Female ensemble (featured vocals) Male ensemble (featured vocals)	Act 1 Scene 4 – 'Many a New Day', 'It's a Scandal'
Female ensemble (featured vocals) Full ensemble (featured dancers)	Act 1 Scene 6 – 'Out of Your Dreams', 'Laurey Makes Up Her Mind' ballet
Full ensemble	Act 2 Scene 1 – 'Farmer and the Cowman'
Full ensemble	Act 2 Scene 3 – 'Oklahoma!'

your specific needs. Once you have drawn this track up, look for areas where you can create smaller featured moments. In this example, the Dream Ballet leaves scope for different characters in the form of the 'sexy girls' that Jud Fry sees in his postcards that come to life in Laurey's dream. Those roles could involve a core group of dancers that breakout of their ensemble roles and have this character as an addition to their standard track.

Each show will be slightly different but will likely fall somewhere between the two examples above. In all cases, it's important that you track the full show and be secure in what the show requires the ensemble to do at all times.

Communicating with Your Choreographer

In many cases working with the ensemble will mean collaborating tightly with your choreographer. Choreography and dance is an art form that comes with its own very specific language and multiple modes of description. Whilst it's rare for directors to be well versed in French ballet terms or Labanotation, you need to establish a way of communication that works between you, so you can actively describe how a dance should look. I find reference images and videos very helpful in order to show a choreographer the style and tone you're hoping to achieve. Don't just send them a link to the Tony Awards performance of the musical you're directing and ask them to copy that; remember they will have their own distinct style that they want to achieve with the show and won't necessarily want to copy steps that have gone before. Research different styles of dance, especially those outside of the canon of musical theatre and think about how the bodies are moving and the possibility of incorporating elements into your vision.

For some shows, some dances are inescapable, and in some cases written into the contract. For years the only way to license *West Side Story* was to sign a commitment to recreate the choreography. Books with marked-up choreography were part of the rental material and choreographers had to interpret and teach this choreography to their cast. At this stage the choreography becomes a photocopy of a photocopy of a photocopy – the thought of a high school having to contractually 'recreate' Jerome Robbins's iconic choreography is somewhat absurd – so some artistic licence has to be in place for obvious reasons.

Other familiar styles include 'Fosse', 'Stroman', 'Tommy Tune' and 'Michael Bennett'. Your choreographer will likely have their own reference points and will want to decide for themselves if they want to recreate these steps and styles as best they can or instead go down a different track altogether. A production of *A Chorus Line* that doesn't open with Bennett's iconic right-arm, left-arm moment may be seen as being sacrilege, but be aware of asking your choreography simply to replicate a dance from a YouTube video or recording. Instead, think about the ways that you can pay homage to the original style or choreography or moments that simply have to exist in order to satisfy the audience.

SHAPES AND STEPS

When working with a choreographer I sit down and talk about 'shapes and steps'. As a director, I see musical numbers in terms of shapes and want to work with the choreographer on how the number can be built, as well as which characters will be involved. I often start and plot out the song or number visually, drawing on a set plan or similar and communicate any specific shapes I would like them to work with. This may not be your specific skill, in which case feel free to hand over the number entirely, but make sure you communicate any narrative moments that have to be seen and communicated from the start of the number to the end.

It's important to communicate with your choreographer, before they start a number, about WHO and WHAT they have for each number. There's no point in them staging a number with a full ensemble, only for them to later find out that five people can't be in it because they have a quick change and need to be in the next scene. Share your ensemble tracks, as detailed above, and make sure they know if things update or change in relation to who can / should be in each number. It's also important they know what is on stage at that time, what set is present and most importantly, what space they have to work in.

MOVEMENT

Choreography is not necessarily just dance steps. Many musicals use movement and principles of choreography that don't focus just on dance steps but also how characters walk, move and exist in space. Many actors are trained in the world of practitioner Rudolf Laban and his approach to how actors move and communicate. Amateur actors aren't likely to have encountered his work, but I would encourage you as a director to have a working knowledge of his principles, if you can. Think about how your characters walk, hold themselves and move across the stage in a way that communicates meaning, as well as how they dance. Even a musical that doesn't seem like a dance musical on the surface will be enhanced by having a choreographer or movement director working with the cast on how they move in space, adding an authenticity to the world they're inhabiting and helping communicate character. So often I see amateur musicals where little-to-no work has been done on the movement elements, which in turn means the characters feel two-dimensional and untruthful.

PERSPECTIVE: WORKING WITH A CHOREOGRAPHER, BECKY EAST

The role of the choreographer in musical theatre isn't just about bringing physical movement to the stage, but meaningfully advancing storytelling, deepening plot lines and driving character development – this is why a strong partnership between director and choreographer is essential. As a choreographer you have to remember that you're working to serve the production as much as the director. It's not just about coming up with dance moves that look pretty and impressive, dancing should be used as the narrative drive within the overall concept for the show. Think

Creating and Maintaining an Ensemble Character

At this point you'll know the various tracks involved for all of the ensemble players throughout the full show. Some actors may have two to three different characters that interchange and others may have one core central character that they maintain throughout.

CREATING AN ENSEMBLE CHARACTER

The primary thing to encourage your ensemble to do is to own their character. The more ownership they have over their role, the more they will enjoy the experience of bringing the show to life and the more three-dimensional the production will seem. No one wants to feel like they are just a number in an ensemble. If your show doesn't have defined characters it is your job within the ensemble rehearsals to find these and bring them to life.

COMMUNITY

Many musicals are about community and it is within that community that most of the ensemble roles lie. Looking at a traditional structure and shape of a musical in the most basic form reveals how important that community is in creating the world of the show. None of the principal roles can exist within a vacuum. Tracy Turnblad is deliberately written to be different and 'othered' from the community in the same way that Dolly Levi is a heightened operator within the community she lives. Without said community, she would have no one to 'meddle' with and, in turn, no one to contrast with, in the same way that Tracy wouldn't have anyone to appear different to.

The protagonist's journey in most musicals comes from their being an outcast or outlier in the community in which the show is set. Most musicals successfully establish this with a song or scene early in the show that establishes that community so the audience 'read' the world of the show. Quite soon after that is established comes the protagonist's 'I Want' song, in which their principle desire for the rest of the show is portrayed front and centre. It is that journey that the audience then invests in. Through comparison and interaction with that said community, either with help from or a desire to fit into it, the show creates a narrative arch that forms the backbone of the show itself (see Table 2.8).

Table 2.8 Community and Conflict in Musicals

Show	Protagonists	Community	Conflict	Resolution
Oklahoma!	Laurey, Curly, Jud	Farmers, cowmen and ranch hands	Laurey is an outlier in the community having not chosen a man. Jud is an outlier and shunned for being different and reclusive.	Laurey and Curly marry, Jud is killed. The community embrace Laurey and Curly and protect Curly from criminal proceedings.
Fiddler on the Roof	Tevye, Golde, Daughters	Villagers	Tevye's daughters don't fit into the traditional roles and want to marry outside the community. Community is threatened by Russians.	Those characters who don't fit within the traditions of the community are shunned. The community is dispersed to America and beyond.
Hairspray	Tracy, Edna, Penny, Seaweed, Motormouth	Teenagers who 'conform' with looks and styles; the Black community who are repressed in Baltimore	Tracy vows to dance on national television, interracial dancing appears on TV.	The community sees what can be overcome by working together and accepting people of all sizes, races and types.
Honk!	Ida, Drake, Ugly	Farmyard animals	Ugly goes missing after being shunned by the community for not looking and behaving like one of them.	Ugly becomes a swan, teaching the community not to judge based on appearances, but to accept everyone regardless of looks.
Carousel	Billy, Julie	New Englanders, mixed community of different people	Billy is seen as being trouble and Julie is judged for having married him, which creates generational prejudice within the community.	The younger generation learn to not be held back by the mistakes of their parents and that they too can fit in with the wider community.

Note the similarities in each of these cases. The conflict forms the basis of the show with the resolution ending happily in all cases, usually through acceptance of difference.

In doing the above, you'll show your actors the importance of the ensemble in laying the groundwork and foundation for the story. Without 'Tradition' as an opening number, there is little drama to be had in *Fiddler on the Roof*, as the audience won't understand what is expected of Tevye's daughters and why their decisions are so important to the rest of the show. Without understanding the world of Ascot, the Opera and the Embassy Ball, Eliza Doolittle's journey from Flower Girl to Princess won't be affecting or have any level of stakes attached.

Plotting the Ensemble's Journey

Draw a chart that tracks where the ensemble fits into the overall narrative structure. Identify any different groups that appear in each scene, and monitor their purpose at that moment. You should then be able to track the progress of the ensemble and understand how they relate to the protagonist(s) and mark out different stages in their overall narrative journey.

As you'll see from the example in Table 2.9 using the ensemble from *The Music Man*, the purpose of the ensemble develops throughout the structure of the show to act as a backdrop to the narrative progression of the protagonists. In a show such as this, the ensemble is primarily the citizens of River City, which in turn is a large, expandable track from which multiple characters can be drawn.

WHO *ARE* THE ENSEMBLE?

Rather than assign numbers to cast members (Citizen 1, Citizen 2), encourage each actor to think about the community you want to show on stage. This example is perfect to show how much work can be done to shape the full community, from the named characters of Mayor Shinn and Mrs Shinn through to the named characters of the Ladies Dance Committee and beyond.

Table 2.9 The Ensemble's Journey

The Music Man Scene	Ensemble Present	Ensemble Purpose
1.1 Train Opening ('Rock Island')	Salesmen	Introduce the nature of travelling salesmen and con-artist Harold Hill.
1.2 Centre of Town ('Iowa Stubborn / Ya Got Trouble')	Citizens of River City	Show the hostility of the town to outsiders and to each other. Show how Hill manages to whip them into a frenzy as part of his plan to dupe them.
1.5 Gymnasium ('Columbia Gem of the Ocean', 'Seventy Six Trombones', 'Ice Cream')	Citizens of River City	Show the hierarchy in the town and the 'establishment'. Continue the frenzy and show they have been convinced by Hill's plan for a boy's band.
1.6 Street in front of Library ('Sadder But Wiser Girl', 'Pick a Little')	Ladies Dance Committee	Show the gossipy, small-minded nature of the townsfolk, their established power structure and how they have treated Marian in the past.
1.7 Library ('Marian the Librarian')	Readers and Dancers	Backdrop the courting of Harold and Marian.
1.11 Centre of Town ('Wells Fargo Wagon')	Citizens of River City	Show how the community has changed and their excitement for the band instruments and uniforms as they have fallen for the scam.
2.1 Gymnasium ('Shipoopi')	Citizens of River City	Social dance showing the community becoming loosened due to Harold's presence.
2.7 Assembly Room ('Finale')	Citizens of River City	Show how the community have been 'thawed' and come together to accept Hill's 'think system' resulting in his acceptance and their blessing of union between Hill and Marian.

Ensemble Exercises

Exercise: Power Structure

During the first rehearsal or an early rehearsal, ask your ensemble to work as a full group to come up with a visible hierarchy within the ensemble. They should answer the following questions:

1. Who is our community?

2. What do they represent?

3. Who leads our community? Does this change or shift over the time of the show?

4. What is our main goal and purpose?

Ask the ensemble these questions and get them to vocalize their answers together as a group. Use this to discuss ideas within the group and encourage participation from everyone. Try not to lead this too strongly yourself – you should be inviting feedback from the actors as to how they see their roles.

Once these discussions have taken place, ask them to collectively visualize the power structure within the ensemble as a whole. Play the status game described near the beginning of this Act. On the second round ask them to debate their status within the community they have established.

When they have formed a line and debated their status, ask for a freeze-frame image that shows the collective status of the full group. This may be a centralized image or show a triangular structure or something entirely different. Set a time limit for this to be worked out and take a photograph of the result to share with the company and discuss what you see.

Development Exercise: Who Am I?

Usually early on in the process I would ask the ensemble to go away and do some 'homework' on their character within the community that they have previously debated. This is often a good task to set directly following the exercise above, whilst the discussions are fresh. You should encourage the group to answer these questions in their own time and come prepared with their answers written down on a small index card or similar. Depending on the show, this may be a good exercise to do digitally and build a digital 'profile' that fits the world of the show, for example.

Name:
Age:
Occupation:
Marital Status:
Gender:
Sexuality:
Family:

As well as asking for the answers to be written down I would also ask for the cast to find a photo of a person that they can use to visualize their character. It doesn't necessarily have to be photo realistic or suitably period, the idea is that they start to draw a picture of the character in their head who exists and comes to life from the page.

At the start of the next ensemble rehearsal I would ask everyone to share these and briefly present their character to the group. Encourage them to do this in the first person, assuming the role that they have created or are going to play. You can do this one at a time or even better through 'speed dating'. Create two circles one facing out of the room and a larger one facing in. As the circles rotate, each character will have 1 minute to 'speed date' other people in the room, introducing their characters as they go. Use index cards for prompts so that everyone receives the same information. Once you have done a full revolve, share within the circles so that everyone gets to 'meet' each of the other characters.

BECOMING THE CHARACTER

It's easy to be cynical about the level of development an ensemble role demands particularly in relation to principal characters. Some casts may be resistant to this level of detail, but it is your job to communicate why this is important. Think of it simply as creating a 3D picture out of a 2D image. The historical role of the ensemble is to support and move as one and, more importantly, to not pull focus from the main narrative, or as one infamous fictional director said: 'don't pop the head, Cassie'. A committed and three-dimensional ensemble will add depth to your production and will enhance the scenes that they are in, which will be visible to the audience as a whole, either consciously or subconsciously. Whilst knowing what your particular character had for breakfast will usually not translate onstage or 'read', it will enhance the tapestry of the world you're attempting to create.

It's also worth saying that within the world of amateur theatre more focus is often placed on the ensemble due to it holding the vast majority of society members. Most of your audience will be connected to someone involved in the production in some way, with the majority being someone from the ensemble. This results in increased audience attention, so the more work you can do on broadening individuals' role within the scope of the show, the better. Giving your actors ownership of their ensemble role will also result in a more meaningful rehearsal and performance process for them. Rather than feel like a number, allowing them to develop their characters and finding individuality will create more focus and dedication in the company as a whole and provide a richer experience for everyone involved.

PHYSICALITY

One of the questions you may be asked by actors is how they can develop their characters when they aren't given moments of direct and solo communication with the audience. Rather than relying on speech and voice, physicality becomes the most important method of communication for an ensemble in order to differentiate themselves and stand out from the crowd. Whether it be an ensemble of factory workers in *Made in Dagenham* or street vendors in *Brigadoon*, the crowd can be as distinct and unique as possible.

Photo Exercise

- Once you have done the exercise above and each member of the ensemble has their own index card of key stats, ask them to each bring in a photograph sourced from the internet or book that shows a crowd of anonymous people. This may be a crowd that directly relates to the show you are rehearsing or simply a crowd taken at random at any point in history. Share these photos amongst the group and find two to four images that show different and contrasting crowds, or ensembles of people.

- Divide the ensemble into smaller groups and give each group a photograph. Give them 5 minutes to discuss the image, paying particular attention to physicality. Their goal is to replicate the image the best way they can, first as a frozen picture and second as a 'moving' image, where sounds and small sequences of action can be encouraged.

- Get each group to share their frozen image with the company. Depending on the photo, this will most likely be a naturalistic image candidly taken of a group. After the freeze-frame has been established, ask the group to extend their physicality to stretch from a naturalistic centre to an exaggerated version of the character in the photo. Encourage them to extend this to the most extreme version they can manage before relaxing.

- Once every group has shown their images, discuss the similarities in the physicality and what it meant for each of these to be 'extended'. What were the effects on those watching? What was clear? How did it feel? At what point did it become 'too much'?

Directly following the above exercise, centre the group back on the world of the show. Using their individual stats and characters, repeat the exercise above but as a whole group within the world of the show in which you're creating. This may naturally divide into separate groups (for example *South Pacific*: Seabees, Nurses, Officers). If so, you can start with separate images in these groups but quickly move into one full ensemble image. If you're working in a room with mirrors this will work well, but otherwise take a photo of the stage picture and share this with the group immediately so everyone can see the image that has been created.

Occupation

One of the most significant character traits that will affect physicality is a character's occupation. In the community that your ensemble is representing, 'work' will be a major identifier for characterizing the world of the show. *Oklahoma!* features ranchers, cowboys and farmhands; *Hello, Dolly!* features waiters, hat makers, shop clerks and merchants; *Kinky Boots* features drag performers and factory workers. Even if your ensemble is listed as 'villagers', different occupations and social structures will be built into the overall picture of the show that you are trying to create. Make sure everyone in your ensemble has identified their occupation – creating their own if it is not specified – and understands how this specifically relates to their physicality, then ask them the following questions:

1. Describe your occupation in as few words as possible.
2. What are you wearing to do your job?
3. Which body parts are involved with doing your job?
4. What impact does this job have on your body – how you walk, how you stand, how you hold yourself?

ACT OUT YOUR OCCUPATION AND PROCESS

Once everyone has answered these questions and shared with the group, ask them to find a space on their own and show their job in action by miming it. This can begin in slow motion or occur in real time. Ask them to focus on the *effort* involved in the job. Does it require lifting, carrying, holding, moving? Identify these movements and how the body creates and shows these elements of repetition. Put on some background music – not from the show itself, but something that creates a beat or pulse. Ask them to establish a routine of movements that can be sped up and slowed down at your instruction, or minimized / maximized to different scales.

Once they have relaxed, ask the actors to focus on which part of their body they found themselves leading with. How did they hold their bodies and how did this change as the working movements took place? Encourage the group to explore this further by walking around the room at a neutral pace and with a neutral gait. Refer to this as a 'neutral position' and ask them to maintain this, expanding to the full size of the room.

Whilst they are walking, ask them to strongly visualize their character, paying particular attention to the part of the body that they will lead with. This could be a nose, a head, an ear, a hip. Any part of the body they discovered was 'engaged' in the previous exercise. When you clap your hands, they should immediately adopt the form and physicality of their character whilst continuing to walk around the room. The aim of this exercise is for each actor to be able to quickly access their character and go from their 'neutral position' to that of their character as efficiently as possible. Strong visualization, including their chosen physicality, will allow this to flow back and forth with ease. Experiment by clapping your hands to switch between the two positions quickly, varying the speed of the room and allowing interaction between actors as it naturally occurs.

The above exercise can be done at the start of each ensemble rehearsal to allow development throughout the rehearsal process. Encourage your actors to experiment with their physicality until they adopt one that feels natural to their character, but allow them to change this in time as they learn more about the show and their role.

Repeat the photo exercise above, but this time – rather than using an external photo as stimulus – use the world of the show and the chosen characters. Ask your actors to find a strong frozen image of their character, building on their previous work. Their physicality should represent the character elements they have discovered and come together as a full stage picture.

Family

Another key defining element that helps solidify the ensemble is the family relations between them. Many amateur companies will have cross-generational casting, some including children and others with older roles. Once everyone has shared their character profiles, look for links between the characters that can come together to form family units. Think about the make-up of the world you're representing and which units would be most appropriate. The citizens of River City Iowa for example would most definitely sit within nuclear units, where single men and women would have a particular stigma attached to them. In fact, Marian exists as an outsider in the community because she is an unmarried adult woman. Having other women in the ensemble who are similar will take away the difference she feels and make it feel less impactful as a whole. Think about the links that exist between the family units and the opportunities you have within the numbers to showcase these.

Staging 'Iowa Stubborn' with ensemble members existing in isolation would of course work, but think how much more effective it would be to be able to show the expanse of the community as it exists within nuclear family units. Not only would it provide a contrast to Marian who is unmarried, but it would softly emphasize the world in which Harold Hill is about to enter. The same can be said of the 14th Street Parade in *Hello, Dolly!* Showing an ensemble full of married couples dancing together will only emphasize the world that Dolly Levi sees, meaning her realization that leads to 'Before the Parade Passes By' is much richer, as we understand her fear of being alone and her decision to re-enter the world. Communities will also include aunties, grandmothers, cousins and so on, particularly if the world of the show exists to show 'small town' life that the protagonist is more often than not trying to break out of. Considering how each member of the ensemble connects to another will provide a richness and texture that will enliven each ensemble scene and show a tapestry of the community you're hoping to show.

Some musicals may require the opposite of the ensemble in order to show a world of isolation and loneliness that a protagonist is operating within. Musicals set in New York or a big city are often good examples where connections between ensemble members should be deliberately opaque and distant to reflect the world in which the lead characters find themselves. Shows such as *On The Town* or *Saturday Night Fever* require a buzzing city of missed connections and isolation in a world that reflects a form of anonymous chaos against which a lead character can fight in order to overcome their primary obstacle. In these cases, be wary of creating too many connections between ensemble members and always remember that the ensemble should always be used to reinforce the story you're trying to tell.

Musicals are largely built on heteronormativity with traditional narratives focusing on the pairing-off of a lead male and female, often as well as a secondary male-female couple. It's rare to see same-sex ensemble pairings in ensembles for a variety of systemic issues surrounding the time and context of when shows were written. Think about the texture of the world you are creating, especially relating to your context and overall concept for the show itself. Any same-sex pairings within an ensemble, particularly in a show set at a particular time, will make a statement. Think about what that statement is and don't just use it glibly. Drew McOnie's direction of *On the Town* at the Regent's Park Open Air Theatre in London in 2017 featured a same-sex pas de deux during the 'Lonely Town Ballet'. Without changing a word of the script or note of music, an extra layer of ensemble characters was created, opening up a different context and sparking a conversation about LGBTQI+ people in New York in the 1940s. Nicholas Hytner's revival of *Guys and Dolls* at the Bridge Theatre in 2023 similarly featured an ensemble moment set in a gay bar during the Havana sequence. As Sky and Sarah explore the nightlife, Sky takes her to an environment that reads as a primarily gay venue depicting same-sex dancing to which Sarah reacts and starts a physical fight.

Be aware that every choice you make has consequences. In the above example, Sarah's anger towards an ostensibly gay character made me think of her role within the Salvation Army and its stance on LGBTQI+ people in both a contemporary and modern context. In choosing to highlight this moment, Hytner makes an active choice in foregrounding this discrimination, which in turn can give audiences a different 'read' on the character as a whole. If you're directing a show such as *Elf* or *Ghost the Musical* set in the present day, creating same-sex partnerships within your ensemble will have a different effect, so it's important to remember that context is key.

Relationships and Tensions

Once you have begun to build a network within the ensemble community the next step is to create an interconnected web of relationships across the whole ensemble and principal roles. Ask actors to consider who else in the room they know, who they are close to, who they interact with regularly and so on and to vocalize that and share ideas. A show such as *Promises, Promises* or *How to Succeed …* is set largely within the confines of an office structure. This is an easy world for a hierarchy and relationship web to exist.

Invite actors to identify three other people within the ensemble – one who they like and would be friends with; one who they hate, dislike or are scared of; and finally one they either know a secret about or have a secret desire for. This scenario works in almost all ensembles and helps elevate relationships that can be utilized within different scenes to great effect. What you are trying to avoid is an ensemble, in whatever show, existing merely as a block of people with no aim, individuality or purpose. Many shows are written with the ensemble supplying background atmosphere to enhance the narrative in relation to the principal roles. Whilst you don't want the ensemble to pull focus or distract, you do want them to create a three-dimensional stage picture and world that augments that of the story. Ensemble roles are often woefully underwritten in librettos, leaving much open to interpretation and development. Professional actors may find it easier to create their own backstories and narratives that can feed into the overall picture, but in my experience amateur actors can often struggle to know how to make this work and feel realistic and relevant to the story. Posing these questions and asking them to play them at any given time can help give them ownership of their character. Experiment by asking them to ramp these feelings up and down on a scale of 1 to 5. Maybe in their first scene their relationship to someone they dislike is more obvious and is something that softens by the end of Act 1. It may then take a turn and by the end of Act 2 they have transitioned from disliking to harbouring a secret desire for the other person.

This exercise should also be extended out to the ensemble's individual feelings towards the principal roles. You should ask every ensemble character to identify their feelings towards the principal characters they appear in a scene with. This may differ accordingly and should develop throughout the show. It may not be necessary for every single ensemble member of River City to have an immediate reaction to Harold Hill, so experiment with different members of the ensemble softening towards him throughout the arch of the show. Some members of the World Wide Wickets Corporation in *How to Succeed ...* may feel more sceptical towards Finch and his ascent up the corporate ladder, whilst others may find themselves drawn to his charm and charisma at a much earlier point. Again, differentiating these feelings within the ensemble will make for a richer tapestry within the group as a whole and give the ensemble actor more ownership of their character and journey in the show, as well as taking some of the labour off your shoulders.

Improvisation

I'm a big fan of improvisation in the rehearsal room. It's a word that many actors dread and can immediately conjure up feelings of embarrassment, self-consciousness and fear. 'Improv' is well-ridiculed in popular culture, although its roots in performance are well-documented and effective at bringing actions, behaviours and feelings to the foreground. At its essence, the idea is to allow actors space to 'play' without focusing on specific blocking. It's a low-stakes approach to rehearsing a scene that allows scope for characters to be developed, relationships to blossom and feelings to be found organically. As I discuss below in relation to book scenes and working with principals, improvisation allows for the natural behaviours to come to the fore without being distracted by the functions of a scene and specific blocking that can hinder a performance from developing.

Improvisation is not, however, restricted to scenes of determinable and clear actions, which are usually reserved for principals. There is much fun to be had with ensemble scenes that in turn can unlock performances and again create ownership for the actors within a framework that supports the world you're creating onstage. To get your actors used to improvisation, I begin with the below exercise that is done in isolation, before encouraging interaction with other members of the company.

DAILY ROUTINE IMPROVISATION

Ask all of the cast to find a space in the room where they have enough space apart from each other. Ask them to visualize and unlock their character, building on the physicality work above.

Find a pulsing piece of lyric-less music to play underneath. Ask each actor to think about an average daily life in the world of their character. As the exercise starts, ask them to start by beginning their day, improvising and miming at a sustained and regular pace.

Encourage them to act independently, not interacting or looking at others in the room. Control the speed that they walk through their day by guiding them through the following steps, changing as to what is appropriate in the context of the role they are playing. The below is an example you could use for a show such as *9 to 5 the Musical*:

1. Waking up, getting dressed, showered and ready for work
2. Commuting to work, encountering various obstacles in the way e.g. forgetting keys; missing the train; starts to rain; lose their bag; stand in dog-poo, etc.
3. Arriving at work, finding their desk, attending a meeting, breaking the photocopier, getting trapped in the lift
4. Going out for lunch, trying to find somewhere to eat, forgetting their wallet, bumping into an old friend
5. Finishing work and commuting home, getting stuck on a subway, finding that they have left their keys in the office, having to repeat their journey
6. Getting ready for bed, preparing for work the next day.

You will guide them through this daily routine as a collective, varying the speed and intensity as you see fit. The reason I find music that underscores the activity, is so that this doesn't happen in silence and can help drive the action and give a pulse to work with. It doesn't matter how wild this exercise gets or over-the-top the actions are. The idea is that each new 'event' you describe is a surprise and the actors have to react and mime their handling of the situation as their character. What you're hoping to achieve is to make each actor comfortable with thinking on their feet and exploring actions in a safe environment where everyone is too busy with their own exercise to worry about looking at each other. This should loosen inhibitions and get your actors used to the idea of making decisions for themselves.

This exercise can be repeated over and over at different stages of the rehearsal process. Sometimes it works as a nice warm-up activity to engage the full company and re-introduce everyone back into the world of the show. You can be as specific or as general as you would like. Try to keep it somewhat linked to the world of the show so that everyone can begin to attach some elements to their character, but it is largely the thought processes that you're looking to unlock.

IMPROVISING ENSEMBLE SCENES

Once you've introduced the elements of improvisation to your ensemble, move from the general to the specific. It would be time-consuming and ultimately restricting for you to give each member of the ensemble an exact thought, action and behaviour for every moment of a show. Instead you could look at creating a framework and shape within which ensemble members can choose their own actions, behaviours and events within the overall structure of the scene as a whole. This will utilize much of the work described above and will rely on ensemble members having done their work beforehand that they can build on and bring to the table.

Take for example the auction scene in the second act of *Oklahoma!* This is a scene that utilizes the full ensemble in the background, coming off the back of the company number 'The Farmer and the Cowman'. The scene itself holds an important function within the plot that has been suggested from the opening scene where Curly and Laurey discuss the box social and who will bid for each basket. It's important that the scene delivers the necessary tension building up to Curly outbidding Jud Fry so he can save Laurey from being 'won' by him, but only after he has sold his saddle, horse and gun. This is a long scene that relies on careful staging to build and grow tension, with the ensemble acting as a vital medium to show the community in front of which Jud embarrasses himself, leading to the show's conclusion.

Your focus on directing such a scene is primarily the script and the back and forth between Aunt Eller as auctioneer and the various men bidding on the picnic baskets. You should encourage the ensemble to react appropriately but at the same time you want to develop a natural and realistic reaction to the events.

IMPROVISATION EXERCISE

Break the scene down as follows:

> **Setting**: An auction where picnic baskets are being bid upon by men to 'win' a girl.
> **Characters**: A divided ensemble of farmers and cowmen who have come together to raise money for the schoolhouse despite underlying warring factions between the two sides.
> **Event**: The group has to decide how this will be organized, set up the auction and decide on a process.

The natural instincts of the actors will be to stick closely to the script and some will even find themselves saying lines and imitating what they think should be said, according to the book. Encourage them to not worry about the exact events but instead only the key event outlined above. How will they order themselves? Where will people stand? Who will take charge? Who falls into which side of the divide? Who can each person trust? Present this scenario above and ask for them to act it out both physically and vocally with each person contributing to the scene.

Once the improvisation has played itself out, shout 'freeze' and introduce the next action into the group by reading it out. Give them a second to consider and then 'unfreeze' the action and let it continue.

Action: A dangerous and suspicious outsider enters the group wanting to bid on a girl.

Watch as the group decide how to proceed and which direction they choose to take it, before adding the next action:

Action: One of the community challenges the outsider to a duel, with the winner getting to pick their girl.

Whilst this action deviates somewhat from the narrative direction of the scene, it will give the actors enough scope to think through their behaviours and actions as well as their relationships to the characters. Continue the improvisation for as long as it can be sustained, and feel free to keep adding new actions that potentially take the scene in a different direction.

Unfreeze the group and ask them to reflect on what happened during the improvisation. Hopefully they would have all felt loose enough to lean into the exercise and explore their feelings and emotions. What you're looking for is the *behaviour* that each actor found themselves exploring and inhibiting. Ask them the following questions:

1. How did your character feel?
2. What did your character do?
3. How did your character react? For example, did you step up to lead the group, did you recoil, did you shy away from conflict?
4. How would you describe your character's behaviour?

You don't need to necessarily share each of these answers within the group, but ask the cast to really focus on their answers. You may repeat the exercise in the same way with the same actions and events, but this time ask them to behave the opposite way to how they behaved the first time. Ask the same questions again and ask them to identify any new behaviours that they found themselves doing.

Improvisation is about making choices and exploring the limits of these within the scene. You may have found some of the reactions too extreme or over the top, so discuss with your ensemble what worked and any reactions that you would like to harness or refine. If there were specific moments you thought that worked particularly well, highlight those and ask the actors to replicate these or build on them as you begin formally working on the scene. What's most important is to get the ensemble to memorize their behaviour, particularly in relation to each new action, as you will build on this as you block the specific scene.

The same exercise could be done with any show or scene that includes an ensemble. Take for example one of the opening scenes of Act 2 of *Thoroughly Modern Millie*. Millie Dillmount returns to work at Sincere Trust to tell the ensemble of stenographers that she is completely over her love of Jimmy. This propels into the number 'Forget About the Boy' in which the ensemble encourages her to leave her feelings behind. You can replicate the exercise above in the following way:

Setting: An office during working hours.
Characters: Office workers of different rank busily working in a shared space.
Event: One office worker tells the others she has broken off her relationship but doesn't know how to react.

With a simple premise, ask your actors to improvise the event and see in what direction they take it. Are they upset? Do they care? Are they indifferent? Do they like the office worker? Does someone else harbour feelings for the person she has broken it off with? Does someone try to convince her to get back together? Again, try not to be restricted by the needs of the scene as written, which builds to the song and collective claim to 'forget about the boy', encouraging natural reactions and behaviours as though the event happened on an ordinary day at an ordinary office, away from the specific setting of the show itself.

Ask your ensemble the same questions as above, establishing behaviours and what worked for the scene as a whole. Perhaps someone took it in a different direction and convinced the character to get back together with her love. Perhaps something altogether different happened. The important thing is: there is no right answer.

Bringing into the Scene

After improvising these scenes you will be in a stronger position to stage them. Ideally you'll have learned what has worked well and which behaviours occur naturally to the ensemble within their own worlds that they have created. Go back to the scene and begin to stage it as written. This time you'll want to give the ensemble a structure to work in, broken down through the events as written in the script itself.

Go through the scene you are staging and itemize the key events that occur within it (see Table 2.10). Talk the ensemble through the structure of the scene and let them know the framework of how you want them to generally behave and react, as identified below.

The questions will help drive behaviour as the scene progresses. There may be moments in the scene that you want to feel collective and unified, and other moments may be more open to interpretation where variety is key. Identify questions to ask your ensemble in relation to each action, identifying any events that require unanimous answers or collective group-think to focus an audience on a necessary event or moment. In the above example, identifying a moment of maximum tension is key to bringing your ensemble together. Whereas your questions will have invited individual and different responses that create a more natural reaction to the events, the

Table 2.10 The Structure of a Scene for the Ensemble

Event	Ensemble Behaviour Framework
Auction gets started, Aunt Eller is established as the auctioneer.	Rowdy excitement as the auction starts following the dance number and call for unity between the Farmer and the Cowman.
Final two boxes are left and identified as Ado Annie and Laurey's.	What do you know about each of these girls? Do you want to bid on their boxes? Do you know them? How do you know them? Do you have a stake in who wins them?
Bidding begins on Ado Annie's, her father encourages Ali Hakim to bid on it with his gun. Will Parker becomes jealous and tries to counter-bid.	What is your relationship to Ali Hakim as an outsider? How do you view Ado Annie's relationship with Will?
Ali Hakim manages to convince Will not to bid, keep his money so he can then have the $50 needed to marry Ado Annie	Are you invested in who gets to marry Ado Annie?
Bidding begins on Laurey's hamper, Jud starts to outbid others and becomes the likely winner. Aunt Eller tries to stall.	How aware are you of Jud Fry? Have you heard the rumours of why he came to work here? Have you had any interaction with him? Why is Aunt Eller stalling the bidding?
Curly enters to outbid Jud.	Tension begins. Who is going to win her? Why is Jud a threat?
Curly needs to sell his saddle to match Jud	Do you think this is a good idea? Do you want to buy the saddle?
Curly needs to sell his horse to match Jud	Stakes are being raised, focus is increasing. Why is it important that Curly wins Laurey's basket?
MAIN EVENT: Jud is the winning bid, saying he is giving all of the money he has in the world.	What will happen if Jud wins? Is Laurey safe? Is this a fair auction? Moment of maximum collective tension.
MAIN EVENT: Curly offers up his gun, selling it for $18 and becoming the highest bidder. Eller closes the auction.	Moment of maximum tension continued. Collective ensemble reaction to enhance the focus of this moment.
Tension is broken by a call for them to shake hands.	How do you feel? Scared? Nervous? Pleased it's over? Do you have any sympathy for Jud?
Jud pulls Curly to one side to show him the 'little wonder'.	Do you know what the little wonder is from the previous scene? Have you lost interest as the party begins to dissipate?
Aunt Eller calls for music and the party to continue.	Where are you going next, what is your next aim for the party?

ensemble must come together and focus on the moment of tension through stillness, focus and collective fear of what may happen which will enhance the atmosphere for the principal performers and focus an audience on the main event of the action.

Not every ensemble scene will require such detail, but the above is a good example of when improvisation can lead to a collective understanding of the behaviours that underpin a significant moment. Whilst you want to encourage your ensemble to find their own behaviours to play, you will also want to create a structure and framework within a scene to stop it going off in multiple directions. Remember, your primary function is to tell the story and the ensemble are a key part of that and should enhance, rather than cloud, the action of a scene.

Playing Three Words

Another exercise that can enhance an ensemble's sense of purpose and individuality is a simple premise that boils down behaviours to three simple words. Ask your ensemble to find three words that describe and sum up their character. These should be adjectives that are generally easy to understand and convey. They could include excitable, horny, bashful, nervous, lethargic, suspicious, etc. The list is endless. During a run or rehearsal, ask them all to lock into one of these words and 'play' the word to a moderate degree. It's more fun if they don't share with you (or each other) what the word is and in turn they deliver their lines, singing and movement with this word at the forefront of their mind. As long as it doesn't change the material aspects of the character or interferes with either the action or other people it can be a fun way to extend improvisation into a set routine or blocking that otherwise may be falling flat or coming off as two-dimensional. This exercise was apparently used in the original production of *Cats*, as director Trevor Nunn and choreographer Gillian Lynne encouraged the tribe of cats to play a word to keep the show, their reactions and their characters fresh.

Directing Child Actors

It's not unusual for amateur theatre groups to involve a number of child actors as part of the ensemble, or in some cases, in leading roles. Shows such as *School of Rock*, *Oliver!*, *Annie* and *Elf the Musical* all feature child performers and are popular due to the fact they are recognizable titles that bring in audiences. Often the need to perform a show with roles for young people is purely financial; having young people in the cast often means more audience members come to see the show as the extended friends, family and school groups will be more likely to support the production and buy tickets. Try not to make this a driving factor. Speak with the committee about the expectations of the group and how they have worked with children in the past if you are unsure.

Child protection labour laws differ around the world, but in the UK are quite strict in terms of expectations and safeguarding. A child under school leaving age will likely need a child performance licence that must be applied for by the person in charge of the event at least 21 days before the event. Licensed chaperones should be arranged by the company, which in turn will introduce rules and regulations for all involved with the production. The best way to understand what is involved is by signing up for training through the NSPCC (https://learning.nspcc.org.uk/training/protecting-children-entertainment-chaperone-training). There are rules on how many performances a child can partake in, based on their age, as well as regulations on rehearsal hours and any additional work that falls within regular school hours. As a director, it shouldn't be your job to organize this part of the process but you should speak to your producing team about the logistics and make sure that your committee know ahead of time if you intend to involve children.

Children in leading roles may find themselves carrying a huge show on their shoulders. *Annie* and *Oliver!* for example feature many large roles for young performers, which can't take place without them. In many ways the exercises above and below can be used just as they are, but you may find you have to adapt your manner and behaviours. It's important to manage the rehearsal room carefully, especially with a mixed company. You should watch your language and interactions and make sure that the adult company is always aware when you have children's calls by marking them in the schedule. There are many books and resources available that focus specifically on drama games and activities for young people so I would encourage having some of these up your sleeve for every eventuality. Below I've listed some top tips in terms of directing young performers:

Tips for Directing Child Actors

1. **Speak to them on their level**: no child wants to feel patronized or frustrated so make sure you adapt your body language, tone and mannerisms depending on who is in the room. There may be a huge age gap between the oldest and youngest members of your company and you have to guide each of them through the process together. Don't confuse them by referencing theory or instructions they won't understand, instead try to connect with them and make suitable references. They may need more active encouragement to know they are 'doing it right' so always reinforce your ideas, correcting gently but praising frequently.

2. **Offer breaks**: consider your overall schedule and don't rehearse too late in the evenings. Try and start the rehearsals with the young company members and keep them for 1 to 2 hours max on an evening. Make sure you factor in more frequent, shorter breaks to keep the focus.

3. **Be incredibly clear in your direction**: unlike adults who will be willing to explore their roles more independently, children will tend to want very clear and specific direction. Try not to be opaque or vague in what you ask them to do; you may find yourself having to physically place yourself in the scene and demonstrate a lot more.

4. **Repeat, Run, Repeat**: I would always run everything twice as many times as I would with adults. Reinforce the work you have done and schedule time for regular recaps especially if there have been gaps in the schedule. Running scenes over and over, especially if you have different 'teams' of children, will mean they are more comfortable overall. Unlike adults, children tend to enjoy repeating scenes over and over.

5. **Don't compare and contrast**: you will likely have two 'teams' of children sharing the performances across the production. You may even have split the lead roles to fit in with the performance rules attached to young people. You must avoid comparing children, either in front of them or with other cast members. You will naturally have a preference for one 'team' or set of principals but you should never make it clear. Encourage each team to watch and support each other but don't invite conversations about who is better and never hold up one child or team above the other as an example.

6. **Don't apply too much pressure**: in some cases there will be a lot riding on the shoulders of some of the child performers. Don't remind them of this in a nega-tive way, instead celebrate the fact they may be the lead or playing the titular role but in a supportive way. Be mindful of their life outside of the rehearsal room – school, exams, other extra-curricular activities and try not to inflate their role to be bigger than the production itself.

7. **Make sure they enjoy the process**: remember, the process should be fun and enjoyable for everyone involved. You may be shaping a child's lasting love of the theatre. This will no doubt be a formative experience and one they'll remember for the rest of their lives, so make sure this is positive throughout.

8. **Plan for every eventuality**: I would encourage teaching songs as a group to ensure as many children as possible are familiar with the music and words in the event that you may need emergency cover. Children can get sick, lose their voices and even have their voices break in a very short period of time and so I try to cover myself for every eventuality. Split-casting main roles would mean you won't find yourself without a lead should the worst happen. Having infor-mal understudies and other young performers who know the parts well will help you should things go wrong.

Many of the principles above can be used when working with principal actors, but there are a number of different ways you can approach the lead characters and those who carry most of the show on their shoulders.

Directing Principal Actors

Many of the fundamentals and exercises above can be repeated and used with prin-cipal actors and I would encourage working together, as much as you can, as a full company. One of the common problems within the rehearsal process is that there is often a divide between the principals and the ensemble, due simply to the nature of the show and the practicalities of the rehearsal schedule. Your principal actors need a different kind of attention, and whilst it's easy to naturally expect them to require less time than the ensemble, often the opposite is true. I don't think I've ever directed a show where I've managed to successfully spend enough time with the principal performers. Often the actors are more experienced, they may have trained or may have done the roles before. You're probably familiar with the phrase 'the squeaky wheel gets the grease'. In most productions, the ensemble is the squeaky wheel. Principals are too often left to their own devices in favour of co-ordinating the larger number of people. Whilst this may be efficient timewise, you have to create a bond with your principal performers that allows them space to deliver, but doesn't just expect them to arrive performance-ready.

Try not to favour one set of people over the other. The ensemble should never be made to feel like they're draining your time and similarly the principals should never be made to feel neglected. Balancing your time and energy between the two is diffi-cult and requires a lot of diplomacy to make the full company gel. There are many shows where the principals and ensemble simply never appear onstage together, and so may find themselves never interacting, either onstage or off. Relationship building offstage is as important as on, and much of this is cemented whilst actors wait around, take breaks or pause backstage waiting for the cues. This is not only an important time to bond socially, but also as a coherent company, where each can be supported by the other. After all, you're all working on the same show and should be rowing in the same direction.

Some shows are worse for this division than others. Identify this early on, before rehearsals begin and even address it during the first rehearsal. To combat division I would encourage regular check-ins and sharing sessions, using the ensemble as the audience for principal scenes and vice versa. As I identify in the section on schedul-ing, I favour a schedule that allows maximum crossover, so that the two groups can regularly meet, despite maybe working in isolation. Consider how lonely it can be for a principal performer. Whereas the ensemble get to work together, crafting backstories and three-dimensional tableaux, the principals are usually carrying the book scenes and interacting through solo numbers and duets. There is an isolation and loneliness inherent within some roles that can naturally make a performer feel on the outside of a wider group. Spending 5 minutes as you transition from one call to another to share what you have been working on will make all the difference and keep everyone feeling included. As long as this is in agreement with the performers and not too early in the process, it can help tear down walls between the two groups and give you much-needed live feedback that can help shape the performances going forward.

The pressure on principal performers to deliver can be huge, and so having 'show and tell' sessions throughout the rehearsal process, rather than when it comes to runs, will make all the difference. Particularly for scenes that include moments of vulnerability where a lot of pressure is on the performer (Lola in *Kinky Boots*, Rose in *Gypsy*, etc.) it can help the performer feel supported and also helps the ensemble feel connected to the wider pieces of the puzzle you are collectively solving. The key is making sure these happen at the right time – don't make a principal perform their number to the whole cast after one 30-minute rehearsal in the second week of the process. It will knock their confidence and potentially not show them in the best light. Equally, keeping it a surprise or trying to build anticipation for the scene until right at the end of the process will only add pressure to the principal and heighten the division between the two groups. Remember – everyone is on the same side, and it's your job to consistently balance the two.

Table Work

One major distinction between principals and ensembles that I find useful is what is called table work. This traditionally means sitting with the lead actor(s) and simply talking through the script, their characters and the wider themes of the show. This is usually collaborative, and is a conversation rather than a lecture. Remember, your principals are likely experienced and will bring with them ideas, thoughts and feelings that you can use. They may offer a different perspective on their character that you haven't considered. By talking between you, and the wider group of principals, you can explore ideas that help illuminate the show as a whole. Until this point, directing will have likely been an isolating experience. Your head will be spinning with thoughts and ideas, but it's most likely that you haven't yet communicated these ideas or even spoken them aloud. By doing so, articulating your thoughts and ideas and defending interpretations, your understanding of the piece as a whole will develop and harden.

Ask your actors open questions:

- What do you think about XYZ?
- Why does your character do this?
- What does your character want?
- How do you see this scene?
- What is your intended motivation?

Although time may feel precious in a rehearsal room, these sessions will ultimately serve you well in the long run and are never a waste of time. You may feel that you have to focus on blocking a scene right away and that time sitting around a table talking is wasteful, but that is never the case. I schedule these at times when the ensemble may be learning a vocal part or dance. You can continue to have these discussions right the way through the process – ask yourselves the same questions and you'll see how your ideas have changed as your understanding has grown deeper.

Some musicals may lend themselves to table work more naturally than others. Some of the best rehearsals I ever had were working on *Sweeney Todd* and *Nine*, where we sat around for a full rehearsal and just talked. Lighter shows and musical comedies may not feel as easy, but even Shrek, Princess Fiona and Elle Woods have deeper meanings that are worthy of discussion.

Principal Rehearsals – Discussing a Scene

With principal rehearsals, I find that each rehearsal usually begins with a form of table work where we talk about the scene we are looking at and discussing where it fits in the overall context of the show. Before you even think about blocking, you should sit together and lead an active discussion of the scene you are about to look at. Start by reading the scene together, focusing on and identifying key events and actions, making notes of any character points or questions the scene presents.

Questions to ask / discussion topics:

1. Where are the characters, both physically and emotionally? Who is up, who is down and why?
2. Where have the characters come from directly before this scene? Where do they go directly after?
3. Who has the power in this scene? How does it shift and why?
4. What is the function of this scene? What do we learn as an audience? What happens in terms of plot and character?
5. What does Character A want from Character B? How do they achieve this?
6. What are the stakes of this scene?

This list isn't exhaustive – feel free to add as many questions as you feel are needed at this point. The reason for doing this before you attempt blocking is to open up the scene and invite a dialogue with the actors about the direction of the scene as a whole which they can then play with. These questions don't have to be answered immediately, or indeed in this order, and after time they will become natural to you to ask without having to list them. You don't need to write down answers or commit anyone to their answers; the idea is that these things can shift as you play the scenes – there is no 'right' answer, particularly when it comes to elements of behaviour. Your actors may not agree at first with each other, and that is to be encouraged. The aim of the rehearsal is for you to all end on the same page – you don't want a scene where your actors don't agree on who has the power and how that shifts, but the question can be an active discussion for you to explore within the rehearsal itself. In fact, if your actors disagree then you have an excellent starting point to explore within the scene itself.

Your initial discussion may raise questions that you want to identify and work through, which is exactly what they're intended to do. For example, imagine this is the first scene between Mrs Lovett and Todd in *Sweeney Todd*. Directly following her song 'The Worst Pies in London' the pair embark on a long scene that includes exposition for both of them, cementing their relationship and co-dependency. Whilst the scene is very well written, it leaves you and your actors with much to discuss. Who has the power, and when does this shift? When does Mrs Lovett recognize Todd as Benjamin Barker – immediately, midway through the song or at a later point? Does Todd question why Mrs Lovett has kept his razor so easily accessible after all of these years? Does he question why she knows the story of his wife Lucy and his daughter Joanna? None of these questions are obvious, or indeed answered, leaving much open to interpretation. Discuss these moments and look for clues within the text and lyrics that can support your arguments.

Improvisation and Experimentation

Having had these discussions and opened up the scene, you can build to improvising the action and behaviours contained within it. Concentrate on finding the behaviours and different actions that lead to these rather than worry about movement. Put down the script and improvise the scene, both in character and out of it. Encourage your actors not to commit too early to decisions that may limit other decisions. Every choice an actor makes shuts one door and opens a window. At this stage, your actors should keep as many doors open as possible without limiting their possibilities, for both themselves and their scene partners. Your role as a director is at this point to guide your actors through these doors and encourage them to step back through and find a different one to open and unlock.

Often you'll find actors commit too early out of insecurity and it's difficult to encourage them to explore other options, such as vocal inflections, intentions, line delivery and movement. You should explain that at this stage it's a playground and no one needs to get anything right the first time. Actors tend to be perfectionists, and trying to get them to experiment can be tricky, but persist and challenge them. The easiest way to do this is to offer a completely opposite and alternative choice to what they have already delivered. If they've played the scene elated, ask them to do it subdued and suspicious. It may sound counter-intuitive, but getting them to play the complete opposite will make them think and question their initial choices which in turn may throw up something altogether different and possibly revelatory.

Encourage your principals to continue through a section of a scene without stopping to question or second-guess themselves. Ask them to commit to the moment rather than withdrawing or worse self-editing. Even the most accomplished actors self-edit as they go, backtracking on choices mid-flow and breaking character to apologize and say that something hasn't worked. Get them to instead play it out – if a choice is wrong, correct it mid-cause or stick with it to its natural conclusion. At least that way you'll know if it fully fails.

Your job throughout this experimentation is to look for elements that work and 'extract' from the experimentation things that have worked. Discuss with your actors what feels right, what they think worked and what didn't. Rather than tell them how you want something to be played, invite them to bring their ideas and guide them gently towards your overall motives. Beginning a scene by saying exactly what you want, where you want them to move and how you want them to communicate will instead just limit your actors and they will feel constrained, which will naturally reduce their performance and what they are willing to deliver. Unlike directing the ensemble, you have more scope and time to encourage different interpretations and readings of a scene that will ultimately give the principal actors much-needed agency over their roles. One of the most common complaints I hear principal actors have is being made to feel like a director's 'puppet'. You should guide and lead towards a performance but never push or force.

Types of Performer

THE SHY PRINCIPAL

One of my favourite types of actor to work with are those who aren't necessarily used to being a principal role. You may have given someone a chance on a role for a variety of reasons, they may have impressed in the audition or worked particularly hard and for whatever reason, this is their first time playing a leading role after years in the ensemble. Don't underestimate their excitement and their nerves. Work with them sensitively so as to not emphasize the pressure and don't let them dwell on the fact that this may be their first time as a lead. Nurture their enthusiasm and build them up by boosting their confidence, but try not to treat them too differently to other actors they may be working with. I find conversations and reassurance outside of the rehearsal room can help build a rapport and encourage them to ask questions they may be too nervous to ask in the room, especially if they are around other more experienced actors.

THE EXPERIENCED PRINCIPAL

Many amateur theatre companies have experienced members who are used to getting lead roles and playing them over and over again. In certain environments this can make for a difficult rehearsal process, especially if you haven't worked with them before or are directing a show for this company for the first time. Actors who have played the same role in previous productions can have advantages and disadvantages. In many ways, they will always have discovered the role away from your creative vision and carry baggage associated with a previous production. I would always start asking the actor why they are wanting to recreate a role. Perhaps they had unfinished business in terms of the role, maybe they're trying to prove something to themselves and others or maybe it's just a great role they have wonderful memories of doing. Either way, you'll be competing with a version of the past you have no control over. Don't ignore the fact they have performed the role before – but at the same time – try not to reference it throughout the rehearsal process. I would encourage a conversation during table work about their experience with the show but then try and move away from conversations that begin 'last time I did … ' as it will only infuriate you and the rest of the cast. Depending on how open they are, they may be willing to share various 'pitfalls' in the character or role as written, or practical details about entrances, costumes and so on that could create an efficiency, but in general

I would advise them to treat this as a new experience. Theatre is ephemeral and no two productions will be the same. Push them to rediscover the character and not revert back to previous tropes and shortcut their way to unlocking the character, and you can promise them a richer and more fulfilling experience.

THE 'GO-TO' PRINCIPAL

One of the familiar tropes of amateur theatre is that the same people always get cast in the same roles, and, if they are on the committee, pick shows purposefully for themselves, their friends and relations. Whilst there are certainly elements of this in societies, your job is to cast according to who is best suited to the role as you see it. Growing up I saw the same couple play almost every role from Captain von Trapp and Maria to Curly and Laurey whether they were right for it or not – they were just the established leads in the society and whichever show was picked would see them take on the principal roles, regardless of suitability. I would generally try to avoid these societies, but you may well find yourself directing for them, in what feels more like a rep company than an amateur theatre group. Experienced leads in this situation can revert back to type rather than try and explore a character or relationships afresh. Encourage them to push their range and not dial in a performance they've already delivered three seasons ago, just with a different wig and costume. Actors who are consistently cast may not feel the same level of excitement as those coming to it anew, so encourage them to push their own boundaries and 'play' as much as they can in rehearsal.

THE TRAINED PRINCIPAL

Some performers in amateur theatre are ex-professional or resting actors. Some may be in a transitional phase, balancing a variety of work during a slow patch, but still wanting to perform. Others may have trained long ago and left acting behind them to pursue a different career. Either way, these actors will likely come to the room with a degree of professionalism and thirst to be challenged and pushed. Director training focuses primarily on understanding how actors are trained so you can harness that and work with them alongside the 'toolkit' they have assembled. Be inquisitive and ask about their training and experience, without making too big of a deal, else it becomes off-putting to other actors. You should not distinguish between 'professional' actors and amateur actors or refer to them as though they are operating on a different plane to the rest of the company. You'll find that some may be vocal about their training in a boastful way, maybe to help them feel distinguishable against an untrained company, or to create distinction. Don't encourage this. Draw on the experience when necessary but don't dwell.

For all principal performers, try not to take their performance for granted. Whether this is a 'shy' principal who is performing for the first time or a seasoned professional – all of them require and appreciate being told they have done a good job. Don't ignore their performance, even when they finish a song for the hundredth time. Reiterate what has gone well, give praise where it's due but never fall into the trap of overindulging them. As rehearsals grow their performance goes from 'wowing' in the room through to becoming second nature, but the actor still needs to be reassured that what they are doing is good and hitting the mark.

Blocking, Staging and Direction

BLOCKING VS STAGING VS DIRECTION

The three terms above are often used interchangeably, but to me they have quite different meanings. Throughout rehearsals you may find yourself undertaking a mix of the three and I find it important to define the terms so you and your cast are on the same page about what is expected and your method of working.

Blocking: physically placing actors on stage in relation to set and props.

Staging: getting these thoughts and emotions into the body and physicalized / verbalized in relation to the character and other characters.

Direction: understanding a scene and character, searching for meaning and intention. Exploring feelings, emotions and behaviours and how they relate to both events and actions.

Know the difference between each of these words and how they fit alongside each other. Understanding how they have to work together in order for a piece to come to life is important, but you'll need to balance how you work each of them together with your cast.

Not Blocking Too Early – Direct, Stage, Block, Direct Again

In my opinion one of the biggest mistakes you can make with directing principal actors is blocking too early. Blocking (that is telling actors where to stand and move) should come once the initial scene work described above has been done. Too many directors begin a rehearsal by giving exact and explicit instructions on when to move, exactly when to cross, when to tilt their head and so on. You don't need to devote time to this. If you do the above you'll find these moments naturally and your actors will respect you more for not making them feel like chess pieces or battleships. Offering loose blocking can be helpful, beginning a scene by telling actors their playing space or which side of the stage the scene is taking place or any specifics about their surroundings and so on, but never begin a scene by notating where and when they should move before you've let anyone play. Actors hate this. It'll reduce their performance and make them feel as though they have no agency, as well as diluting their trust in you as a director.

Direct, stage, block and direct again is a mantra I work with. Blocking is the dullest part of the process for everyone and if you've done the first two things well, it will fall into place naturally. You may need to refine certain elements in relation to the wider picture – who needs to enter from where, where actors are in relation to furniture and so on – but it shouldn't be your primary focus. I generally go into a rehearsal with some simple blocking sketched out, particularly for larger scenes, but when working with principals my expectation is that it will become clear within the playing. You may wish to begin a scene with a simple piece of blocking (Mrs Lovett is standing behind a counter, Sweeney is sitting downstage on a stool). That should be enough for your actors to begin with. Let them explore when and how they interact and come together, when Sweeney feels right to stand and so on. Actors tend to have excellent instincts and if you've done the work on finding the behaviour, this should come naturally and your time can be better spent on more fulfilling moments of rehearsal.

Blocking Charts

At this juncture I want to shed some light on different elements of blocking to consider as you approach a scene. Obviously this will differ hugely from show to show, mainly due to the demands of your space and the set design, and I won't be able to address specifics. The following will at least give you an overview of things to consider and more commonly encountered problems with blocking.

Figure 2.1 shows a traditional stage layout of a proscenium stage, detailing the main stage positions for blocking purposes. This is a basic layout that identifies

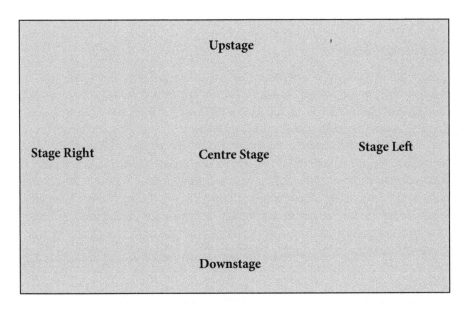

Audience

Fig. 2.1 Stage Layout – Proscenium.

the key areas of the stage that your actors will be operating in. Revisit your notes from your site visit and think about what you learned by watching a show in the space.

- Where is the 'strongest' part of the stage? Think of this in relation to a character delivering a song but also entering and exiting. As Western audiences traditionally read from left to right, our minds and eyes are naturally drawn to action occurring Stage Right before anything else.
- Where is the 'weakest' part of the stage? Is there any section where audiences can't see so well or have worse sight lines?
- What set elements will be in position for each scene, i.e. how much space will be available for each scene? Does this change within the scene itself or song?
- Where does a character enter and exit from? Go back to your 'world map' and think about the direction of each entrance and exit, what's the internal logic of where they have previously been and where they are going to?
- Is your stage balanced? Think of the stage being balanced from the centre, how do you balance blocking across the full stage so that focus doesn't 'tip' in one direction or another?

The best piece of advice I can give is to make a 2D or 3D cut-out of the playing space and experiment with blocking positions ahead of rehearsal. This is particularly helpful when staging musical numbers. In the past I've used everything from pennies to board game markers and even cut out figures to signify cast members and move them around in the space.

Rehearsing in Space

One of the most common mistakes I've found amateur directors make time and again is rehearsing in a liminal space that doesn't reflect the stage experience. From the very first rehearsal you should aim to block and stage scenes within the size and shape of the playing space you will be working in. There may be times, usually during choreography, where it is beneficial to learn something in a wider space before bringing it down, but even this method has significant drawbacks. Depending on your rehearsal room and location it may prove tricky to give your cast an accurate stage size. If this is the case, I would strongly suggest finding a more appropriate venue where you can rehearse comfortably within the stage parameters. We have all been to shows where you can see the cast have rehearsed in a much smaller space as the blocking doesn't accurately reflect the playing space and there is much dead space on the stage that goes unused. It is unfair to expect your cast to 'grow' into a space with just one or two days of tech and dress rehearsal. You should have a show rehearsed with precision so that it can lift from rehearsal room onto the stage in the most seamless way possible.

The easiest way to do this is to always measure out the stage in your rehearsal room. At the bare minimum, you will know the width and depth of the stage. If you don't know this, ask your designer, stage manager or even committee to make sure you have the most accurate information. Many venues will also publish this online, usually on their 'hire us' section of their website where technical specifications and stage plans will usually be available to download. Remember these measurements, write them in your notebook and even better, commit them to memory. Whilst you may not always know the exact size of set detail, trucks or set pieces, you should always know the width and depth of the stage and start every rehearsal by measuring this out.

If you have a stage manager who attends rehearsal, this will usually be their job. Armed with masking or LX tape, ask them to mark out the stage floor plan in as much detail as possible, using different colour tape if possible. Marking up entrances, staircases, raised platforms and so on will also be hugely helpful, although this can be time-consuming. For every job I have had in amateur theatre I carry a tape measure and tape, and turn up to rehearsal 10 minutes early to mark out the stage in the most effective way possible. It is worth the time and the work and your cast will thank you for it. If tape isn't possible for whatever reason, mark out the stage with four chairs, one in each corner. Even this is better than nothing and expecting your cast to guess where they are in relation to each other and replicate it at each rehearsal.

Set Models and Demonstrations

If you're lucky enough to have a designer on board you may be able to show the cast a set model, or set diagram of the production. If you're working with a set company they should have images and set plans of what they are providing. Showing these to the company as early as possible and sharing the images on your social media groups will help them visualize the production and make sense of staging and blocking. Where a scale model is available, have this at the rehearsal to show the cast and demonstrate any moving elements. If you have a 3D drawing or even 2D diagram, talking it through with them will be beneficial. It will help the whole production feel much more alive even at this early stage.

Rehearsal Number Line

After years of turning up early armed with a tape measure I came up with a portable way to ensure that any rehearsal room we were working with could be efficiently and consistently marked out. Having worked on a number of productions where rehearsals took place in several different halls and venues, having something to hand became necessary to establish each room in the same way every time so the cast could get used to a level of consistency. I took inspiration from seeing shows on

Broadway where the 'number line' was visible from the audience whilst looking down at the stage. Along the front of the stage runs a number line, beginning with '0' marking the centre and numbers going up in 2 every 2 feet in both directions. The numbers face the cast on stage so they can see at ease their marks and locations on stage throughout.

As staging has developed in professional contexts, some productions now use electronic versions of the line or rely on different colours to indicate their location horizontally across the stage. Dance-heavy shows also use vertical lines to indicate the depth of the stage running from downstage right and left to upstage on either side. The effect then gives a grid system to the stage, somewhat like a battleship board, where people, set and properties can be placed.

Whilst you're unlikely to need a line to work in such detail and your blocking to be that specific, using a horizontal stage number line means that you can always have the full measure of the stage in feet and also have your cast know where they should be stood within their blocking. I have made numerous versions of these in the past which are portable and can be transported easily to each rehearsal location. I then roll it out along the front of the stage space, with the numbers facing the cast and the space is transformed.

Observing Rehearsals

Many directors panic about where to place themselves within the rehearsal room environment. I always favour a small table at the front centre of the space, giving

---

MAKE YOUR OWN NUMBER LINE

Numerous companies online now sell versions of this, but I have found it cheaper to always make my own.

1. Order a roll of black vinyl, usually around 30 centimetres in width. This comes in different sizes, I find you'll rarely need more than 45 feet.

2. Buy white wheelie bin stickers in varying numbers, working out how many of each number you will need by drawing it out on paper first.

3. Roll out the vinyl the full width and lay a tape measure alongside it. Mark out every 2 feet with a small piece of white tape.

4. Stick the numbers to the vinyl 2 feet apart, starting at '0' in the centre of the roll. I mark the divisions out, usually from 2 to 20 on either side, depending on the width of your stage in feet.

5. Securing the line with tape at both ends and in the centre keeps it in place, and the white numbers are easily seen against the black vinyl roll, creating an easy to use and transportable number line that can be used time and again.

a clear overview of the full playing space. I find a table vital for me and a team to make notes, hold scores and scripts and other items we may need such as blocking charts. There are some who find the concept of the table as a visual demarcation between cast and creative team, acting as a 'boundary' that restricts collaboration. I would say that whilst that can certainly be true, it presents an organized room and shows the cast that the director and team are serious in their approach to the rehearsal about to take place. That said, I find a lot of the time when working with actors I am more present in the space and in front of the table, or communicating on my feet in their space. However you feel comfortable, it is important to understand that a table is a physical boundary, which on occasion can provide much-needed distance, but does go someway to reinforcing traditional hierarchies that you may be fighting against. Consider using a mix of methods by establishing the table as a base and working with actors on your feet and in 'their' space.

It's important when measuring out the stage that you establish the onstage and offstage areas of the space you are working in. Cast who are waiting in the wings or watching should be out of the way, to the sides or behind the table. It's important that these spaces don't 'bleed' as it will be distracting to those working in the space as well as to you and the production team. I also encourage that bags, coats and personal items are kept out of view so as not to get lost in the space or provide distractions. As you get closer to the performance, the stage manager will most likely assemble a props table on the side of the stage where actors can get used to collecting (and returning) props that are needed for each scene. Trying to keep the space as organized as possible and free from clutter will keep everyone mentally together in the space, allowing for the most constructive rehearsal environment.

PERSPECTIVE: ADVICE FROM A STAGE MANAGER, SUZANNAH CHEEK

It really helps if a director has a clear vision of what they want the production to be like before the rehearsal process starts, this includes: having realistic ideas of how they want the set to look, being aware of the possibilities and limitations of the space that they are working in and then being able to communicate these ideas but being open to other people's ideas. Visuals can help us understand the effect and feeling the director wants to portray. The director needs to understand that there is a budget and be open to suggestions of how to create similar effects without it blowing the budget. Think about how you want to split the budget and not just blow it all on a 2-minute dance number.

Effective communication is key, keeping everyone in the loop with any changes that are made. Rehearsal reports are really helpful especially when members of the team / cast are not at rehearsal. Holding regular production meetings to ensure everyone is on the same page and so you are aware of what each department is doing, which then avoids last-minute changes if you decide you don't like what has been produced. Having a rehearsal schedule mapped out helps everyone to try to stick to it and manage rehearsal effectively in order to maximize the time you have. Often, there can be a divide between creative and technical team members; encourage your tech team to come to rehearsals so that they get a better understanding of the production and feel like they are part of one team, not two split teams.

Blocking and Staging Charts

To keep a record of blocking I use a mixture of charts, which ultimately turn into 'the book' that the stage manager will keep on file and will be referred to throughout the tech and performance process. Working with the designer or production team I will create a blank diagram of the stage, which I can replicate either digitally or in print. This usually holds the basic set and stage space onto which I can draw and notate for each scene and keep track. Figure 2.2 shows an example of where I've used these charts in the past to keep track of different scenes. I will mark actors and track their movements as well as draw formations of actors and set pieces as they develop throughout a scene. These can be colour coded for each actor so you can easily track progress and be as detailed or minimal as you would like. For ensemble-heavy shows I tend to use more diagrams to keep a handle on where everyone is, working mainly in pencil to update the inevitable changes that will occur throughout rehearsal.

There are many digital ways to make this experience efficient and helpful to the full cast, although you will no doubt have your own preference over physical vs digital copies. When working with physical files I usually photograph them and upload to the cast shared drive so everyone has access to them and can keep track. They can be handy as references for cast members who may have missed a rehearsal or want to keep their own 'books' to keep track of tricky movements throughout the show. Using an iPad or tablet can be a great way of digitally drawing these files that can instantly be shared and updated, so you may find that this is your preference if you're more tech-savvy. Either way, making sure you write down blocking in a way that makes sense to you, to be able to recall and communicate it at a later date, is key. What you'll want to avoid is a constant back-and-forth with actors claiming that you previously told them to enter from stage left, or cross on a different line and so on. Write everything down and document it in a way that makes sense to you and then you'll efficiently be able to keep track of the show.

Stage Write is an app that was created for directors and choreographers which offers a digital app-based product that does this work for you. It's a relatively expensive solution and can be quite fiddly to get your head around, but it does the job and allows you to share it with the cast and production team seamlessly. It's generally

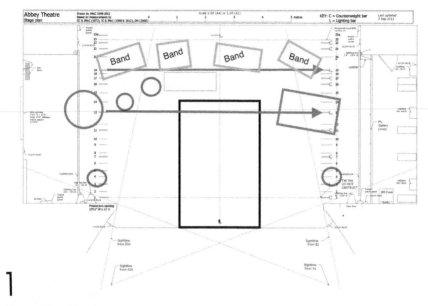

Fig. 2.2 Blocking Chart.

designed for professional theatres and productions that are very tech-heavy or have lots of movement. They offer a free trial, so I recommend you download and have a play with it to see if it's something you think you can work with.

Directing a Book Scene

As discussed above, a book scene refers to the section in a show that contains script and dialogue rather than music that is sung. There are exceptions of course where the music and lyrics intertwine their way through an otherwise spoken scene, but for the purpose of this section I will focus on directing the dialogue. Many of these moments include underscoring and music that creates the tenor of the scene and musically connects or joins the parts of the musical together. As previously noted, the strength of book scenes vary widely from musical to musical – some shows feature strong dramatic moments with realistic dialogue that develops character and advances plot. Others are more functional and are designed to keep the momentum of the show going and will offer you less to work with. Oscar Hammerstein was, in my opinion, a beautiful and underrated dramatist who knew exactly how to structure a musical, balancing song, lyrics and dramatic function. It is his musical *South Pacific* that I have chosen as an example to highlight how to approach two different examples of book scenes; one that leads up to and includes music and lyric and another that is strictly dialogue-only.

THE BOOK

Fundamentally in musicals the book scenes (i.e. the spoken dialogue in between the songs) are largely functional, written to move the action forward usually from one song to the next. The history of musicals shows a wide variety in the quality of books. It is often said that it's the hardest ingredient to get right in a musical out of the score, lyrics and book and is frequently cited as a reason why many musicals fail. Read any contemporary review of even the biggest shows throughout the twentieth and twenty-first-centuries and pick out how many times the book is mentioned. Rarely will you find it spoken about in positive terms; more often than not it is blamed for the reason the second act in particular falls apart. Stephen Suskin's excellent book 'Second Act Troubles' gives a fascinating overview of the problems found within musicals that famously and infamously flopped, and more often than not it is the book that is to blame.

Musicals such as *Gypsy*, *West Side Story* and *Guys and Dolls* are often quoted as having 'strong' books when considering hit musicals of the twentieth century. Sometimes the lyricist writes the book (e.g. Oscar Hammerstein), other times the composer (e.g. Meredith Wilson, Lionel Bart) serves triple duty and is credited with the whole show. Whilst this may be a unique talent reserved for only the most celebrated in the musical theatre community, it is largely restricted to shows that are seen as 'through-composed' such as *Hamilton*, *The Last Five Years* and *The Wild Party* (La Chiusa). The frequent misunderstanding that shows without spoken dialogue don't have books mistakes the work of the composer in writing the show and constructing it as a complete piece. As musicals grew more complex in form and style during the 1970s and beyond, more weight was placed on 'the book', which in turn saw more playwrights turning their attention to musicals. Neil Simon (*Sweet Charity*); Alfred Uhry (*Parade*); Terrence McNally (*Kiss of the Spider Woman*); Dominique Morisseau (*Ain't Too Proud*); Quiara Alegría Hudes (*In The Heights*); Lynn Nottage (*MJ The Musical*) and James Graham (*Finding Neverland*) are all writers from across decades who made their names with straight plays before eventually collaborating on a wide variety of musicals. The trend very much continues today, as producers look to hire writers from legitimate theatre to pre-empt and overcome problems that could occur in terms of structure, style and dialogue. As audience tastes become more demanding and musicals themselves continued to push boundaries, more weight became placed on the importance of the book and the creation of shows to an expected theatrical standard. Even more trivial shows that you may be directing such as *9 to 5*, *Shrek the Musical* and *Made in Dagenham* feature books by established and celebrated playwrights – Patricia Resnick, David Lindsay-Abaire and Richard Bean respectively.

Structure

Musicals are structured in generally similar ways, more often than not in a two-act structure that pulls from traditional narrative structures of a three-act drama. In reducing a musical to two acts, the exposition and development are included in Act One, ending on a problem or choice for the lead character that leaves the audience going into the interval with a reason to return. More often than not a secondary character or secondary plot arc is introduced midway through the first act, which in turn is resolved before the main plot is tied up at the end of the show.

MUSICAL STRUCTURE

A. Exposition – introduction to the world of the show

B. Introduction to the protagonist and their 'want' or essential need

C. Development or 'problem' in relation to the protagonist

D. Secondary Plot – introduction of another central couple / character or device

E. Decision point – Act break

F. Reintroduction to the problem

G. Further Development

H. Secondary Plot tied up

I. Resolution / Denouement

Table 2.11 is a somewhat simplified structural analysis; it shows, in the main, how the musical's book is designed to move the story forward within a pre-established structure. As musicals progressed in terms of style and content, the established structure that audiences came to expect was developed and changed as writers began to push the boundaries in relation to the form. Concept musicals for example use an inherently different structure, usually in relation to their overall premise.

Take the musical you are directing and plot the key structural points within the show as a whole. Draw up a list of scenes and take note of where the musical numbers fall and which scenes don't include any songs.

Table 2.11 Key Structural Points within the Show

Structural Letter	*Crazy For You*	*Hairspray*	*Damn Yankees*
A	We are introduced to the Zangler Follies in New York.	'Good Morning Baltimore' – establishing Tracy's world.	The world of baseball is shown in relation to married spouses, 'Six Months out of Every Year'.
B	We learn of Bobby Child's want to be a dancer on the stage and the pressure from his Mother and Fiancée to be a banker, 'I Can't Be Bothered Now'.	Tracy's desire to dance on TV and the restrictions in her path, 'The Nicest Kids in Town', 'Mama, I'm a Big Girl Now'.	Joe Hardy can't express his love for his wife Meg and is more involved with the Yankees winning the Pennant, 'Goodbye Old Girl'.

C	Bobby is sent to Dead Rock Nevada to foreclose on an old theatre where he meets Polly and falls for her, 'Shall We Dance?'	Tracy falls in love with Link, 'I Can Hear the Bells', and is stopped by Velma from dancing in the Corny Collins Show.	Joe Hardy sells his soul to the devil, Mr Applegate, to get his wish. Transformed into a young baseball player who can save the team, 'Shoeless Joe'.
D	Bobby disguises himself as Zangler in order to win Polly and to hide from his Fiancée who has followed him to Nevada. The town needs to attract more visitors to save the theatre so decides to put on a show.	Little Inez and Seaweed are introduced, bringing the themes of discrimination of Black dancers and singers into the main narrative. Secondary couple of Eda and Wilbur established.	Applegate's assistant Lola is introduced as a foil for Joe, tasked with seducing him or living her life in eternal hell, 'A Little Brains, a Little Talent'.
E	No one attends the show, put Polly encourages everyone to not be negative as she sings 'I Got Rhythm' as the real Zangler arrives in Nevada, which will lead to a comic problem for Bobby.	Tracy and cast must decide whether to accept the status quo or rally against it with protest action, 'Big Blonde and Beautiful'.	Joe becomes a baseball star and the Yankees are on track to win the Pennant. Applegate fears losing his bargain, releasing false information about him that leads to him being forced into court and having to decide if he will go back to Meg.
F	The town is reminded that they face closure unless they find more visitors and money.	'The Big Dollhouse' shows us the women locked up following their protest march.	The baseball team contemplates how they will win without Joe as fans are furious at the news, forcing Joe to go back to Meg, 'The Game'.
G	Bobby is sent back to New York after finding out that Polly is in love with Zangler, not him.	Tracy and Link declare their love to each other as they escape. They all plan to integrate the Corny Collins Show, 'Without Love', 'I Know Where I've Been'.	Joe faces a trial as Applegate stalls the proceedings to try and ensure he defaults on his deal.

H	Bobby's Fiancée falls for a local innkeeper, taking that problem off his hands.	Edna and Wilbur affirm their life together, 'You're Timeless to Me', and Edna gains confidence in herself.	Lola meets Joe in the place of 'Two Lost Souls' where the world's most famous lovers meet. Applegate considers simpler times, 'Those Were the Good Old Days'.
I	The town puts on a good enough show to attract more visitors and save the theatre. Bobby and Polly declare their love for each other and everyone ends happily together.	Tracy and her group take over the Corny Collins Show with Tracy being declared the winner of Miss Baltimore. They celebrate the show becoming integrated from now on, 'You Can't Stop the Beat'.	Joe hits a home run, securing a win for the team but turns into his older self. He proclaims his love for Meg which in turn destroys Applegate and Lola who can't fight true love.

Take a look at the scene structure below that Hammerstein devised for the first act of *South Pacific*:

ACT 1

OVERTURE

Scene 1: The Terrace of Emile de Becque's Plantation Home

DITES MOI

A COCKEYED OPTIMIST

TWIN SOLILOQUIES

SOME ENCHANTED EVENING

DITES MOI (REPRISE)

Scene 2: Another part of the island

BLOODY MARY

Scene 3: The edge of a palm grove near the beach

THERE IS NOTHIN' LIKE A DAME

BALI HA'I

CABLE HEARS BALI HA'I

Scene 4: Company Street

Scene 5: Inside the Island Commander's Office

Scene 6: Company Street

Scene 7: The Beach

I'M GONNA WASH THAT MAN RIGHT OUTA MY HAIR

SOME ENCHANTED EVENING (REPRISE)

A WONDERFUL GUY

Scene 8: Company Street

Scene 9: Inside the Island Commander's Office

Scene 10: Another Part of the Island

BALI HA'I (reprise)

Scene 11: Inside a Native Hut on Bali Ha'i

YOUNGER THAN SPRINGTIME

Scene 12: Near the Beach on Bali Ha'i

Scene 13: Emile's Terrace

WONDERFUL GUY REPRISE

THIS IS HOW IT FEELS

I'M GONNA WASH THAT MAN ENCORE

FINALE ACT 1

The first act alone is made up of thirteen scenes, of which six feature no songs or music. Ten songs are introduced in this act and reprised in functionally different ways throughout the full structure of the act. You can identify by just looking at this breakdown where the book scenes are placed – largely in the middle of the act during the 'development' section of the show where the various narrative strands are coming together. *South Pacific* has a somewhat unique structure compared to contemporary musicals and again when compared to Hammerstein's own work. As you can see, four songs and a reprise are included in the long opening expositional scene, including the 'hit' song 'Some Enchanted Evening' which will go on to be reprised throughout both acts in different ways. It takes until Scene 2, approximately 25 minutes into the first act for the 'establishing' song to begin ('Bloody Mary') in which we are introduced to the wider world of the musical and the secondary and tertiary characters. Hammerstein front-loads the early scene not only with some of the score's most memorable melodies but also with a record number of events and actions where information is learned by both the central characters of Nellie and Emilie and also the audience. As we will examine below, the internal structure of the book scene is designed to carry each of these musical moments, flowing some-what seamlessly between the numbers.

Whilst unusual in a wider context, this structure fits in with Hammerstein's own boundary pushing structures that make up his most famous musicals in his wider body of work with Richard Rodgers. *Oklahoma!* for example begins quietly with the offstage voice of Curly McLain singing 'Oh, What a Beautiful Mornin' as he enters Aunt Eller's farm before a similarly introspective scene featuring just three characters. *Carousel* opens with a pantomimed prologue that evolves into a smaller expositional scene between Carrie, Julie and later Billy, leading into the famous 'Bench Scene' where the pair fall in love. Hammerstein as a dramatist not only is responsible for establishing what the twentieth century came to describe as the 'integrated' musical of the Golden Age but at the same time was the first to break his own rules and expand audience expectations.

The structure of the first scene of *South Pacific* leads many critics to find fault with the show as a whole due to its 'small' start that features too many songs in a small, single scenic space. It's worth considering the wider context at the time of writing, as composers of the era found themselves often writing for specific stars. In this example, Mary Martin and Ezio Pinza were the major draws so audiences would not have been too upset by seeing (and hearing) their material so early in the show. Other musicals are designed with 'star entrances' to do the opposite and prolong the arrival of the above-the-title star to build anticipation, especially with a property with not as much to offer as *South Pacific*. British director Trevor Nunn experimented with the structure of the piece in his 2001 National Theatre revival which starred Lauren Kennedy and Philip Quast. Rather than open at Emile's home, the musical begins with the ensemble of Seabees singing 'Bloody Mary', placing the introduction of Emilie and Nellie after the introduction of Cable, Billis and Bloody Mary. Whilst officially sanctioned by the Rodgers and Hammerstein Estate, the structural change was largely seen as a negative move and subsequent productions have stuck with the author's original intentions. Remember – structural changes can only be made by approval with your licensing company and are highly unlikely to be granted for an amateur production.

Function

One of the first things to ask when approaching a book scene is: what is the scene's function? As you can see above, scenes can include one song, many songs or no songs. Work out how many the scene has and ask yourself the question of why that is the case. Traditionally, book scenes without music were often written to cover a set or costume change and would often happen far downstage in front of a curtain or drop. These are sometimes referred to as 'traveller' scenes in older librettos. More often than not, they follow directly on from a large production number where many cast and scenic items will have been involved. Often their function is very much practical rather than necessary. Look out for these scenes and mark them in your script. Often they can read as being clunky and somewhat dull, other times they are used to quite clearly move a situation along and feature one character sharing information with another or learning something that will propel the action forward.

QUESTIONS FOR EACH SCENE

1. Who is in the scene? List the characters.

2. When was the last time these characters came on stage? Where have they come from? Where are they going?

3. How many characters speak in this scene, and who do they speak to?

4. Does anyone feature in the scene without speaking?

5. *What is the function of this scene?*

Write the answer to each of these questions at the top of your notebook or in the margins of your script. Try and have a clear answer as to the function of the scene as the writers have intended it. Few scenes are wasteful and unnecessary. To work out the function, ask yourself how the scene travels from A to B:

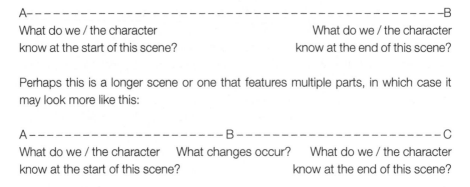

Perhaps this is a longer scene or one that features multiple parts, in which case it may look more like this:

In each case, ask yourself:

1. How did we get INTO this scene?

2. How do we get OUT of this scene?

The answer to this may be very simple; this is not a trick or a challenge. The most obvious answer is usually the right one.

- Why are the characters here?
- What is their 'need energy' entering the scene – i.e. what does each character want?
- What obstacles are in the way for the character to achieve this goal?
- What do the characters learn at the end of this scene? What do the audience learn at the end of this scene?

After answering all of the above, the function of the scene should appear clear. Take for example Act 2 Scene 4 of *West Side Story*:

1. **Who is in the scene? List the characters.**
   A-Rab, the Jets, Anybodys, Anita (enters mid way through) followed by Doc.

2. **When was the last time these characters came on stage? Where have they come from? Where are they going?**
   Anita has last been seen in the previous scene in Maria's bedroom where she has learned about Maria and Tony sleeping together. She tells Maria that Chino has a gun. She is tasked with going to the drugstore to warn Tony and telling him to wait until Maria comes for him. The Jets have last been seen together in 'Gee Officer Krupke' following The Rumble in which Tony killed Bernardo.

3. **How many characters speak in this scene, and who do they speak to?**
   The Jets speak to each other to discuss their plan. They speak to Anita as she enters, leading to her attempted rape and 'taunting scene' music. Doc saves her by entering and stopping the action.

4. **Does anyone feature in the scene without speaking?**
   Some of the Jets don't have lines but are part of the action.

5. **What is the function of this scene?**
   For Anita to mistakenly tell the Jets that Maria is dead, leading to Tony thinking she has been killed by Chino.

1) **How did we get INTO this scene?**
   Transition from Maria's bedroom into Doc's store. Almost immediately in real time. (Scene is marked at 11.40 pm, previous scene marked 11.30 pm.)

2) **How do we get OUT of this scene?**
   Transitions in real time (11.50 pm) into the cellar of Doc's drug store where Tony has been hiding.

- **Why are the characters here?**
  The Jets are hiding Tony from the police and planning their next move. Anita enters to pass on a message from Maria.

- **What is their 'need energy' entering the scene, what does each character want?**
  Anita wants to pacify Maria and communicate with Tony. The Jets want to protect Tony and in turn create an obstacle for Anita.

- **What obstacles are in the way for the character to achieve this goal?**
  Anita face the physical obstacle of the Jets who taunt her and attempt to rape her. The Jets are faced with indecision at what to do.

- **What do the characters learn at the end of this scene? What do the audience learn at the end of this scene?**

  Anita learns that the Jets are not to be trusted and to go with her instincts on protecting Maria, prompting her to lie. The Jets and Doc learn that Maria has been shot by Chino (although this is not true) which is vital in terms of passing on the misinformation to Tony. The audience learns that mistake at the same time as the characters and can see how the end will then play out.

As you can see in the above example, by asking yourself these questions and answering them systematically the function of the scene becomes clear. This particular scene is very much a climax of the second act, leading up to the final death of Tony, so its function is front and centre for the action. All scenes have a function, and by asking yourself these questions and answering with your cast, it will always become clear.

Events, Actions and Behaviours

However you wish to approach a scene, the core ingredients remain the same. I work from a system of Events, Actions and Behaviours that dictate how I direct any scripted scene. I'm going to demonstrate how these are identified, documented and developed and how I would use this to then work with actors.

First I register and note down the **events** within the scene. These are the basic moments of dramatic function where something changes. Events tend to be physical – a person entering or leaving the space or doing something that creates a change within the scene. These tend not to include dialogue that discuss characters' needs, wants or motivation or discussions about what is happening to others offstage. I describe them as the most basic events happening within the scene on a functional level that result in something *changing*.

When reading a scene, mark in pencil every time a new event occurs, as outlined in Table 2.12. This will give you a clear reading of the structure of the scene and allow you to see how busy the scene will be. Scenes with lots of events will require different pacing and are often there to move the narrative forward. Those with fewer events are usually more character-driven scenes that signify a deeper learning moment for the audience rather than a slew of actions.

Once you have your list of events, describe the action happening in between each event as the 'action'. This may be something that a character does, feels or has done to them. The action should describe the event and read more narratively. If you were to just read the events after each other they wouldn't make for interesting reading, but the action should tell more of the narrative. The purpose of this is to attach the action to the specific event that has caused it. Someone has entered a room – why? What action does that create? Someone opens a window – why? What action does that instigate? The point being, scenes are made up of events that in turn create action. Identifying both of these will lead you to the next step – that of behaviour.

Table 2.12 Events, Actions and Behaviours in a Scene

Event	Action	Behaviour
Jets run into the drugstore	Action asks after Tony, we learn he's down in the cellar and that they're protecting him by trying to hide from the cops	Anxious, nervous, protective, on-edge, scared, apprehensive
Anita enters the drugstore	A mambo is turned on from the jukebox as the Jets feel threatened	Enraged, bitter, angry
Anita approaches the cellar door	The Jets begin to rally together against her	Anxious, frightened
Anita is blocked from the cellar door by the Jets	The Jets become more threatening and intimidating	Threatened, scared (Anita), emboldened, entitled, protective (Jets)
Anita is pushed into a wild 'savage dance' and encircled by the Jets	The tension escalates becoming physical against the beat of the music and the Jets assault her	Heightened versions of the above
Anita is pushed into a corner and Baby John is lifted and dropped upon her	An attempted rape happens, pushing Anita to the ground and assaulting her further	
Doc enters from the cellar	Doc, as the only adult, stops the assault and reprimands the Jets	Furious, enraged, disappointed, desperate
Anita frees herself and gets up	Anita is holding back tears and yells at the Jets	Terrified, violated, disgusted
Anita tries to leave but is stopped by Snowboy before shaking loose	Anita faces off against them, telling them the opposite of what she has come to say, impacted by their behaviour towards her	Stronger, determined, deliberate
Anita leaves the drugstore	She slams the door and runs away leaving them to take in the 'news'	Furious
The Jets file out of the drugstore after her	Doc yells at the Jets and they leave, ashamed	Disappointed, ashamed, embarrassed, defensive

ADDING BEHAVIOUR

Behaviour allows acting to occur. Understanding a character's behaviour, often on the most basic level, allows you to realistically portray the actions presented in the script. If the event is *what* is happening, the action is *how* it happens, the behaviour is *why* it happens. All three of these elements need to come together in order to effectively convey the meaning of a scene and present a well-rounded moment. Your first task is to identify the behaviours, following on from the work you have already done above. Each character may behave differently and there's often no 'correct' behaviour or one that is universal for all. Encourage your actors to discuss this and be part of the decision rather than force a behaviour on them.

Discuss as a group the specific behaviours, noting why and where these shift and which actions they are attached to. Often it's easier to 'play' these base behaviours removed from the world of the scene as opposed to attaching too much contextual baggage to them. If your actors are struggling, encourage them to work backwards to find out how to act that way, starting with the behaviour first.

HOW TO FIND THIS BEHAVIOUR? IMPROVISATION

Take the behaviour Anita feels as she approaches the cellar door – that of anxiety and fear. Take your actors out of the world of the show and set up a simple improvisation to find and explore that behaviour, loosely attached to the event but not directly related to it:

Actor 1 Scenario: something you want is behind a locked door but you are scared of approaching it as you are unsure what will get in your way.

Actor 2 Scenario: you are trying to protect something behind a locked door and need to ensure that Actor 1 doesn't reach it, but you aren't allowed to touch them or have physical contact.

Let the scenario play out, intercepting different actors (and adding more actors on either side) as you wish. Focus on the behaviours that occur and how Actor 1 gets what they want and Actor 2 prevents them. The scenario can extend and develop, but the key ingredient is understanding the different wants and needs of each actor.

Dramatic scenes are often built from a similar basic scenario to the above. One actor wants something from another actor and has to work to get it from them. This in turn creates drama. The situations may vary drastically (Elle Woods wants Warner to marry her; Curly wants to take Laurey to the box social; Max Bialystock wants Leo to join him as a producer) but the base behaviours are often incredibly similar. Each character has a want and a need, more often than not, one that is introduced in a less-than-subtle song usually within the first 15 minutes of the show. Identifying this on a show level for each character and then again from scene to scene will help you keep focused and give each actor their energy from action to action.

Once this has been established and improvised, try running the scenario again, but this time within the world of the show and the specific scene. Rather than try it straight away with the exact lines, have the actors assume the characters but free from the exact beats and lines. This should be a midway position between the out-of-context improvisation and the scene itself. The purpose is to carry on the improvisational techniques that help find the specific behaviours before attaching them directly to the text.

Scenario: Actor 1, Anita, is trying to get a message to Tony who is hiding in the basement of Doc's store. Actors 2 (and 3, 4, 5, etc.) are preventing her from reaching him and trying to stop her in her tracks.

Let the improvisation play out and don't be afraid if it takes a different direction to the text of the scene. Let the actors play the behaviours to find out how it feels to be anxious, scared, threatened and so on, without them having to rely on the text of the libretto.

Once you have done this, feel free to discuss with your actors how it felt to find and play the behaviours. Think about how they can play these within the scene itself and find any takeaways from the improvisation that they would like to use in the scene itself. Go back to the script and use these elements within your scene to elevate the moment and don't be afraid of going back to improvisation should you find yourselves stuck.

Text vs Subtext

It's often tricky to understand the difference between the text and the subtext and many actors can get hung up on the challenges between the two. The simplest way of describing it is the text is what is on the page and the subtext is what lies underneath. Often this is constructed deliberately, with the subtext being the 'unspoken thoughts' the characters feel but aren't shared in the dialogue. There can be different reasons as to why certain directors chose to heighten and articulate the subtext, often to draw out cultural relevance or contextual elements that enhance the vision or concept. Subtext is most frequently expressed through song and lyricists have a long tradition of hidden meanings through song lyrics which even extends into the melodic structure or even the orchestrations. As a director it's your job to guide actors in finding and presenting this to an audience in a sophisticated way that's not overly complicated and contradictory to the action on stage but also enlightens the meanings beneath the text.

Look at the scene you are staging and closely read the text, asking yourself the following questions:

1. What is being said?
2. What is not being said?
3. What can be inferred by an audience?

Subtext for subtext's sake can be galling and grate against not only the piece's original intention but also your overall concept as a whole. As you make one decision and open one potential door, other doors then become closed, so it is prudent to think through each of these decisions carefully and explore in rehearsal before you settle on a particular interpretation of the material itself.

Subtext can be a large part of a director's overall vision for a show, fitting into a concept as discussed above. For example the character Bobby in Sondheim and

Furth's *Company* is written as a bachelor turning 35 amongst their married friends. A director may choose to explore various reasons as to why this is, one obvious one being his sexuality. Although generally denied by Sondhiem in multiple interviews, there is a queer-coded reading of the piece that is possible, which in turn creates a subtext that you as a director may wish to bring to the front. Despite not being directly addressed in the original libretto (although future revisions would try to address it) the current licensed version allows scope for a director to pull the subtext to the fore, making the audience consciously question Bobby's rejection of heterosexual marriage, without changing a word of dialogue.

Beware of forcing a reading onto a particular show through embellishing the subtext, or allowing room for subtext that isn't necessarily there. In many cases, you need to trust the author's original intentions. Ask yourself why the subtext exists, it could be that contemporary attitudes meant various readings were coded a certain way, seen in the work of a dramatist such as Noël Coward who was expert at giving dual readings to his plays, largely to get past the censorship of the Lord Chancellor. Sometimes digging deeper into a scene can unearth more problems than it solves or makes the drama deeper and heavier than originally intended which in turn can capsize a show.

From Book to Song

One of the hardest elements for a bookwriter to overcome is the transition from spoken word to song. It is often said that in musical theatre songs are born from a character's need to express themselves when speech is insufficient, thus a song begins. Depending on how well-crafted your musical is you may face different challenges in getting your actors to make the transition as natural as possible. Character songs rarely start cold, unlike larger ensemble numbers that often begin scenes and acts with a brief fanfare of arrival. A character song or a song between two characters is usually carefully plotted to transition from spoken dialogue into the song itself without feeling unnecessarily blunt or awkward. In most cases, the work has been done by the arranger and book writer to identify the exact moment underscoring or song introduction should begin. Look out for these marks in the libretto and co-ordinate the cues with your musical director and you'll likely not end up in a situation with an actor waiting for beats before their singing starts.

The music starting is an event and should be marked as such in the script and treated as a moment of change. Consider both your blocking and a character's reaction to the music, using the introduction not as a moment of pause, but as an extension of the thought the character has or is going to have.

'Mister Snow' in *Carousel* features an expert introduction for the characters of Carrie and Julie, where a thought is picked up in the orchestra leading to Carrie questioning: 'Julie! Julie! Did you like him?' which begins the opening recitative of the song and the first theme ('You're a Queer One') that eventually leads to Carrie's narrative monologue song in which she describes her new beau. Study the text before this song as an example of how a song arrives:

A Section

Carrie, Spoken: 'Julie, Julie! Do you like him?'
The orchestra begins the theme underneath the dialogue as Carrie probes Julie into speaking about her encounter with Billy.

B Section

Carrie: 'You're a queer one, Julie Jordan ... '
Carrie takes on the orchestral theme that will recur throughout this section and be used once again by Billy later in this scene as he similarly reads Julie. Carrie reacts to Julie's indifference, transitioning from a recitative-like structure into a developed musical theme.

C Section

Carrie: 'When we work in the mill ... '
A new musical theme is introduced, again one that will be used by Julie and Billy later in the scene, acting as a sort of pre-reprise of what is considered the 'verse' to the song 'If I Loved You'.

D Section

Carrie: 'You're a Queer one, Julie Jordan'
Carrie repeats the theme from the earlier section after Julie rebuts her reading of the situation, affirming her feelings towards Julie and her 'read' of her friend's reason for absentmindedness.

E Section

Carrie: 'Julie, I've been busted to tell you something lately'
The action shifts away from Julie in spoken dialogue, leading directly into the question that will fuel the rest of Carrie's song. Note how it shifts the focus from Carrie's observations of Julie towards herself, as Carrie tells of her new found love.

F Section

Carrie: 'His name is Mr Snow ... '
The song itself begins in earnest, with no further interjection, but instead a description of Carrie's feelings, externalized to Julie.

Considering this whole section shows Hammerstein's skill at song placement and development. Julie is the primary character in the show but instead of her song taking the usual 'second song slot', instead it is afforded to Carrie, which in turn reflects back on Julie and means our reading of her actions appear in direct contrast to that of Carrie in the next scene where she falls for Billy. Compare with Hammerstein's own work in *Oklahoma!* where the two female couples are framed quite differently. Although Laurey's song 'Many a New Day' arrives after Ado Annie's 'I Can't Say No', the audience have had enough exposition of Laurey's desire and drive in the first scene with Curly. In *Carousel*, it is the secondary character who we learn about first, with Julie being presented only by other people's perceptions of her 'You're a queer one' … both by Carrie and later Billy, long before we get to hear any internal thoughts from Julie expressed directly to the audience, which in fact doesn't occur until the second act in 'What's the Use of Wonderin?'

Hammerstein could have indeed begun 'Mister Snow' at the E section, with Carrie telling Julie she has something to tell her, prompting her to ask the question that leads straight into her reply: 'his name is Mister Snow … '. Instead he builds the book scene into the musical themes in such a way that the transition from speech to singing appears natural, with both characters falling in and out of singing as they ask each other questions, before the F section begins and the song itself takes over.

In directing this movement from book to score you need to be sensitive to the physical needs of your actors and the naturalism you wish to present to the audience as a song arrives. The common complaint from those who hate musicals often comes from the dislike of songs arriving out of nowhere which can be jarring and challenging to the overall tone and drama you are presenting. Some shows are better than others, but by identifying these transitions in such a way, you'll be able to guide your actors into the best way to handle these delicate transitions.

Directing Musical Numbers

Many experienced directors panic at the prospect of directing a musical number. Some see a song as being fundamentally different to the script, which they are much more at home managing and directing. Sometimes directors hand over anything with music to the choreographer, other times they block where an actor should stand and leave it to them to 'park and bark', not wanting to get in the way of the song itself. Directing a song is as important, if not more so, than directing a book scene and should be handled with the same level of care and attention. A show does not stop when the singing starts, even if that is one person on stage singing a solo number out to an audience with even the most basic of lyrics.

As director, it is your job to work with actors on songs to the same level of detail and attention to ensure that they are successfully delivered and interpreted. In a pre-production meeting, it's a good idea to discuss the responsibilities with the musical director and choreographer in terms of the songs to establish who exactly will be responsible for each part of the show. As I discuss later, these roles have a degree of flexibility, but even in dance breaks and fully choreographed numbers it is expected that a director will have thoughts on how these should be interpreted and delivered. It is common for actors to spend time on music calls with the musical director to learn their material and go over notes, rhythm and timings with other actors. A good musical director will also spend time with the actors on discussing the meaning of the song and talking about how to bring it to life. As a director, I find it important to be part of these conversations and like to be in the room when actors are learning their music. Discussing a song with the MD before a rehearsal will help ensure you are on the same page and can work together effectively to bring out the best performance possible from your actors.

Types of Songs

Musicals feature a mix of different songs that each have a different function in both the score and the drama. Space does not allow a thorough investigation of how musical scores are constructed – there are many books that do this brilliantly, listed in the Bibliography and Further Reading. Whilst the above sections discuss some elements of structure that shape the demands of a musical score, this section will instead focus on the different types of songs you will encounter and different approaches each type requires from a director and actors.

ESTABLISHING SONGS

Examples: 'Good Morning Baltimore', 'Tradition', 'The Jet Song', 'Comedy Tonight'.

Many musicals begin with a song that directly addresses the audience and invites them into the 'world' of the show. These songs are important for establishing the status quo and the world that the audience is about to enter into. The examples above set out 'rules' of the show – most importantly they establish the tone and set the expectations going forward. A strong establishing song will do the work for you, opening the curtain on the world of the show in a tone and style that is consistent with the piece as a whole. 'Good Morning, Baltimore' for example paints the cartoon-es-que world that Tracy lives in, following her morning routine and introducing the people she meets along the way. It's larger than life, it's inflated and not naturalistic.

1. Identify the tone: Is the song funny? Does it contain jokes and direct audience address? Does it include visual humour? Don't play against the song, identify the key elements and lean into these.

2. What narrative elements have to be established or told? Make sure they are clear and the staging isn't too busy that they get lost. Remember, audiences take time to 'settle', both in terms of what they are watching and what they are listening to.

3. Identify any key lyrics that must be communicated effectively for the rest of the show to be understood. Don't allow them to get lost. 'The Ballad of Sweeney Todd' directly invites the audience to 'attend the tale' but also includes key bits of information about his character that need to be heard.

4. What is the mood of the show as it opens? The Prologue and Overture of *Follies* sets a different, slower mood than the opening of *Hairspray* or *Oliver!* Does the show grab the audience by the collar or ease them slowly into it?

More often than not these songs will require staging and/or choreography, so you'll want to make sure you speak to your choreographer and collaborate on how best to stage these moments. These can be epic in nature (think *Titanic*, *Ragtime or Hunchback of Notre Dame*) and used to introduce a lot of back-story that builds to a certain point in the narrative where the protagonists can then begin their journey. Plot out each action and event as you would a scene and focus on the storytelling contained within the lyrics and key moments that drive the number forward. These numbers likely include the full company, introducing various groups and characters, often simultaneously as their paths cross and build to a 'conclusion' of the number. Make sure you plot each group or character throughout the full number – run through it from each of their perspectives and know where everyone is at all times. Do they leave the stage, do they remain in tableau, do they exit and return as something different? Make sure you have tracked their full journey through the number and understand how each of them fits into the number as a whole.

DIRECT ADDRESS
Examples: 'Climb Every Mountain', 'Cockeyed Optimist', 'You'll Never Walk Alone'.

Direct address songs are usually performed to the audience or another character and can include elements of narration or passages of time. There can be some crossover between these and establishing songs, or even internal monologues, which by their very nature are directed outwards or towards another character. These songs are usually answers to questions posed by another character, 'teaching' moments or moments of instruction from one character to the other. As such, they are usually still and smaller and have a greater reliance on a character's vocal abilities. Think about how best to stage these moments by asking yourself:

1. What is the character expressing and who are they expressing it to? Another character on stage, the audience, a group of people?

2. What is the intended outcome at the end of the song? If the song doesn't have a function it's unlikely to be necessary to the show, in which case it would have been cut by the creatives. Think about what is happening at the start of the song and what you're expecting to happen at the end of it.

3. What does your actor require to be able to deliver this song effectively? Ask your actors. Can they sing this song sitting down / behind a desk / lying on the floor / swinging from the fly bars? Make sure your actors are comfortable with the delivery of the song and can successfully deliver it in the way you have staged it. If it's not comfortable, or won't be comfortable after rehearsing it, change the staging.

Often the hardest part of this type of song is for the actor(s) not singing. If the song is good enough, it will have beats, actions and moments for an actor to identify or storytell. If this is a solo number they will most likely command the stage and focus the attention. However, you can't leave your other actors high and dry standing reacting with nothing to do. When staging the song make sure you call everyone who is onstage for that moment to the rehearsal – don't fall into the trap of thinking you can slot them in later just because they are not singing. 'With One Look' may well be a huge solo direct song for Norma Desmond, but the actor playing Joe Gillis has to be on stage the whole time occupying the same world in which Norma is singing her song. This song is addressed *to* Joe and comes from a scene directly before it where Norma is convincing him she is suitable to play the 16-year-old Salome. The song is as much about Joe learning about Norma's talent, her self-perception and the world in which she exists (both in her own mind and otherwise) and although he doesn't sing, his reactions are vital to the success of the number. Having all the actors in rehearsal as you explore the song and craft the staging is vital to the success. The actor singing needs to feed off the energy of those onstage and the actors not singing need to understand the journey the actor is taking and respond accordingly. 'Climb Ev'ry Mountain' is as much about Maria overcoming her fears as it is Mother Abbess telling her to return to the Von Trapp's house. One can't exist without the other.

INTERNAL MONOLOGUES
Examples: 'Soliloquy', 'Somewhere That's Green'.

Like a monologue or soliloquy in a play, these songs are internalized thoughts that are externalized and presented to an audience away from other characters in a show. They aren't heard by others in the world of the show and can include information or feelings that are held back and not expressed, thus remaining unexplored outside of the relationship between the character and the audience. As such, they can be used to invite the audience into a 'secret' that others in the world of the show don't know, putting the audience ahead of the action as it unfolds onstage.

These songs can appear at any moment in a show but are often found up-front in the first 20 minutes or so following the 'establishing' number. They can fall into the category commonly known as 'I Want' songs in which the protagonist expresses their primary goal / want / dream / ambition to the audience (or other characters) which in turn propels the narrative forward. However, not all 'I Want' songs are internal monologues – many include other characters, a mix of direct address and even some movement / action. Identify those internal monologue songs that involve no other characters and provide 'hidden' information and ask yourself the following:

1. What is the text and subtext of the lyrics? What is being asked, longed for, requested, identified, etc., in the song as a whole?

2. What does the audience learn about the character throughout the song and how does this affect our relationship with them?

3. Is this song reprised, and if so, how is it different? (See below.)

Finding the Beats
The first thing you should do is identify the journey of the song and discuss this with the actor. If you're lucky, the song will be such that the answers to the above

questions will be clear on a close read of the lyrics. Treat the song like a piece of text, reading it aloud with the actor as you would do a monologue and identify what the song is doing, what it is saying and how it is doing so. For example, breaking down 'Soliloquy' from *Carousel* reveals the following beats:

1. **Questioning**: 'I wonder what he'll think of me … ' – Confronted with the news of Julie's pregnancy, the song begins with speculation as to what his new relationship with his son will be like.

2. **Action**: 'I'll teach him to wrestle' – Moving out of speculation, Billy identifies how and what he will do with his son.

3. **Imagination**: 'Bill … I will see that he's named after me' – Billy solidifies the image from an abstract concept of a new born child to an exact replica of himself, painting a strong image to the audience of how he sees his son in his image, focusing on looks as well as attitude. Here he introduces the idea of being able to shape the behaviour of your child, going some way to exploring his subconscious and offering an insight into his own 'taught' behaviour.

4. **Projection**: 'I don't give a damn what he does' – Billy expands the vision beyond a baby, projecting his whole future, right up to being President, giving an 'American Dream' vision of his child's potential and future prospects, unbridled by his surroundings.

5. **Realization**: 'Wait a minute … what if … ' – in imagining his son with a girl, it dawns on him for the first time that he may in fact have a daughter. The initial reaction is panic, as he fears he has to be a 'father' to a girl and won't be able to have fun.

6. **Imagination**: 'My little girl' – the song repeats musically and thematically as Billy imagines the best for his girl in the world.

7. **Determination**: the song ends with a declaration of intent that he will be the best father possible, change his ways and offer the best to his child.

By breaking the song down in this way you can identify the changes of mood and tone present and the overall arc that the character goes on. The lyrics are supported musically by recurring motifs and themes that help the actor, and the audience, connect these dots and go on the journey together. Boiling the journey down into the most basic formula possible, you get:

IMPETUOUS FOR SONG: A character finds out they are having a baby.
Questioning – Actioning – Imagination – Projection – Realization – Imagination – Determination.

FEAR – EXCITEMENT

ANSWER: The character journeys from fear to excitement through this whole song.

Now you have this roadmap through the song you can begin to explore delivery with the actor, drawn from those core emotions attached to each section. Identifying behaviours will once again enlighten the performance. Ask your actor HOW they behave when they imagine a rosy future? HOW they behave when they want to appear determined and so on, and focus on conveying these emotions vividly and honestly. Don't be afraid of improvisation, away from the context and lyrics of the song, just as we have explored with scene work above. Your job is to get the actor to access these core behaviours and be able to access them within the world of the song, and transition from one to the other realistically and seamlessly.

Not every internal monologue song will be as complex (or as well written) as the above, but in each case you can follow the same exercise. You may discover that there is just one or two emotions in the song, which is absolutely fine. Many examples of this type of song project just one emotion to the foreground as a 'moment' within the wider show. Not all will have the same journey or narrative path, but all of these songs exist for a reason that can be discovered by answering the questions up front.

STAR TURNS AND SMOKE AND MIRRORS?

These songs are often tricky to stage as they rely heavily on the performer and their delivery. Many of these songs are written to be performed on a solo, empty stage with just the performer ('Rose's Turn', 'If I Were a Rich Man'). Traditionally, they were written with particular stars in mind – a larger-than-life moment that requires a bravura performance by the central actor, unfussily staged, giving the audience a moment alone with the performer. In the amateur world, they therefore can be exposing moments for the actor performing them and can highlight certain flaws in their performance. With these songs you need to ask yourself honestly about the skills and capabilities of the performer, as this will dictate how you stage the number. There's a temptation to leave the actor alone in a spotlight, as per the original production and its point of delivery. With any luck you will be fortunate to have actors that can deliver the material in the way it was written and originally intended, but there are times when you may have to 'smoke and mirror' through staging to hide some of their weaknesses.

Many of these songs require an audience to connect with the lyrics. Look at the song we've just broken down above. The audience needs to hear the lyrics and connect with Billy's character. It's an intentionally static song that requires a lot from the actor, so having them roam the stage, through different locations or interacting with other characters would pull focus and be distracting. Knowing when to distract the audience is a skill, and one that depends on the actors you are trying to protect in serving the text and narrative as a whole. I once saw a production of *Ragtime* where the second act show-stopper 'Back to Before' had the actor playing Mother battle her way through an ensemble with umbrellas, creating stage pictures and surrounding her like it was a follies number. Despite the skills of the actor and their ability to deliver this monologue song it was an odd decision and one that pulled focus from both the song and the performance. Directors tend to panic in moments of stillness and worry that leaving a solo number to be performed alone on a stage is a cop out and doesn't show their work. Never panic about stillness. Often shows are written in such a way that a moment of 'calm' is required by the audience. Trust the material and trust your performers. Directing a cohesive and nuanced performance by an actor of a 'still' song requires just as much skill as a large performance show-stopper.

FAMOUS SONGS AND EXPECTATIONS

Most musicals feature famous songs that audiences know and connect with. Often this may be outside the world and context of the show itself, but other times the song and its original staging may be so ingrained into the minds of audiences, any deviation will be met with disappointment. These songs can range from production numbers ('Steam Heat', 'Cell Block Tango') through to interior monologues ('If I Were a Rich Man') and come with their own baggage (or 'ghosts') that can mean you feel creatively wedded to a certain vision and delivery. If you have a strong conceptual vision for your show you may be able to see this through in how you conceive the production as a whole. More often than not it's futile to play against the audience's expectations of the number, and you have to weigh up the case for deliberately playing against it vs creating something entirely new.

DIEGETIC VS NON-DIEGETIC

These two terms to describe music and songs are often mis-used and misunderstood. The terms themselves come from the film world to describe the music or score as experienced within the world of the film. Diegetic music concerns that which appears within the world of the show, experienced and heard by the characters as music. Non-diegetic music is therefore music or songs that don't function as music within the world of the show. Most musicals feature non-diegetic music, i.e. the characters sing songs unconsciously as extensions of the script. Other characters don't respond as though the actor has 'burst into song'; instead it's a natural extension of the world of the show. Diegetic songs tend to come from a specific place – a bar, a nightclub, show act and so on. Many musicals mix the two, especially those set within or around the world of showbiz. *Cabaret* is perhaps the best example of this, mixing songs that are being performed by Sally Bowles in the Kit Kat Club such as 'Mein Herr' or 'Cabaret' with other 'book' songs such as 'Perfectly Marvellous' and 'What Would You Do?'. *Cabaret* is constructed to flip seamlessly between the two types of song and each are written to serve the world of the show and the performance of the characters. When Bob Fosse directed the Oscar-winning film adaptation he reduced the score to just the diegetic songs, which kept the musical world of the club separate from the more naturalistic narrative.

Identifying the difference between these songs will be your first task, and it's rarely difficult to do. Any show that requires a performance will be signposted as such, and it's your job to differentiate this moment from the rest of the show so the audience understands how the two types of songs operate together. In some of the better musicals, the songs can even have dual meanings. The title song in *Cabaret* for example, performed directly post-abortion by Sally acts as a performance in the club as well as a wider commentary on Sally's situation. A clever book writer and lyricist won't shy away from making this obvious, but it's worth a close reading of the lyrics to identify any parallels that may not be immediately obvious.

Often diegetic songs don't enforce the narrative, use character names or further the plot or story. Think of 'Take Back Your Mink' and 'A Bushel and a Peck' from *Guys and Dolls* – both are performed by Miss Adelaide as part of her nightclub act and can end up being showstoppers themselves thanks to clever choreography and staging. You should create seamless transitions between the two different types of songs within the internal logic of the piece as a whole.

OVERTURES AND INSTRUMENTALS

Musicals of the Golden Age and post-Golden Age were generally designed with overtures in mind. Most of the time this was practical, allowing audiences time to get to their seats and settle as well as introducing key themes and melodies ahead of time to an audience with the hope they would 'lodge' in their minds. At a time where Broadway music was very much part of the 'hit parade', sheet music sales and cast albums were key sources of income for composers and producers, with the hope that the biggest artists of the day would cover a song from the score and introduce it to a wider audience. Overtures and entr'actes were therefore created to reinforce this music and create an audio introduction to the musical world of the show. Think of your favourite overture – it should evoke the world of the show, set the tenor of the piece and build anticipation ahead of the curtain going up.

As musicals modernized, overtures became rarer. It's common for twenty-first-century musicals to open with a 'bang', and as scores reduced their instrumentation to smaller ensembles, their impact was lessened over time. If you're directing an older show you will, however, be more likely to encounter an overture, and so you'll have a decision about how to handle it. Before I make a decision I would ask myself the following questions:

1. What is the first scene directly following the overture? How long does it take following the everture to get to a musical number? If there's a strong opening number ('Call on Dolly') then the overture may not be necessary. Other shows that start smaller, such as *Camelot*, *Brigadoon* or *My Fair Lady* benefit from the overture before much more intimate first scenes, which are led by solo songs.

2. What size orchestra are we having? Whilst they can be beautiful and beguiling, they can also be extremely exposing. Attempting the overture to *Gypsy* with a 5-piece band may highlight the fact that you have minimized the musicians, which isn't a great thing to do within the first 5 minutes of a show.

3. What's the expectation of the venue / company? I worked with a company for multiple shows and realized there was a strong tradition of latecomers arriving after the 7.30 pm start time. Excuses included parking, transport, the location and general audience habits. I decided that including the (optional)

overture in *West Side Story* – which would therefore give the audience time to trickle in and settle down – was better than many of them arriving through the danced prologue, which requires a lot from the company and could do without the distraction. Although it wasn't ideal, sometimes you have to identify a problem and try to mitigate, rather than change it.

Once you've decided if you're going to keep the overture, your next decision is how to stage it. Depending on your performance venue you may or may not have a pit and velvet curtain. Often audiences enjoy these minutes to prepare for the show and that time watching and focusing on the music can help the audience 'settle' and tune into the world of the show and the experience of being at the theatre. Director Bartlett Sher in his revival of classic musicals at New York's Lincoln Center certainly leaned into this during revivals of *South Pacific*, *The King and I*, *My Fair Lady* and *Camelot*, showcasing the 30-piece orchestra performing the original orchestrations, which in turn set the tone for the production as a whole. Daniel Fish's revolutionary revival of *Oklahoma!*, however, did away with the overture, beginning with the first song – both giving very different effects. Think about what you want from your audience and how you want them to connect with the show in the first instance.

Not all overtures have to take place with the curtain down – you could consider creating a visual picture to go alongside the music. Rather than do this arbitrarily, think about what is potentially missing from the start of the show and what can be gained from adding exposition to the piece. When I directed *How to Succeed ...* I noticed that the show (as licensed) began quite softly with Finch behind a window frame listening to the world of the book. The first number therefore was just a solo number taking place in a specific location that doesn't offer a strong enough window into the world of the show. Given that for the show and its inherent satire to work in the twenty-first century, it's vital that the audience immediately understand they are in a very specific time frame, I worried that it was too slow a start for this to be established. I therefore used the overture to show a visual 'heightened' world of late 1950s New York. Working with the choreographer I established a narrative showing the full ensemble of office workers waking up, commuting, arriving at work and preparing for their day, all at a sort of frantic and embellished pace. This helped set up the office hierarchy and set the tone of the piece that this was going to be quick, satirical and painted in bold colours with a wink to the audience throughout. I found that this meant by the time the first song began the audience had accepted the world of the show and more importantly the tone of it, knowing not to take it seriously and framed it visually in the colourful, slightly embellished world we wanted to show.

Much of my inspiration came from 'Runyonland', Frank Loesser's opening to his previous musical *Guys and Dolls*. Written as a sort of danced overture, it serves the same purpose, introducing the audience to the visual and musical tone of the piece ahead of the first song 'Fugue for Tinhorns', which doesn't bear any relevance to the characters or plot. Not every show requires this. The overture from *Gypsy* for example wouldn't naturally lend itself to visual storytelling, although the overture to

My Fair Lady would allow you to expose the world of Eliza's London, with its different class structure – the flower sellers and opera goers – in a way that helps the story-telling. Think about what you want to achieve and ask yourself if staging the overture enhances this or threatens to take it away.

Entr'actes are also less common and are often cut or vastly reduced in length. I find they are often good to re-awaken an audience post-interval and refocus attention on the show, but rarely include enough material to warrant a staging. Other instrumental passages will likely be described in the libretto in terms of the action supposed to occur. Sometimes this will be rich in detail (Hammerstein's instruction / description of the 'Prologue' for *Carousel*) or other times include only slight instruction ('The Shriner's Ballet' in *Bye, Bye, Birdie*). You should identify the author's intentions in these moments and establish a clear list of narrative points that you wish to explore. These are the moments where you have the most freedom, as you aren't necessarily wedded to interpreting and performing the text as described. Think about what the music is doing and how it functions in the scene. Is it used as narrative exposition? Is it used to develop a story or show the passage of time? Something like 'LA to Los Angeles' in *Gypsy* has a very clear function, to show the growth of the characters of June and Louise, and although you have freedom to show how this happens, the narrative function is clear.

The 'Prologue' for *Carousel* offers an excellent example of how you can use your innovation to stage your concept and ideas within the show itself. Read the description from the libretto and plot out what has to happen in order to get from point A to point B, just as you would ordinarily do with a song. Hammerstein describes it as 'pantomimic action' synchronized to the score, but specifically states it is not to be danced as a dream ballet (that comes later in the show). The printed libretto offers around five pages of description as to the action, setting up the fairground complete with a bear being led by a ballerina against the backdrop of Julie and Billy meeting for the first time. Whereas much of the description centres on the dynamic between Julie and Billy, as well as Mrs Mullins the owner of the carousel, much can be left to the director's imagination. Lonny Price's production at the ENO used this moment to attempt to humanize Billy and explain his (later) problematic treatment of his daughter. We were shown a flashback of young Billy growing up and crucially being hit by his parents, the inference being that this behaviour and aggression was learned behaviour directly related to his childhood. The scene still functioned in the same way, introducing the main characters and Julie to Billy, but took it further to act as a precursor to Billy's aggression in an attempt to justify his actions.

In Jack O'Brien's 2018 Broadway revival the same scene was interpreted differently with almost supernatural 'flashes' as the two characters locked eyes and the rest of the ensemble froze, highlighting an almost otherworldliness to their meeting, something that would again be highlighted later in the production. Nicholas Hytner's iconic 1992 National Theatre production chose to focus on the millworkers, grounding the show in that industrial image that then transformed spectacularly into an umbrella-style carousel which then set the tone for the whole production.

Boiling down the core actions of the number:

- We see a fairground scene with carousel
- Billy is working at the carousel, attracting attention from the women
- Julie goes on the carousel and is attracted to Billy
- Ms Mullins notices them and isn't happy
- Billy and Julie connect.

The action itself is simple and leaves a lot of scope for a director to enhance their scene over the six or so minutes of music. Once you have identified the core actions that have to happen, you can explore the additional staging and framing. Go back to your concept research and ask yourself what it is you want to show during this moment: what's your core concept and how can you use this section to highlight it? Who do you have to highlight and focus on during this number? What's the world of the show that you want to deliver?

Map out the full number, writing in prose, describing exactly what you want to happen. In this example, I would write my own version of Hammerstein's prose, describing the core actions and what you hope to achieve and establish before you then attach the actions to the music.

Similarly, narrative ballets / instrumentals such as the dream ballet in *Oklahoma!*, *West Side Story*, *Brigadoon*, *On the Town* and *Fiddler on the Roof* offer scope for you to explore the show in relation to your concept. Each has a description within the libretto of the core actions, often aligned directly to particular passages of music that specifically create different sounds and timbres. You aren't, however, bound to producing these moments as described – the music cannot be touched, but the interpretation of these moments is up to you. Be creative and use these moments to explore and enhance your concept as a whole.

REPRISES

Reprises are moments where songs are repeated at a later point in the show, usually within a different dramatic function. It's common practice in most musicals to reprise a tune from earlier in the show, but changing the action and function of the song as a character has learned new information or situations have changed. In each case, identify *what* has changed and *why* it has changed. Why is the composer using this music again? More often than not the reprise is delivered by the same characters. 'People Will Say We're in Love' offers a similar musical moment when sung by Curly and Laurey in the second act of *Oklahoma!* But the situation is now that they are ready to accept and confirm their feelings for each other, inverting the lyric to 'let people say we're in love', propelling us towards their offstage wedding. Reprises are often moments of learning or discovery, and don't have to always be performed by the same people. Think of how 'Look at Me, I'm Sandra Dee' is used in *Grease*. Rizzo introduces the song to mock Sandy during the first act, highlighting and satirizing her naivety. In the second act, the song is reprised by Sandy herself, owning the song and inverting the original meaning as she waves 'goodbye to Sandra Dee', showing that she has changed (rightly or wrongly) to mould herself into the kind of female Danny Zuko requires.

Meredith Wilson's use of reprise in *The Music Man* is often cited as the cleverest way of showing characters changing their feelings. The music to Marian's ballad 'Goodnight, My Someone' is a waltz-time version of Harold's anthem '76 Trombones'. The change is slight, but audiences don't usually notice the musical similarities between the two songs until Act Two, where the two songs are performed together and 'blend', showing Marian's submission to Harold and Harold's realization that his feelings towards the librarian are genuine. Identify how composers have framed each of these moments and understand what they are saying to an audience.

ACTION SONGS

Examples: 'A New Argentina', 'What You Want', 'Poor Professor Higgins', 'Let's Have Lunch'.

Many musicals use songs to move through passages of time and show character developments in a truncated form. These action songs can be longer sequences that incorporate a number of different elements, from sections of interior monologues to reprises, duets and production numbers. The first thing to do is identify where these sequences begin and end, before identifying the key overarching story element that it is trying to tell. From there, I would break down the number into sections, identifying character, plot, location and important narrative elements. From this, you may wish to share with your choreographer certain sections that they will be working on and the transitions between them, in order to present a cohesive and entertaining number from start to finish, that serves both narrative purpose and effective character development.

For example, consider the number 'What You Want' from the musical *Legally Blonde*. This is an excellent example of an action song that moves from various locations with a simple through-line, designed to show a passage of time at truncated speed. For any action song of this type, I would break it down as shown in Table 2.13:

This method is called song-mapping and allows you to see all of the elements of the number placed together in one easy chart. Rather than feeling overwhelmed by the scale of the number, you can instead see the full map and the multiple elements that are involved. This will not only help you envision the number in your head in order to make creative decisions, it will also help you schedule the various elements for rehearsal. It's unlikely that you'd be able to stage this whole number in one rehearsal, so breaking it down into these scenes and elements will help your cast work on this in smaller chunks, before putting it all together. By identifying different responsibilities within the creative team, you and the choreographer will be able to agree on who is responsible for each section and how the two elements can come together cohesively. Have conversations before you begin staging the number of elements that you would like to work together on and how the various sections will transition, particularly as different characters move from one to the other.

Table 2.13 Song-Mapping an Action Song

Song Section	Characters	Location	Narrative	Responsibility
'Wait a sec! This is the kind of girl Warner wants …'	Elle and Delta Nu	Delta Nu house	Elle meets Vivien, decides that in order to be taken seriously she needs to attend Harvard Law School	Director – staging coming out of the scene
'Law school?'	Elle's Dad, Elle's Mum, Elle	Elle's family home or golf course	Elle presents her plan to her parents who are less than impressed but say they'll pay for it if she gets in	Director – transitioning straight into new location
'Hey everybody, it's the spring fling beer bash extreme!'	Elle, Sorority Girl, Frat Guys, Grandmaster Chad, Academic Advisor	Sorority House / Elle's bedroom	Elle knuckles down to study whilst the sorority girls and frat guys party around her. This scene is a mini transition in itself, moving through time until Elle grades 175	Choreographer – to create transition into this sequence, stage the background scene. Director stage Elle, etc.
'So, Gentlemen'	Harvard Professors	Harvard Admissions office	Harvard Admissions team deliberate incoming students, assessing Elle's application	Director – to stage office scene. Costume change for Elle / Delta Nu / ensemble
'I'm what you want Harvard'	Harvard Professors, Elle, Delta Nu, Pilot	Harvard Admissions office	Elle bursts through the door to deliver her personal essay with Delta Nu / Ensemble	Choreographer – looking after dance break / cheerleading section as full ensemble enter to dance

Scenic / Costume Elements

Once I have made a chart such as Table 2.13, I'll share it with the wider production team to speak about the transitions between the scenes and the various scenic elements that will be involved. It's important to have these conversations as early as possible, sharing your song-mapping chart so that everyone understands the speed required between each of these transitions. Looking at the various locations, the song isn't designed for full scenic changes between each one and so you'll have to work with your designer on suggestive elements that can be brought on to suggest the different locations at speed and with ease. Think about how you will show the transitions of time and space. Should it be filmic, moving seamlessly from one location to the other? What happens when a location is finished with – do you leave it visually on display to add to a collective sense of space trailing in Elle's wake? All of these options (and more) are available to you, but only by tracking this out will it be clear what is possible.

The same can be said for costumes. Create another column on your table and track the changes, for both the lead characters and for the ensemble. You need to ascertain how many people you require in each scene, and more importantly, costume changes that may be required in fast transitions. Remember on Broadway each show has a team of professional dressers and specifically designed costumes for this exact purpose. Having a full ensemble change from sorority / fraternity clothes into a semi-marching band (in this example) is ambitious, so you may find it easier to split your ensemble to cover the two scenes or work to build the number with enough time for changes between sections. I've yet to see an amateur production of *42nd Street* where the ensemble manages to change in time to get back on for the different sections in the song 'Dames' …

Narrative Plotting

Many action songs are simple in what they are trying to achieve, but others have more intricate sections that require in-depth plotting and preparation. 'A New Argentina' from *Evita* is one example that springs to mind where the narrative elements are not clear from just reading the lyrics and a director needs to work hard, not only to identify the different narrative elements but also to communicate those to the cast and more importantly, the audience. As written, the song spans multiple times and locations, showing Eva and Peron discussing their plans for the future and how they plot to take control of the country. The politics within the musical are softly plotted and it's easy for them not to make sense to those who haven't read a programme note or Wikipedia synopsis. For a song such as this, I would repeat the above exercise, but give careful attention to the narrative elements you wish to show and those plot points that are most relevant. Given the verse / chorus structure of the song, it's easy for it to be staged in a way that lacks specificity, but you should aim to create as much narrative flow as possible that builds to the climax of both the number and the end of the act.

Another example of a song such as this is the 'Montage' section of *A Chorus Line*. For this number I broke it down similarly to the above, using both the tracks from the complete recording of the show and also bar numbers from the rental material. From here I could identify with the choreographer not only who was responsible for each section, but show the narrative journey throughout the whole piece.

The 'Montage' acts as a transitional centre to the show where multiple stories are put together to address the theme of growing up. The song 'Nothing' occurs within this section, despite it being one of the show's most well-known numbers and existing firmly outside of the context for which it is written. However, as part 3 of a 10-part structure, you can see how it is framed and functions within a much wider section and, although it still has the ability to be a show-stopper, should be considered part

Table 2.14 Narrative Plotting in an Action Song

Section	Songs	Characters	Track Time	Bar Numbers	Notes
1	'Hello Twelve' / 'Gonorrhea' / 'Four Foot Ten'	Connie, Mark, All	**Track 8:** 0.30 – 4.00	1 – 112	Staging
2	'Hello Twelve'	All	4.00 – 5.20	113 – 156	Dance
3	'Nothing'	Diana	**Track 9:** 00.01 – 04.15	1 – 175	Staging
4	'Don Theme'	Don	04.15 – 05.05	1 – 29	Staging
5	'Hello Twelve'	All	05.05 – 05.59	29 – 68	Dance / Staging
6	'Little Brat'	Judy	06.11 – 06.45	69 – 92	Staging
7	'Mother'	Maggie, Judy, Diana, Al, Cassie, Sheila, Don, Val, Greg	06.46 – 08.44	92 – 136	Staging
8	'Greg Theme'	Greg	08.56 – 10.14	137 – 165	Staging
9	'Hello Twelve "jazz"'	All	10.15 – 11.41	165 – 221	Dance
10	'Finale'	All	12.56 – 13.58	269 – 303	Dance

of a wider whole. This song is like a mini-musical within the larger musical, designed to break the frame of the single-character narratives told to Zach on the line and give a collective response to the question of growing up. Each section includes its own story within the wider narrative, and identifying that and allowing it to come through will keep your overall storytelling neat and focused.

PRODUCTION NUMBERS

Examples: 'Be Our Guest'; 'Who's That Woman', 'Put On Your Sunday Clothes', 'Consider Yourself'.

Production numbers are often some of the most well-known and memorable moments of a musical. They are usually plotted into the structure of a show at a point where audiences need a form of release, are not taxing for an audience and often don't move the plot or narrative along a considerable amount. Some shows will have multiple production numbers designed to show off different elements, from large ensemble dance routines to set pieces and scenic elements that help bring the show to life. In Jack Viertel's essential book *The Secret Life of the American Musical* he discusses the fact that musicals depend on 'rhythmic energy shifts', arguing that 'quiet thoughtfulness must be followed by noisy energy, and vice versa'. Production numbers therefore become 'the noise' that can have different purposes, from shedding light on the culture and emotion of the setting ('There's Nothing Like a Dame') through to numbers that exist for pure joy, to 'recharge' the audience and give the show a fresh jolt of energy ('With a Little Bit of Luck', 'Who Will Buy', etc.).

If the writers have done their jobs correctly, the build and 'rate of release' will be inherently written into the number and shouldn't take much study for you to find it. Jerome Robbins described this as a 'release of ideas', saying that as soon as an audience has understood a visual idea and absorbed it, a new one must be presented. It's a balance between an idea getting established enough to provide pleasure and not outstaying its welcome for the audience to get bored. Multiple visual ideas should be carefully mapped out so as not to overwhelm and confuse an audience as to what they should be looking at, and move on to build to a visual climax with a strong enough release for the audience. Often these numbers are busy, using the full stage and full company. You have to consider exactly what you want the audience to look at and when. Anything vital that has to be seen must be noted and framed as such, as well as any important lyrics the song may contain that cannot be missed. Usually these songs are written with over-stimulation in mind and the lyrics are often strong, repetitive and include a catchy chorus.

The first thing I would do is 'song map' similar to what I described for an Action Song. Go through the score and identify the different sections of the number, putting focus on who is singing, how it builds and any moments of specific action that are happening. Usually these numbers begin life as simple songs that are then extended by dance arrangers and vocal arrangers to provide the necessary 'release of ideas' from the original production or revival. Licensed material will feature the 'official' version of the number that you are obliged to perform, but note that this may be different to a professional version you have seen or even the cast recording that you have been listening to. The first thing to do is sit with the musical director and go through the score to make sure you're literally all working from the same song sheet, and remember – you must perform the version that you have licensed. If the material differs vastly I would ask the MD to play and record the number so you have an accurate reference before you start preparing the number. I find that for older and classic shows this is more of a problem, where revivals have had official licence to update and revisit numbers that are then committed to recordings.

Directing Scene Transitions

Scene transitions are often the most forgotten part of a show for directors, but if done well can elevate a production and eradicate an amateur feel and help a show appear slick. As your focus and energy will quite rightly be on scenes involving actors, you mustn't leave consideration of how you take an audience from one scene to the next until the technical rehearsal. Remember, the entire show is a journey and your job is to take the audience along. Think of the show as kicking a ball in the air – you start with a jolt and watch it cruise to a height before slowly coming back down to earth on a clear trajectory. You don't ever want that ball to drop, as you'll lose momentum, pace and energy. A bad scene transition can bring your ball crashing to the ground, meaning you have to literally keep starting again to get from A to B, making for a disjointed and unsatisfying journey.

Start by listing your scenes for each act and identify the different locations, number of scenes and their placement. Count the pages in the script to find the overall rhythm of the act and see where your breaks and beats will land. Make notes of the locations involved and more importantly any props, set pieces and other technical elements that are required. Having this written out in a table will mean you can easily share this with your technical crew, from set designers who will need to look after the scenic elements as they transition through to the sound crew and lighting team who will be responsible for bringing the transition to life.

Older shows were written with less care over transitions and relied on frequent blackouts in a structure similar to: 'Scene / blackout / set change / next scene / blackout'. Usually scene change music was written (or indeed improvised in the first instances) to cover these changes and varied in length depending on what was required. As discussed above, smaller scenes (often called 'traveller' scenes) were written deliberately to be performed in front of the tabs, as far downstage as was possible in front of a curtain or painted gauze. This allowed the larger scene to be changed behind, ready for the next location and big number. As Broadway evolved and changed, directors such as Michael Bennett changed audience expectations by creating cinematic scene transitions in shows such as *Dreamgirls* (1981) where blackouts weren't used and instead one scene bled into the next, similar to what can be achieved on film. Shows became 'slicker', written specifically to allow these transitions to take place and keep the pace of the show, which in turn dictated scenic design, musical arrangements and more.

I have never been a fan of seeing stage crew on stage moving set and props. Instead, I usually utilize the cast and block the scene change, including any set change, into the choreography of the scene. This generally depends on the technical requirements of the venue and the size of the stage – as a general rule the larger the stage and venue the easier it is to disguise stage crew and 'distract' from the change, largely as your scenic requirements will likely be more complicated.

DISTRACT METHOD

If space allows and you are faced with a large scene transition, I'd advise distracting the audience as your first option. Remember, as a director your job is to identify and influence where you want your audience to look, and nowhere is this more important than when you have somewhere you *don't* want them to look. As a scene ends, think about where the next location is and where the narrative is going. What has just happened – has the scene ended on a high or a low? Do you need to break the tension, add pace or remind the audience of a secondary plot or a secondary character? Remember, as nothing is specifically written between the scenes you have the freedom to do what you wish – so long as you don't add any dialogue or music you can utilize whichever cast members you wish. For example, consider the scene breakdown in Act One of *Sweet Charity*:

SYNOPSIS OF SCENES – *SWEET CHARITY*
ACT ONE
Scene 1: The Park by the Lake
Scene 2: Hostess Room of the Fan-Dango Ballroom
Scene 3: Fan-Dango Ballroom
Scene 4: New York Street and Canopy in front of the Pompeii Club
Scene 5: Interior of the Pompeii Club
Scene 6: Vittorio Vidal's Apartment
Scene 6a: The Same
Scene 7: The Hostess Room
Scene 8: The 92nd Street 'Y' Information Booth and Elevator

There are a number of difficult scenic transitions between each of the different locations. From Scene 3 in the Fan-Dango Ballroom you have to take the audience to the next scene, in front of and then inside the Pompeii Club. No matter how big your set budget may be, the feel of these scenes has to be completely different from each other, from the sleaziness of the Ballroom and 'Big Spender' through to the sophistication of 'Rich Man's Frug' – it's important that Charity feels 'different' in these settings as she's swept up in the world of Vittorio Vidal. The libretto simply says 'the dance hall moves off and the New York Street moves in'. If only it was that simple. Directly before this transition Charity has been performing 'Charity's Soliloquy' in which she dances with a 'customer' Marvin, giving the audience an insight into her life as a dancehall hostess. Looking at the lyrics of the song, there's nothing that specifies it has to fully take place in the club; instead it can establish itself there and quickly move to a non-specific every place as the audience is distracted by Charity's internal monologue and performative slow dancing with Marvin. By this point the world of the Ballroom has more than firmly been established – you can therefore begin the scene transition much earlier than the libretto suggests, building in enough time for one scene to 'dissolve' and the other to be ready behind it as the song ends.

Think about beginning the song in the original setting of the ballroom. The key thing is the audience understands how this world works – a customer pays money and selects who they dance with. Once that has happened and Charity begins to dance with Marvin there is not necessarily much more to be gained by remaining in that location. What we DO need to focus on is Charity's description of how this transactional relationship works through the lyrics in the text. Work with your choreographer on keeping this movement tight and isolated – it is a sort of 'lap dance' after all – and make the two of them our primary focus. Place them in a spotlight downstage, travelling across the front of the stage which gives you time to 'distract' the audience from the scene being changed behind them. By the time the number ends and the 'playout' section of the score begins you'll have banked enough time to begin the next scene afresh. This may not work specifically for every single transition, but look for an easy opportunity where these can happen earlier than the libretto suggests, taking the song or moment out of a specific location and distracting the audience as they continue to perform.

A similar effect can be had by bringing on other characters for crossovers or walkovers, lighting them at the front as the stage behind them changes. Sometimes these can be ensemble members or characters we don't need to see again or invest in; they literally are there to distract. The transition between Scene 5 in the club to Vittorio's Apartment is simply covered by 'Scene Change Music' according to the libretto. The audience have just seen the dancers in the club react to Charity collapsing, leading to her being led to Vittorio's apartment. As the principal characters leave the stage and the location shifts, why not use the dancers to distract, showing them move from the Club? Where are they going? We don't care or need to know, but you can continue the energy from the scene and extend it into the transition in order to distract. Keep their aloofness, make us wonder where the party is going and keep us in their world until the next scene is set and ready to begin.

OWN IT

Another method or transition is somewhat the opposite – that of owning the theatricality of the scene transition. This method usually works better in smaller spaces, especially those in the round / thrust or promenade where the traditional trappings of theatrical disguise are harder to utilize. Rather than pretend that the audience moves from one location to another in a realistic or natural way, instead own the theatricality and have your cast change the scene in full view of the audience. As long as this convention is established from the very beginning and used consistently an audience will buy into it and not feel affected by the shifts. Choreographers Susan Stroman and Chris Wheeldon have both utilized this to great effect in shows such as *Crazy For You* and *An American in Paris*. Rather than have the cast simply pick up a chair or table and awkwardly strike them, instead they choreograph the movement and make a virtue out of them moving the set so that instead it becomes a beautiful extension of the world of the show.

Thinking of the example above, you could just as easily move from Scene 3 to Scene 4 without distracting the audience and instead taking them along with you. On stage you have a full cast of Ballroom Dancers and male customers, transitioning from the Fan-Dango into the Club. As Charity sings her soliloquy, experiment with them interacting with Charity and Marvin as the world around them transforms. Perhaps it's an insight into Charity's head: as she thinks about her life and setting, maybe she wishes it would dissolve away. The cast around her physically remove the world she finds herself trapped in as she tries to disassociate from it. Suddenly the full scene is within Charity's head as she actively tries to distance her mind from it and the physical world that has been established gets removed. Utilize your cast and think of a reason why they are involved in the moment – it won't take much of a leap to rationalize this and have them creatively be a part of the transition.

You may find yourself using a mix of methods throughout the show, but I would generally try and stick to a general tone that remains consistent. If your cast haven't been involved in any set changes for the whole show, it will look jarring for them to suddenly change the set in a scene late in Act 2. Think about your relationship to the physical world of the show and how theatrical you want this to appear.

You may well find yourself having to make difficult decisions during the tech rehearsal when it appears that transitions take a lot longer in real time than you think. Planning as much as you can ahead of this will ease this pain, but speaking with your musical director about the music that's required to cover the change and options on how to extend this will save you a lot of time. Whatever happens, the stage shouldn't be silent, keep the music playing until the next scene is established and maintain as much energy as possible. Think on your feet when problem-solving these issues live and utilize your cast as much as you can. It's much easier to cut parts of transitions than add to them during a tech or dress, so over-prepare as much as you can. Remember, everything is quicker in the rehearsal room. Those desks on wheels will take 3x as long on stage. Bringing on a chair? Double the time. If you can reduce this then great, but give yourself as much padding as possible to cover as many eventualities as possible.

Directing a 'Problematic' Musical

Directing *around* the problems without cutting or changing the text can be difficult, but it's not impossible in all cases. Your collective interpretation of certain characters and how the text is played are all choices left to you and your actors and you can be creative in your approach. One of the main ways in which a show dates itself is generally its attitude to the sexes and male-female relationships. Many musicals are structured around narratives that are outdated, usually around a female protagonist's want and need to find a man. Whilst this drive forms most of the plot and narrative, the character's agency can be controlled in performance and their attitude towards the male character even within the content of the show itself. As a director, talk to your cast about these elements of the plot that may feel uncomfortable and consider how they could be approached in a contemporary manner. Musicals are presentational in nature and can sustain a level of remove from the audience that allows them to exist as a commentary on the time in which they were written rather than act as a naturalistic commentary on the world as it is now. Look for ways in which you can heighten the areas of the show that can sustain it, think about how the show has the potential to be read as a satire or allegory of the contemporary world. The humour of *How to Succeed …* for example comes at the audience laughing at the heightened world of late 1950s New York corporate culture. Enjoying the piece as a satirical comedy doesn't mean audiences are endorsing the behaviours of the characters, as the musical frame itself is clear that this is a commentary, albeit heightened and in many ways ridiculed, of what a contemporary audience would recognize.

Case Study – *Carousel*

One of the most frequently cited popular amateur musicals that's known for being problematic is *Carousel*. As Billy Bigelow returns to earth for one day, he strikes his daughter Louise. When she tells her mother, Julie, her response suggests that it's possible to be hit hard by someone you love and not feel a thing. This is often taken as being an apologist for domestic abuse, as Billy's 'redemption' comes at the end of the show as he sees his daughter graduate and is led to heaven. There are numerous ways this section of the show can be staged without changing the script or narrative and countless productions have offered their own way to get around this problem.

Think about what it is you want your audience to take away from this action and work backwards on how to achieve it. Should they be disgusted by this revelation? Should they be sympathetic towards Julie? Should it be a clear commentary that this behaviour is unacceptable or do you want to create more nuance?

Once you've identified the effect you wish to create, you can investigate different ways of directing that moment to create that desired effect. If the text itself is the non-variable, you need to identify the variables that you do have at your disposal to build a sense of what is possible:

- **Tone:** How does Julie say this line? Is it serious? Is it designed to pacify Louise? Could it even be sarcastic?
- **Staging:** Can Julie sense or see Billy? How does this make a difference to her words vs her actions?
- **Body language:** How is Julie standing while saying that line – what is her body saying? Is it saying the same as her words or is she offering a different reading through her eyes and body language?

- **Reactions:** How does Louise react – does she accept this wisdom or does she look at her mother in horror? Could her reaction, body language and staging suggest that she doesn't accept this definition and isn't pacified by her mother's explanation? Who else is on the stage, how does the Star Keeper react? Is there any ensemble on stage to offer commentary through their presence, look or presence? How does Billy react? What is his body showing and does he communicate any non-verbal remorse?

- **Lighting and sound:** How can you utilize sound and lighting effects to draw focus or dictate feelings for an audience? Should this moment remain naturalistic or be more expressive? Could you use colour? Could you underscore it with some form of sound?

- **Foreshadowing / explaining:** As you've read above, previous directors have explored Billy's upbringing and repressed trauma through the prologue specifically for this moment. Is there a way of prefacing this in terms of justifying the behaviour?

- **Concluding:** Think about how the audience views Billy at the end of the piece, specifically in the next scene. Is it clear his behaviour has gone unchallenged? Does he find redemption? Does he have a 'positive' end?

As you can see in this small example above, every behaviour and action can be interrogated, considered and understood differently. Whilst some musicals have more sustained moments or characterization that should be addressed, the above serves as an example as to understanding what you can do within the limits of the licence through creative direction.

Directing Sensitive Scenes

Musicals frequently deal with real-life situations and scenarios that can be hard-hitting and should be treated with a degree of sensitivity. As discussed above, these should have been identified in your pre-production work, so that the full production team and cast aren't surprised by anything that arises in the script. These may range from moments of intimacy between two or more characters through to drug abuse, mental health issues, rape, suicide, racism, domestic violence and death depending on the show and its context. Rather than shy away from these and hope they resolve themselves during rehearsal, being up-front in conversations about the show as well as how these will be handled during the pitching process will mean they can be handled in an organized way.

Find an Expert

Whilst you are the director, you're not expected to be an expert on all of the issues that the script may contain. Think about relevant support groups and charities that will have online resources to discuss the issues at hand and remain sensitive in your conversations around each of the topics. Identifying any potential triggers within the script will help you support the cast – remember that you will never know the full extent of the lives your company lead and what different people may find triggering. Signpost and announce when certain scenes will be rehearsed and communicate with your company about the issues that the show will be dealing with – even consider crowd-sourcing help and support from across the company.

Intimacy direction is commonplace in professional productions and books, and guidelines have been written on the subject. Educate yourself and understand why they are necessary. It's unlikely that your budget will stretch to hire an intimacy director, but for shows where this is a key factor I would encourage you to look into this as an option, even if it's for a specified number of rehearsals. Musicals by their very nature include romance and intimate relationships and it's difficult to find a show that doesn't include a kiss or two between any of the leads. Do not underestimate the stress your cast may have with regards to these moments – speak to those concerned and listen to their thoughts and suggestions on when to work these moments into rehearsal. Remember, everyone comes from different backgrounds and may have many reasons why they don't want to consistently rehearse these scenes, especially in front of other members of the rehearsal. Be sensitive and work with your cast rather than telling and demanding them to show intimacy on cue with no support.

Closed Rehearsals

Acting can be a raw and exposing experience even for professionals and in many way amateurs are less equipped to handle difficult scenes due to a lack of training. I find it's a good idea to have closed rehearsals for actors exploring certain scenes for the first time. Rather than discuss and engage with difficult topics in front of the whole room, it may be easier for these conversations to be kept small and personal. Discourage the use of phones and recording equipment so actors can feel free and uninhibited to discuss the topics, ask questions and more importantly, make mistakes. Some musicals include scenes and discussions of racism and homophobia, for example, which some members in the cast will find difficult, on both the receiving and giving end of the exchange. Think about the human effect of such scenes on the actors themselves, particularly if abuse, bullying or aggression is involved and don't over-rehearse these sections in one sitting. Acting as a villain or a character who has to engage with negative words and feelings can be draining and isolating – you need to work hard to keep the actor absorbed in the company and make a clear boundary between character and performer. Once this moment has been rehearsed, I suggest diving straight into a more lighthearted moment or song to change the atmosphere in the room and let your actors finish rehearsal on a high.

Do Your Research

As mentioned in the first section of the book, preparation is key in these matters. If there is drug use for example you have a responsibility to understand how this forms part of the narrative and how it is used. This doesn't necessarily mean you are committed to presenting a naturalistic approach on stage, but it's important that you work with your actors on the real world concerns around this and the ramifications it may have. Consider how you speak about these subjects in rehearsal – don't make glib or off-colour jokes about any of the themes, even if your natural instinct is to use humour to alleviate tension. Give everything the gravitas it deserves and the appropriate attention to detail.

Putting it Together

Once you've worked on building the show piece-by-piece, you'll get to a natural point where you will want to start running elements of the show together. From your rehearsal schedule you will have identified the order in which you have chosen to tackle the show and how you have naturally progressed from scene to scene. As you move from scene to scene at this point, I always try to piece scenes together slowly, maybe revisiting one of them at the start of a rehearsal before going on to work on the next or following scenes. 'Mini' runs are helpful as they allow you to see how the scenes work together, especially in terms of energy and pacing and for the actors it allows them to get to know the show in real time. There may be logical elements that only become clear when scenes are put together – entrances, exits, and so on – and actors can get used to knowing sections in which they may need to preserve energy in order to deliver a song or solo number. Repetition is key, so the more 'mini' runs you can do of different sections, the stronger building blocks you have for putting the other elements together.

Stagger Runs

Stagger runs usually appear in a rehearsal schedule and can terrify cast members. If they're scheduled too early, it can shock and disorientate a cast or contrarily shock them into realizing how much work they have to do. Whilst mini-runs place certain sections together, stagger runs are designed to flow a whole act, starting from the beginning and literally staggering through to the end. Only attempt these when you know you've done all of the scenes at least once. If you find a section or corner that you may not have done, skip over it and come back. Don't let a stagger run be the first time you all explore a scene or moment as it will raise the tension of the room and create bad blood with the actors who will feel unnecessarily exposed.

Before starting these, explain that you know things may be rough and ready, but the idea is for everyone to get the general shape of the act and to piece certain sections together. Again, it allows for logistical problems to be exposed that are better being discovered now rather than later, and gives a sense of accomplishment to the room of how much ground has been covered. Your principals will likely be nervous at first and may wish to remain on-book, which is fine. It may also be the first chance the full cast have had to see certain scenes or solo numbers, so you'll want the atmosphere of the room to be supportive and encouraging, rather than judgy and tense.

Before you start, talk about any areas you're expecting to be particularly rough. The notes that you make for these should largely be for yourself and the creative team. I wouldn't do a formal notes session for the cast after a stagger run, instead I would absorb them into working notes for when you next rehearse those scenes or songs.

There's a tendency for the cast to completely forget everything you've done the second you attempt a stagger run, mainly due to panic. Remember, everyone can feel quite raw at this stage – you'll keep on hearing things like 'we only did this bit once'; 'I wasn't here for this bit', and so on. Don't become defensive and don't blame anyone for things that go wrong. These are as much for you and the creative team to see where you are with the show, rather than a memory test or challenge for the full cast. Once it's over, talk with your cast about things that went well – encourage questions and comments on anything logistical and make a note to revisit. You'll naturally see those scenes that need more work or revisiting, so note those in your schedule for the upcoming rehearsals. Occasionally stagger runs can feel dispiriting and like everything has crumbled under the pressure. Assure the company that this is the foundation for the show and it'll only get better from there.

Full Runs

There's no particular stage in your rehearsal schedule for runs to begin, as much of it depends on the time you have allowed. I've worked on shows where we have been running weeks in advance, only for the show to suffer and get flat, as well as shows where the final rehearsal has been the first time we've run the show from start to finish. I would try and aim for somewhere in the middle. You want your cast to feel confident, not complacent, that you all have a show and that it's going to be good. That positive energy will help propel you into the final weeks, see an uplift in ticket sales – because the company *wants* people to come and see it – and generally keep everything going in the right direction. When a cast feels under-rehearsed and under-prepared they become anxious and fraught or merely switch off and disengage – at which point it's difficult to get them back on track.

First, I would try to schedule runs on weekends rather than evenings. Running a full show, with warm-up, cool-down and debrief can take 3 hours for even the shortest show, so you don't want it to feel rushed and chaotic. Running a show in the evening should focus on particular acts rather than the full show, although you do need to make sure you give the cast a chance to run the show in one sitting so you can collectively feel the pace of the show as a whole. Allow time for people to arrive, settle and mentally prepare for a run. Don't start a run at the time you've called rehearsal to start, no matter how pressed you are for time. People will be late, running from work and so on, and you need to address and calm the room before you start. The worst kind of runs are those that start and half the cast are unaware, even if they're not in the opening number. You need to ensure everyone is on the same mental page when you start. Run a short warm-up and focus activity. Harness the energy of the group and explain the boundaries and set your expectations for how the run will operate.

EXPECTATIONS

There are different types of run and it's important everyone knows what the aim is before you start. Some runs will benefit from stopping and fixing something that's gone wrong; others will require you to plough on and treat them more like an uninterrupted dress. In the rehearsal room, it's rare to have to have an uninterrupted run, especially if it's still a few weeks out from the show. If you tell the cast that you'll stop and fix, set that expectation from the start rather than set the run-up as a dress and then interrupt your actors, as it will unsettle the room and ruin the pacing.

Think about your *needs*. Why is this run happening? If it's for the sound / lighting crew then running as close to time as you can with minimal stopping is key. If it's a speed run to check lines and cement blocking then you'll want to not stop even if things go wrong. Ask yourself and your creative team what is most useful. I would try and alternate different types of run – start with one where you don't stop to see where the holes are, then follow that with a stop-and-fix run that's slightly more relaxed. When you can see problems that need fixing, ask yourself if it's more efficient to fix it now or save it for later. Think about the fact you have the full cast in the room – it's probably not the best use of time to correct blocking in a duologue or solo song. Fixing an ensemble entry or scene transition, however, would be good use of time, given that it will take time to set up that exact moment outside of a run environment. Some problems only present themselves during a run, in which case this is the time to fix them. Solo notes, acting notes and behavioural tweaking is probably more efficiently done outside of a run, either during working notes or a specific follow up rehearsal.

It's important to set the expectations of the whole room and company before each run. Do you expect everyone to sit silently in the wings watching the run and the sections they are not in or are the cast free to leave the room and use the time and space to rehearse their sections or relax? I would say that during early runs it's important to have everyone in the room watching, mainly for courtesy to your fellow performers and out of respect. Keep an eye on the temperature of the room and how it can be influenced by those not performing as much as it can those on stage. I generally encourage everyone to remain in the room, silently, as best they can as even when they're offstage they're contributing to the success of the run. Explain to the cast that they need to match the energy of the performance as it happens in real time and so being in the room helps you see where that sits and ultimately affects their own performance, however small it may be.

EXPECTATIONS

The ultimate aim of a run is for the show to take shape and the full cast to become comfortable ahead of moving into the theatre. The more comfortable the cast is with what they are doing in space the smoother your tech run is likely to be, leading to a more comfortable first night. However, it is possible to overrun a show to a point that the cast loses interest and complacency seeps into the performance. Unlike professional performers who are trained to give the same performance every night for months on end, amateurs are not engaging with the show in the same way, as the acceleration to show week is short and sharp. There's generally no time for the show to 'settle', no previews and so on, so the adrenaline and forward motion is sharper and more intense with less chance to fix and correct before settling. I'm a firm believer that a show can peak too early and that the energy can fall flat for opening night. You need to maintain forward motion at all times, so numbers and performances keep getting better and keep building each time you run, rather than running out of anywhere to go. Your job is to direct this motion forward and make sure that each run 'builds' on the work of the previous one. Adding an additional element to each run will help give an added edge and purpose. This may be the addition of a few props, then some set pieces, then something simple like a micro- phone-plot, and finally, costume elements and full costumes. Having something new, however small, each time will help the momentum push forward and keep everyone climbing upwards rather than simply plateauing. If you sense plateau or decline, I focus a cast on something new to discover with every run. This may be something simple like telling them to use this run to focus on enunciation or articu- lation or it may be more conceptual asking them to use this specific run to tell the show as if they're delivering it to a classroom of children. Having a singular focus for that run helps avoid boredom or complacency, especially for those in the ensemble who may by this point feel very comfortable with their tracks and the overall rhythm of the show.

LIGHTING RUNS

If your lighting designer can't attend a run of the show I would record one of the final runs and provide it as a reference recording for them to begin to see the stage picture and where certain actions occur. They should be familiar with your set design and stage plan so that they know ahead of time where lights need to be rigged and focused. Given the short amount of time during get-in you should encourage them to be as prepared as possible because in many cases a formal light-plotting session with cast on stage will not be available to you. On your set diagrams, draw out certain areas where action tends to happen and specify any 'special' areas that may require extra attention – spotlights, transformation lighting, strobes, and so on. This will help them prepare ahead of the get-in and will save you vital time during the tech rehearsal. I would also consider key moments of the show and describe specific moods you hope to achieve. Be as descriptive as you can, letting them know how an audience should feel when they see that specific moment. You may have rehearsed a beautifully nuanced scene that's then shortchanged by lighting that doesn't reflect what your actors are trying to communicate and sets a different style or tone that undermines the acting.

Notes – How to Give Effective Notes

You should take and give notes following each run. Generally, these get less and less after each run, so don't worry if you find yourself with less to say. Don't just give notes for the sake of it. Again, think about what can realistically be achieved in the time that's left and don't overcomplicate things by having new ideas days out from the first show that you don't have time to deliver on. Your notes should be for the tech team and creatives, as well as the cast, and should be delivered with the same level of care and attending. When noting a dress rehearsal or tech, remain polite and professional. Ask the tech team what they want you to note. Don't waste time noting sound feedback or lights not coming on – your tech team will know this, and it's not helpful for them to be noted on obvious errors. Of course, ask for clarification and raise questions but do so in a collaborative way, again within the remit of the time and resources that are available to you all.

With amateur theatre, I generally give final notes after the dress rehearsal. For short runs, you don't have time to keep making tweaks and changes and, with maybe just four or five shows you have to let your cast settle into it rather than noting them after every show and changing things. Some level of course-correcting may be needed, especially after the first show with an audience. Laugh lines, waiting for reactions and so on may be helpful, but you have to remember to let the cast enjoy themselves. I would largely only note elements of safety during a run or anything that has had to change out of a practical or technical problem that has arisen during show week. I draw the line at giving notes in the interval or mid-performance. You aren't a football manager – stay out of the way and let the show run its course. Directors who do this I feel are only doing so to assert their authority and remind people they still have control. Show week can create difficult feelings for a director who suddenly feels their work has been released and has somehow run away from them. They go from a period of intense control to having a show taken out of their hands, and so some combat this by re-inserting themselves into an actor's performance by giving notes mid-show to remind everyone of their authority. Don't do this – it's unnecessary and no one, least of all your actors, will thank you for it. I recently heard of a director who sent the cast notes the week after the show had ended. Don't be that person.

Note sessions can make or break a production, especially your relationship with your company. I've seen directors give horrendous notes that have soured the whole experience and undermined their work up to that point, as well as directors give such illuminating notes that the cast naturally feel inspired and can't wait to run the show again. In amateur theatre in particular, they can be intimidating and tricky, and so I've compiled my top pieces of advice:

1. **Preface your note sessions:** no one likes being noted or corrected – it's a natural instinct to become defensive. Notes are public, are the most blatant confirmation of the relationship between actor and director and a point where your view is delivered with a level of authority. Before you begin, explain that these notes

are not personal and come from a place of constructive feedback intended to make the show better. Remind people of this each time and try and keep the tone light and breezy as you can so they don't feel told off, however badly the run may have gone. It's worth also saying that you can't possibly see everything and that there may be things you didn't see during that run or didn't manage to write down.

2. **Be positive as well as critical:** again, positive reinforcement often gets you much further than criticism. Whilst note sessions aren't necessarily there to praise each performance, actors will want to hear that what they are doing is working and so acknowledge things that went well and that you liked as much as you can. I generally offer a blanket statement that there's no time to note everything good, but finding something nice and positive to say about an actor, including those in the ensemble, will help balance anything constructive you may also say.

3. **Deliver them to the actor in person:** this is often very tricky given the nature of rehearsal schedules, but, where you can, aim to do notes together in person. Sending notes in an email or posting on Facebook allows things like tone to get misinterpreted – and they may not actually get delivered properly, which can lead to further confusion. You also can't be sure everyone has actually read them or engaged with them; so in-person, directly following a run, whilst everything is fresh in your mind is the best way to deliver them. Waiting until the next rehearsal won't do you any favours as it'll be hard to remember the specifics, meaning they're unlikely to be addressed.

4. **Know the difference between a 'working' note and a 'corrective' note:** working notes are those that require work and can't be fixed on the spot. They may need rehearsal or clarification, often with the MD or choreographer. Explaining where a harmony was wrong or dance position was out of place is inefficient; instead of describing it, make a note to rehearse that corner and turn it into a 'working' notes session where you get the cast to work through the note rather than just listen to it and take it. A corrective note can be given and acted on without re-rehearsal, for example 'please enter the line before you did today' or 'come further downstage during that song'.

5. **Some notes should be done in person and away from the group:** anything that's vaguely personal or sensitive should be given directly to the actor in private. You'll soon see which actors are more sensitive to notes than others, and learning from that will help you build trust and get the most out of your actor. The same goes for repeated names. Often your brain focuses on one person throughout a run and every little thing they do seems wrong and you end up noting them for every thing they do. If you see their name appear over and over in your notebook, think before you speak. Collate your notes and speak to them outside of the session, otherwise they will be demoralized and feel targeted.

6. **Allow space for questions but not for justification:** tell the group that they can ask for clarifications or follow up with you outside of the note session, but ask that they take the note. It's not a space for discussion or justification – an actor's natural reaction will be to tell you *why* something happened. Sometimes this may be relevant but most often it just wastes time, so encourage them to take the note and follow up with you privately for clarification.

7. **Be brief, clear and specific:** try not to dwell on a note or situation. If someone brought a prop on in the wrong place or forgot to pick up a chair, be specific. Don't launch into a monologue or character assassination on the actor and their inability to move furniture – a simple note, 'James, the chair came on too early, please wait for the next line to place it' is all it takes. Equally don't say things like 'James, you always bring your props at the wrong time … ' as it's not specific and not helpful.

8. **Don't overgeneralize:** again this links to being specific. Giving a note like 'I feel everyone is sort of a bit much in the opening number' isn't helpful. Instead, be direct: 'you all need to bring down the volume in the opening number and also reduce the size of your performance to make it feel more natural'.

9. **Switch places and think about how you would like to be spoken to:** turn the situation round and think how you'd like to be spoken to by your actors. Try and level the relationship and give notes in the way you would like to receive them.

10. **Kill your darlings:** depending on where you are in the schedule you have to self-select the notes that are achievable in the time you have. There's no point giving notes that will change a full scene directly following a dress rehearsal if there's not time to work on them. Working notes that don't come with rehearsal time are not helpful. Equally, don't unsettle your actors by giving them new notes at a time when they don't have the time to work them through. The closer you get to performance the more your notes should be about 'refining' rather than 'redoing'.

Rehearsal Reports

It can be really overwhelming when considering a large production team and making sure everyone remains up to date with changes and on the same page. Unlike professional theatre you're unlikely to have the full team in every rehearsal, therefore certain things can easily be missed, leading to challenges and miscommunication. To counter this, when I'm working on a bigger show I use a system of rehearsal reports that are compiled usually at the end of every week and sent out to the full cast and creative team (see Figure 2.3). These reports are similar to the minutes of a meeting – they itemize primarily what was covered, who was present, who was absent and summarize the rehearsal. Often not much needs to be written, but they are a space where you can note down significant changes and keep the full company up to date with progress. I would note what was not covered that week and why, if more time

Rehearsal Report

Show: Nine
Venue: Abbey Theatre

Report #8: 5 weeks out from show

DATE: w/c 21 August 2023, Tuesday, Thursday, Sunday
GENERAL: 1. Staging of Act one now complete. Set "BELLS" and repeated on Thursday so everyone knows it 2. Did a walk through of Act One for chair placement and re-setting / re-freshing. Ran from beginning to after "VATICAN". 3. Candles didn't make the cut. Will rethink if need to add back in. 4. Full vocal recap happened Sunday as well as looking at Act 2 and "Grand Canal" revisit. 5. 3.7m from the back of the cyc to the front of the stage (without apron). Future tidy-ups: "Overture", "Not Since Charlie Chaplin" for choreo purposes. Re-look at chair placement for "My Husband" now we've got everyone. Please all start to track / write down chair movements in detail
PROPS: Gun required (never fires - doesn't have to be specifically weighted stage gun) - SM has brought options for this. Box needed for Young Guido (various sizes - one for the script) Full 'typed script needed for Young Guido to give Guido Blank pages of script needed for Grand Canal for distribution For the paper drop - thinner fax / script type paper to fall. Fans - 9 pairs of fans needed - Claudia has made prototypes that look great Cigarette & holder needed for La Fleur (not long one, shorter one) Cigarettes / lighter needed for Guido - Guido will use herbal cigs, with two separate ashtrays one either side of the stage.

SET:
Followed up in a separate email. New idea for the back wall and drop hire.
Band to be on floor level but still needs to fit behind Gauze.
Band needs to fit behind the gauze line - LINE 16 for Gauze Legs to be flown in for the 'reconstruction' - these will live on Lines 7 and 11.
Bars 9 and 10 to be used for the 'drop'.
Videos created for the pre-set and the final Reprises scene.
Need to discuss the cyc when we see it set up for the photo shoot. Replacement cloth needed potentially, also need to confirm pinning this down to floor.
Full white strip to be painted on stage floor
Hires: 2 stage lights non practical from Tring (free - to collect show week)
Camera, director's chair (low), light on castors - Greenroom hire

COSTUME:
Smaller hand fans (Venetian style if poss?) for Grand Canal x5
Ridiculous period dress for Claudia (shared with La Fleur) - Hire?
Potentially some form of hats / headpieces in this style ?

LX:
No additional notes

SOUND:
Pre set sound - Director to create

MUSIC:
1. Decided on 8 bars pre-Overture singing starting 2. Number 13 - no vamp on the second page.

NOTES:

Fig. 2.3 Rehearsal Report.

is required in a future rehearsal and so on. They may detail that more time is required for a set change, or that a vamp bar will be repeated multiple times, or the position of a set element has had to change and so on. Whatever it is, noting it down is helpful not only for you to remember, but also for those who weren't present to keep track and raise questions if required.

Feel free to use and adapt this according to the details you find necessary to report. Whilst it may feel laborious to fill in, I find it an important summary that can be completed at the end of the week and distributed to the full cast and creative team. It's also a good way for the committee or members of the society who have a vested interest in knowing the progress but aren't regularly at rehearsals. Get into a routine of emailing these at the end of a week or first thing on a Monday – your cast and crew will thank you.

Enhancing and Elevating Your Show

After you have run your show a number of times, one of the biggest risks you may face is it becoming stale. As mentioned above, there's a fine line between running enough so that the cast are confident and over-running it so that they tire of it. Unless something is different each time, the life of the show can evaporate before you get out of the rehearsal room. While you have to be able to juggle and manage what time is left in your schedule there is always time to continue working on the show and finding ways to elevate it and encourage your cast to keep discovering their characters and making choices. Below I've listed my tips for the period just before you move into the theatre, usually the week before, and methods of keeping your show growing:

1. **Encourage your cast to keep making choices:** at this point they will be hopefully confident on their lines and blocking. My general rule is that actors should be encouraged to keep playing and making different choices, with the caveat that it shouldn't negatively affect anyone else in the room.

2. **Focus on scene changes and transitions:** try to pre-empt any difficult transitions that will emerge during tech and think about how to keep the energy and momentum between scenes. Now you're used to seeing the flow of the show, try to identify any dips where the energy drops or anything that looks messy.

3. **Think about pacing:** to my knowledge, no audience member has ever moaned about an amateur musical being too short. Be wary of the running time of each run and make sure you write it down each time and share with your cast. You should shave time each run as lines get slicker and the cast grow more comfortable. That isn't to say you should be racing through scenes or speeding up tempos, but encourage your cast to be on top of their lines and keep each scene going forward with momentum rather than sitting back and relaxing. Sometimes doing a 'gabble run' where actors say their lines at speed without blocking can help pick up the pace and identify any gaps in line-learning.

4. **Reconnect with the text:** by now it may have been a few weeks since your actors looked at their scripts. Go back to the text and double check that lines are exact and are not being paraphrased, or have been learned incorrectly. It's very common for little errors to have slipped in unconsciously, and if not corrected can cause problems specifically when it comes to other people being on-book and following the script for lighting and sound cues.

5. **Reconnect with the music:** you may find you're sick of hearing the music from the show at this point, but I find it useful to revisit the cast recording(s) that exist and try and think of the show afresh and with new ears. Pay particular attention to the orchestration and any nuances that you may have missed. Again this may expose small inconsistencies or issues with the songs that you might have collectively let slip, or tempos that have shifted throughout rehearsal. Try and think of the score as though you're hearing it for the first time, as many in your audience will soon be.

6. **Thinking 'on' the line:** actors can become *too* rehearsed in their line deliveries and can sometimes fall into auto-pilot. Challenge this by having them speak their lines to each other in a different way as a form of warm-up exercise. I like to go back to the improvisation techniques I spoke about earlier to open up the scenes afresh. Ask them to rehearse scenes without using the text. They will know their characters on a much deeper level, and freeing them from the text will help you find some new choices. Each line should be spoken as if for the first time – thinking 'on' the line as though it's a new thought rather than rehearsed and prepared.

7. **Focus on storytelling:** remind your cast that most of the audience will be coming to this story fresh. It's easy to forget when you have been rehearsing a show for months that this material has to land in real time to an audience who will experience it just once, in the moment. Revisit your very early exercises concerning what the show is *about* and collectively discuss the core elements of the story and narrative that you have to get across. Concepts, staging and choreography may have developed so much that they get in the way of the core focus of the show: that of telling a specific story.

Remember that the run-up to the opening night is a stressful time for the cast who are learning to juggle many aspects and mentally prepare themselves for the run. You have to judge how much new material they are able to take; if an actor is struggling with lines or blocking, it would be counterproductive to start changing and experimenting with various elements that could confuse them. If you're working with consummate actors who are comfortable with the show in its current form, talk to them and ask them for areas where they feel they need specific work. Certain moments are described as being 'eggy' – a word that actors used to describe a moment on stage that feels awkward, not fully realized or just something that isn't working. Identifying and tweaking these moments now will help you collectively make the leap to the next stage beyond the rehearsal room.

ACT 3   Curtain Up, Light the Lights!

Congratulations! You've made it to this point. Show week is the most exciting part of the whole process and what you have all been working towards. It can feel scary but should feel incredibly exciting. Don't let the feelings get away from you; stay focused and unflappable. Things will go wrong, you will run out of time and you'll have to think on your feet, but try not to let this phase you.

Production Week Schedules

As with everything identified in this book, preparation is key. A month out from show week is when I'd usually be expected to come up with a production week schedule that takes into account every separate department. It's easy to feel overwhelmed, but working with your production manager, stage manager and full creative team you can draw up a plan and detailed schedule that breaks down all of the different jobs that need to happen and assign responsibility. Your job should be to manage expectations across different departments, but remember, not everything is your direct responsibility. Confirming the org chart and making sure everyone knows who is responsible for what during show week will mean that you can maximize your time and keep a clear head.

Make sure you are all familiar with any rules and regulations that the performance venue have in place. Each venue will have different rules, and even places that you are used to performing in could have updated policies. Your contract with the venue should be the first port of call when answering these questions, but I would advise making sure you know the answer to the below questions well before show week begins. The more you know in advance the more you can plan for.

1. What are the access times for the venue on each day? This is especially important for the evening of the technical and dress rehearsal.
2. What support do you have from the venue in terms of tech? Who is your technical liaison / manager?
3. Where can items of set / costume and so on be delivered and are there any access requirements?
4. Are there any regulations regarding smoke machines, smoking on stage, fire hazards and fire drills?
5. What do you do if things go wrong – who is your primary point of contact?

Share this knowledge between your team and make sure there's a clear chain of command to streamline questions between the production and the venue.

Sample (Simple) Show Week Schedule

You should draw up a 'simple' show week schedule that offers a broad overview to the cast, creative team, band and crew identifying how the week will run (see Table 3.1). This should be shared well ahead of show week, if not at the start of the process, so that everyone knows the general times things are expected to run throughout the week.

This offers a broad-brush overview of the week, primarily for the cast, who don't require the level of technical detail a wider schedule allows. This is based on a 'typical' amateur theatre show week schedule, taking into account one performance week. The key thing is to make sure this is shared ahead of show week, if not right at the beginning of the process, so you don't run into problems with cast, crew and band not being able to attend.

Sample 'Master' Show Week Schedule

As well as the above, I would create a more detailed schedule that takes into account all of the wider departments and elements that have to come together (see Table 3.2). I would make this in collaboration with my production manager and stage manager,

Table 3.1 Sample (Simple) Show Week Schedule

Date / Time	Location	Required
Sunday 9.00 am	At the theatre	Full cast and production team for 'get in'.
12.00 noon	Rehearsal Room	Band for Band Call.
2.00 pm	Rehearsal Room	Band and full company for sitzprobe.
7.00–11.00 pm	On Stage	Full cast – tech begins.
Monday 9.00 am	Theatre	Director and lighting crew for light plotting. Tech continues.
	Dressing Rooms / Greenroom	Costume crew. Full cast / crew and band – dress
6.00 pm	On Stage	rehearsal begins.
Tuesday 9.00 am	Theatre	Director, tech crew: Tech tidy up / light focusing.
6.00 pm	Theatre	Full cast / crew and band – first performance.
Wednesday 6.00 pm	Theatre	Full cast / crew and band – second performance.
Thursday 6.00 pm	Theatre	Full cast / crew and band – third performance.

Table 3.2 Sample 'Master' Show Week Schedule

Day	Time	On Stage	Lighting	Sound	Band	Wardrobe	Backstage	Misc.
Sunday	13:00	Rigging drops to fly tower	Delivery from lighting company scheduled	Setting band mics in the pit	Not called	Fittings with principals	Setting up dressing rooms	Delivery of props scheduled
Sunday	13:30	Rigging continues	Unpacking delivery	Setting band mics in pit	Not called	Fittings continued	Setting up for sitzprobe	Collect hires from company (Production manager)
Sunday	14:00	Flats set	Beginning to rig hired items	Sound check band mics	Called for sound check	Lunch	Break	Probs table set up
Sunday	14:30	Flats painted	Continue rigging	Sound check band mics	Sound check / head to sitzprobe	Lunch	Sitzprobe begins with full cast	Break

asking all departments to contribute in the weeks before to create a master schedule for everyone to follow.

As you can see, this tracks the week in half-hour increments, detailing what every department is doing and at what time. This offers a strong overview of all the tasks that need to happen, so everyone knows where they should be and the jobs that (ideally) should be happening in each slot. The stage space will be in demand from all departments and it's vital that the timings are discussed ahead of time and a schedule worked out. Tasks like rigging the flies, hanging lights and so on all have to happen in a specific order – there's no point painting the floor before certain jobs have been done as this will block out time that could otherwise be used on stage.

Again, a schedule as detailed as this shouldn't necessarily be the director's responsibility to create, but I've lost track of the amount of times this hasn't been done, especially if you find yourself without a strong production manager and stage manager. Discuss this ahead of time and ask who is in charge of this and offer to help if needs be.

COSTUME CALL

The costume call usually happens just before show week or sometimes on the day of get-in. Depending on what you may have hired, you may not have access to the full costume set until just before the show, but in other circumstances you may have had fittings long before show week as well as having had the chance to do a costume run in the rehearsal room. The costume call is usually an opportunity for the costume designer / wardrobe team to see everyone try all costume elements on and show you as director to make sure you are happy. You won't need to lead this call – instead hand it over to the wardrobe team – but you will need to be on hand to answer questions and confirm you are happy with how things look. Be diplomatic, sensitive and practical. It's probably too late in the day to call for a full new costume, but don't be afraid to note anything that doesn't work from a practical or artistic perspective.

GET IN

The 'get in' or 'bump in' is the official beginning of show week when you're handed the keys to the theatre. You will generally expect your cast to help and be present, although experience shows they can sometimes be less keen about this part of the process. Think carefully about tasks and jobs that they can do and add value – don't just call them for them to hang about doing very little and getting in the way.

BAND CALL / SITZPROBE

This rehearsal is often regarded as the most exciting moment for the cast, but the most stressful for the musical director. It usually occurs at the start of show week, most commonly on the Sunday during the get-in at the theatre. The term 'sitzprobe' is the German term meaning 'seated rehearsal', but in the UK and USA it is more commonly known as the 'band call'. It's the first rehearsal where the band or orchestra and the cast meet and get to perform together, focusing not on staging and choreography but instead on the music. These rehearsals are left in the hands of the MD, and you should very much be a background presence, if not busy elsewhere during the get-in or technical process. Allow everyone to be excited – a good band call usually sets the tone for a successful show week. Your MD will handle any problems that occur and work with the cast and band to smooth out any issues. One of my top tips is to make sure there's some kind of amplification available for the cast, usually a few hand-held microphones provided for by the sound department. The cast will inevitably be excited and naturally try to match the sound of the band and will oversing, straining their voices. Your MD should mitigate against this and encourage the singers to not get too carried away.

As a director I find it helpful to watch the sitzprobe, not just because it's an exciting collective moment but it's an important time to hear how the songs will be delivered on stage. Every show is orchestrated in a slightly different way and depending on your budget or size of band this can vary hugely. Orchestration is in itself an art form, from the work of Jonathan Tunick, William Brohn and Michael Starobin to name just three, they are the final piece of the jigsaw in bringing a show to life. You may be familiar with how each song should sound from the cast recording but please remember that licensed orchestrations can often vary hugely. It's unlikely that you'll have the exact size of band the authors originally dictated and so some choices will have been made by the MD in terms of reducing and doubling across different instruments.

I tend to sit and make notes as I hear the score, paying particular attention to moments that feel or sound quite different. Again, orchestrations are there to tell the story of the song and enhance the author's intentions. You may find small elements of percussion that you can use to accentuate movement or discover whole new passages of songs that have a different feel to them. Don't panic, it's very rare for these to be completely different to what you have rehearsed and imagined but you may find additional moments that can enhance your staging and help tie various elements together. Make a note of anything that surprises you and find a time to talk to the MD after the rehearsal.

The Technical Rehearsal

The technical rehearsal is a chance to address any specific areas of the show that require technical elements to come together. Remember, this will likely be the first time that these elements are rehearsed in space, so things may not go as planned. Scenic elements may be bigger than expected, props may work differently and costumes may look different to what you imagined. It's important to discuss early on the technical expectations for the show and what can realistically be achieved in the time you have. Theatre contracts will have maximum hours you can use the space which must be observed, including regular lunch and dinner breaks for the full crew where no work can happen on stage. If you have a huge set, a flying car or any other technical element that you know will require an extended tech period you need to ensure that this is part of the scheduling from the beginning and try not to bury your head about potential problems. The general rule is if you *think* something will be an issue during tech, it most definitely *will* be. The temptation is to treat the tech like a dress and just hope that you can start at the top of the show and it'll somehow all iron itself out, as if by magic. This rarely happens, and if it does it's often a fluke and unlikely to happen a second time.

The golden rule is to keep calm. It's important to remind everyone what the purpose of this rehearsal is. This is less about the cast rehearsing their lines and dance routines and more about bringing together the technical elements that need to be rehearsed. You shouldn't worry about the quality of the acting or actors being 'in the moment'; instead their focus should be on incorporating the elements of costume, sound, lighting and set that will grow to enhance their performance. Create a policy where genuine problems and questions filter through the stage manager and avoid engaging in conversations with the cast about technical aspects of the show not relevant to them. Don't allow everyone's small problems to become your big problem, talk to your cast beforehand about how to feedback issues and more importantly, when. A hem on a skirt or missing button may feel like a major issue for a cast member, but are highly unlikely to feature on your list of important issues to address during tech.

PERSPECTIVE FROM A SOUND DESIGNER, ADRIAN JEAKINS

Musical theatre sound is a complex balancing act with lots of competing requirements and desires but the basics are pretty clear – the dialogue and lyrics tell the story so the audience needs to hear them! Given this, what the sound department needs as a basis is a really detailed plan of which performer speaks or sings each line, and often it's the directing team that are the only ones that can provide that. It can be tedious to create but it's the key lifeline for the sound team trying to make sure the right microphone is on at the right time. Time in the theatre is always limited so working together in rehearsals is also critical in figuring out both the factual who-what-when but also establishing who is responsible for what and how information should flow when changes are made or notes are needed.

Modern musicals use radio microphones as a matter of course and for many teams the number of independent microphones is key matter of discussion from a budget perspective – simply put, lots of radio mics add up quickly. In many circumstances it is entirely appropriate to share mics, passing them around the company so that all key solo lines are covered. Collaboration between director, musical team and sound team is critical to achieve a plan for this allocation scheme within the bounds of the budget. My key words of caution here are that every swap is an opportunity for something to break. The sound team can generally remotely check that microphones are working correctly and will try their best

SETTING EXPECTATIONS

Before you begin, work with the production team on the vital elements of the tech rehearsal that need to be covered. Create a priority list, the details of which will differ from production to production, and mark down which elements are vital to rehearse. There's no point in starting at the beginning and working through logically if the second half of Act Two features the most challenging technical elements – it is these sections that you should focus on before trying to run in order. Whilst it's much better to rehearse sequentially, you should only do so if you have the time needed to cover the core elements your team have identified require the time being spent on them.

Priority order:

- **Scene changes:** especially those that require drops, flies and physical set elements that need to be timed and require crew to move and set. Mark down frequent changes and sequences that can be repeated and run those first, going from one set to the next with the appropriate music and lighting cues to iron out any kinks. Repeat until the stage manager and crew are confident before moving on.

- **Extended tech elements:** certain shows may have specific technical elements that need to be rehearsed as a priority: the car in *Chitty Chitty Bang Bang*; the church collapse and flying sequence in *The Witches of Eastwick*; Fiona's transformation in *Shrek*, and so on. These will likely have been discussed ahead of time with all relevant departments and plans put in place for how they will run. Make sure these elements are nailed down and correct as a priority – you can't expect your cast and crew to attempt these elements without appropriate technical rehearsal. Try them 'out of time' for everyone to get comfortable with the elements, before speeding up and eventually running 'in time' with appropriate music and lighting.

- **Set placement:** it's important to 'spike' any set element that enters and exits the stage. This is usually done by the stage manager, using different coloured tape to mark ('spike') the precise location. This may be smaller items like a chair or desk or larger set pieces like a bed or bar. The idea being that whoever is responsible for setting these pieces knows exactly where to place them every time and it's not an estimation. Usually these will have to be set quickly in the darkness, so running these multiple times will aid confidence, especially if it's your cast who are responsible for bringing on and striking.

- **Sound:** any sound that isn't 'standard'. Your sound crew will likely work live in terms of programming and setting microphone levels. Any sound that requires a specific cue, relies on a track or an offstage sound should be rehearsed so everyone is clear on where / how it is being produced.

- **Costume changes:** this will likely be the first chance your cast have not only to run through their business onstage, but also to understand their traffic backstage. They will need to learn how far it is from their dressing room to the stage, which costume changes will be quick changes, which they need assistance with and so on. Identify any specific known quick changes ahead of time or any special costume that requires assistance. Wigs, make-up changes and so on are all part of this and should be rehearsed 'in time' if possible so adjustments can be made if necessary.

'DRY' TECH AND PLACING

You may find yourself with time on stage with your cast where you can attempt a dry tech of certain parts of the show that require specific spacing. Often the choreographer will want to mark out numbers silently with the cast, looking at specific positions on the stage and with the set. This may be to address elements that have to change in the space, or just to identify exact spacing in relation to the stage and other elements. Encourage this to happen in silence, usually whilst light plotting or sound levels are being worked on. If your show is dance-heavy, it would make sense to allocate time in your tech rehearsal for the choreographer to take charge and mark out numbers and spacing, paying particular attention to elements that may be difficult or might need adapting.

You and the stage manager should run tech. Position yourself in the front of the house, usually at a table or desk set up midway in the house. Ask for a 'voice of god' microphone so you can address the whole stage without shouting. Encourage silence from the company and stress the limitations on time that you have, setting expectations and explaining to your cast that they may likely not get a full rehearsal, but instead you will focus on the technical elements that are required. The orchestra or band are usually not called for this rehearsal, so it's important to factor in a pianist and sufficient sound for them to be heard on stage and through the monitors. Your sound team will be working on radio mics and cues, so will need to hear the cast at sufficient volume in order to work.

CUE-TO-CUE

A cue-to-cue run is probably the most efficient use of your tech time. Once the key elements are done and everyone is confident that they have been rehearsed, if not perfected, you can start at the top of the show and run what is called a cue-to-cue.

This will largely be called by the stage manager or deputy stage manager (DSM) who is responsible for 'calling' the show from the side of the stage. In these runs you should skip over longer scenes and songs where no specific technical elements occur. Ballads, duets and static songs are usually skipped, even if they have a number of different lighting cues in favour for progressing onwards to a scene change, scene or musical number that relies on multiple technical elements. Simply pause the action by saying 'hold please' in the voice of god, before deciding where you'll continue or skip to. Sometimes cast members may protest as they want to rehearse their song in place, but remind them that this isn't a rehearsal for their performance, it's for the full technical elements and time is at a premium.

DON'T FORGET to nail down how the show begins. This may seem fundamental but I've seen it be forgotten countless times, meaning a stressful and tricky start to the first night. You should have a clear system in place that follows front of house clearance, cast clearance, band clearance and stage clearance. This will then trigger the first cue, which is usually a pre-show announcement and lighting change, followed by the MD beginning the overture or starting music. Run through this a number of times so everyone (especially the MD) is confident on when the show starts and the order of clearance.

KILL YOUR DARLINGS – WHAT IF THINGS AREN'T WHAT YOU EXPECT

As prefaced above, the technical rehearsal will inevitably expose all of the faults in the show and can ultimately feel quite exposing. This is your first chance to see your full vision come together in one piece and it's important to remember that it may not be exactly as you had in mind. Perhaps the costumes are slightly different, the set smaller or lighting not as exciting as you had envisioned. I was once told by a Tony Award-winning director that they shot for 80 per cent of what they envisioned becoming a reality, and even that was sometimes a stretch. At a certain point you have to work with what you have and mentally accept certain elements are the way they have to be. This doesn't mean, however, that you have to give up – lighting cues, scenic detail and smaller elements can all continue to be worked on right through to the last minute, but there comes a point where you have to sit back and accept what is in front of you.

TOP TIPS FOR TECH

1. Keep an eye on the time and remember breaks. As tempting as it will be to keep working, technical crew, cast and yourself will need breaks for lunch and dinner.

2. Be as prepared as you can be and make swift decisions. Stick to your order of priorities and work through everything in a calm and systematic way.

3. Don't lose your temper and don't take things out on the cast.

4. Don't be overly critical of people's work – remember everything on the stage will have been sourced / made / created by someone.

5. Ask the sound department for a set of 'cans' so you can communicate with all relevant parties whilst sitting watching from the house.

Bows and Curtain Calls

Don't leave these to the tech to stage as I guarantee you will not have time. There's an old superstition of not rehearsing these until the last moment, but quite frankly this is one tradition I'm happy to avoid. Speak with your production team about the requirements for the curtain calls – most shows will have specific music written for this and often the bows are timed alongside the various musical themes in the show. In many cases the order of bows is obvious, although with larger shows 'who bows last' can be an area of much contention and debate. The usual rule of thumb is to start with the ensemble bowing in smaller groups, working up to featured roles bowing in a small group and solo bows for principals. If the show is more ensemble in nature, you can avoid the pantomime style 'run-down' bow where every character gets their solo curtain call. Think about an audience and what they want. They will feel cheated if they don't get an opportunity to give Dolly Levi, Madame Rose or Tevye a moment of solo applause, and the actor will likely feel shortchanged. Keep these simple, short and not indulgent – avoid speeches, flowers and other trappings that elongates the process. Make sure you build in applause for the band, musical director / conductor and the technical team before a final company bow that's often underlined with a short musical reprise or song.

The Dress Rehearsal

With any luck you'll have finished your tech rehearsal at a reasonable hour, leaving you a day or possibly two before the first night. In my experience it's rare for techs to finish on time and you'll likely find yourself in a position where you haven't managed a full technical rehearsal, but if your planning has been effective you'll at least know the major technical elements have been rehearsed. A dress rehearsal differs from a technical rehearsal by being presented as an artificial run, as close to 'performance mode' as possible. I would try to start these as close to the normal performance time as possible, calling the cast at least an hour before the show to get into microphones, costumes, make-up and prepare for the run. Depending on how the tech has gone, there may be elements of the show that you expect to slow down or come to a standstill, but try to not project that energy onto the cast. I'm often amazed at how showbusiness instinct kicks in and problems and kinks work through when everyone is in a collective performance mode.

I would assemble all of the technical team for a final check-in on any progress made during the day, any changes or alterations from the technical rehearsal and to talk through contingencies for if certain elements go wrong. Prepare everyone to only stop in an emergency or if health and safety is affected. Assemble the cast on stage half an hour before the performance for a mental warm-up and final brief note session, focusing on technical changes or updates rather than performances. Many cast members might try and resist this as they'll favour their hair, make-up and costumes, but this is an important ritual and key part of the process. Rather than give complex notes, think about the key messages you want to convey. Anything to do with health and safety should be a priority, try not to change things related to performance or introduce 'working' notes that won't have time to rehearse. Your cast will be energized, nervous and anxious to get started so harness that energy and pull everyone together with a short focus exercise. Agree as a collective how and why a show stop would take place and make sure everyone has co-ordinated this with the stage management team to avoid confusion midway through the run.

I suggest sitting in the auditorium and watching the dress, making active notes throughout. I tend to divide my paper up into 'performance' and 'technical' notes so I can separate the two different elements that need to be focused on. Hopefully the run will occur in real time with no stopping. Resist the urge to shout from the auditorium, even to correct something simple. It will only distract the cast and cause confusion. Your stage management team will run the dress including the interval in real time, making the calls as appropriate. Make as many notes as possible, but at the end of the run, release the cast and crew as soon as you're able to. It's helpful to read your notes back and divide them into the following categories: Essential, desirable and non-essential (see Table 3.3).

Remember at this stage you have limited time and capacity to make fundamental changes. Your cast will be near to oversaturation point, so think twice about all of the notes you give them at this stage. You'll be able to judge those actors who want to

Table 3.3 Essential, Desirable and Non-essential Notes

	Cast	Tech
Essential	Anything related to health and safety; updated positions due to changes in set or props; cues related to sound and lights and set items.	Anything related to health and safety; cues related to the running of the show.
Desirable	Spacing in a production number; articulation in a number.	Adding an extra lighting cue to cover an entrance; bringing on the sofa faster for a scene.
Non-essential	Energy entering a scene; inflection on a certain word; colour of apron worn in a number.	Changing the colour of the LED lighting from a green to a yellow in the opening number.

take such notes on board and those who don't, so consider each note carefully and pass on those that fall into the 'essential' category in the first instance before passing on anything further.

The Run of the Show

Opening Night

Opening night will be a frantic, exciting and nerve-wracking time for everyone involved. Remember, the cast will still be looking to you for guidance, wisdom and support, so whatever you do, make sure you haven't mentally checked out. I've worked with some directors and musical directors who have already moved onto their next project and by this stage, show little interest in how the show turns out. Don't be that person – you deserve to pull this show over the finish line triumphantly.

I would repeat my schedule from the previous night: assemble the cast at the half-hour mark and offer a light pep talk, filled with thanks and gratitude, rather than any formal last-minute notes. It's important to come together and reflect on the process and above all remind everyone why they are there and what they have achieved in this time. Even if you've had a rocky tech or dress and tensions have run high, use this as a chance to re-set and re-align the direction of the production to finish strong, and collectively share the moment of opening night. I often do a light warm-up and focus exercise and part on some words about character and telling the story before handing the show over to the cast and stage management team. I generally then like to get out of the way and not project nerves backstage. Withdraw, have a moment to yourself and join your production team front of house. Remember to thank your MD and tell them to 'break a leg' as you leave the show in their care.

Opening night cards and gifts are a nice, formal way to thank everyone involved in the production and write a personal message to each cast member. Depending on your budget you may offer a gift or memento, or even just a photo from the dress rehearsal. Whatever you do, treat everyone evenly. Write a card for every person in the cast and thank everyone for their work and time.

At this stage, different personalities like to approach the run of the show in different ways. I find myself withdrawing, remaining in the background and making myself visible when needed but not overwhelming either backstage or front of stage. Essentially your work is done, but you should remain on hand for any last-minute dramas that may crop up throughout the show week. Withdrawing in full gives a sense of you running away, but being too involved backstage threatens to overwhelm the cast. I find a simple check-in each night before the show to all dressing rooms is sufficient to show everyone you are there and remain engaged in the process, also to answer any questions that may arise. As mentioned above, I don't note performances unless of course it's an essential note due to health and safety or something fundamental has had to change.

One thing you will inevitably notice throughout the run of the show is how the cast responds to feedback, both in the moment and after each performance. Unlike professional theatre where you have a series of previews to judge audience reactions, taper performances and make tweaks, amateur theatre rarely has this luxury. Amateur actors are more susceptible to audience feedback than professional ones, mainly as the audience is largely made up of friends and colleagues and people within the amateur theatre community. Feedback, both positive and negative, will begin to trickle through – and show-week drama intensifies emotions and feelings for everyone backstage. I usually address this in a pep talk, encouraging people to stick to their guns and not adapt their performance based on the feedback of their significant other, flatmate or friend from work. You'll often see actors enjoying audience feedback in the moment and pushing laughs, even competing with others on the stage to see who can gain a bigger audience reaction. There's only so much of this you can manage, but by this stage your professionalism should have set a standard for quality and consistency that the company adopts. If it begins to become a problem that affects other actors, speak to the actor(s) in question and remind them of the process and their responsibility to their fellow company members.

Try to instil other examples of show-week etiquette such as:

1. Arrive an hour before the show to prepare, at the latest half an hour before.
2. Don't leave the theatre in costume or make-up.
3. Don't invite people backstage who aren't part of the show.
4. Leave all costumes and props at the theatre in your dressing room.

Remember the cast will be eager to see you following the show and you should make yourself available to smile, congratulate them and share in the energy. Giving notes as soon as an actor comes off stage is counterproductive. Allow your actors to enjoy their post-show moment and be careful about focusing on any errors or problems that may have arisen.

Reviews and NODA Reports

Sometimes the company will have invited local newspapers, blogs and online outlets to review the show in order to create some publicity for the production. The obvious idea behind this is to sell tickets and extend the reach of the audience base beyond that of people related to the production. I find reviews of amateur performances troubling for a number of reasons. Unlike professional actors, everyone associated with the amateur production has not necessarily agreed to be reviewed as part of this show. Whilst I understand the need for publicity, a negative review or one that favours some cast members over others can sometimes disrupt show week and ruin the experience for some of the people involved. When a professional production opens, producers invite a wide spread of reviewers and this can lead to 20–50 reviews which in turn offers a breadth of opinion. Having just one or two reviews of an amateur production can negatively disrupt company morale and disproportionately place emphasis on the opinion of one or two external people. Be mindful of sharing and discussing reviews that do come out during the run of the show and be aware that not everyone will want to read them. People who are praised or mentioned will no doubt find a way to broadcast this in the dressing room, leaving people who were not mentioned, or indeed criticized, feeling despondent and can ruin their overall experience. Speak with the committee and trustees about how the reviews should be shared and be sensitive, remembering that no one signed up to this process to be formally reviewed by an external source.

In the UK, NODA-affiliated companies will invite a NODA representative to see the production and provide written feedback. From my experience this feedback ranges from a basic school-report-style assessment with blanket comments such as 'costumes were well worn', 'make-up was applied' and 'actors entered and exited with ease' through to more engaged judgements on the achievements of the production overall with some light constructive criticism. Just as with reviews, speak to the committee about how and when to share these reports – usually after the production has finished. I always contextualize these reviews with the caveat that they are written by someone from within the local community who is invariably attached to the company in some way and thus rarely impartial. Even the most glowing assessment is just one person's view and shouldn't be taken as the final say on the overall success of a production as a whole.

Closing a Show

Knowing how to close a show is as important as knowing how to open one. You will be remembered by the cast, company and production team by your words and actions throughout the whole process, right up to the very end. Before the final performance I usually gather the company once again at the half-hour point and have some form of ceremonial finish to the project. This may include exchanging a small gift or 'secret santa' to symbolize the end of the process, or it could be just sharing a memory from show week. Different societies will have different traditions that may or may not include you. Often there's a party or gathering following the final show or get-out. Attend and be gracious, as people will want to thank you for your work and time and you'll want to pass on the same compliments to the full production team and everyone involved in making the show a success. Sometimes this feels awkward but resist the temptation to run off into the night (I've done that many times ...) as you should be proud of your hard work and want to formally close the production for everyone involved.

Get-out

This will be the same process as the get-in but in reverse. Just as before, having a clear plan of what needs to happen is key and this should be something that is co-ordinated by the production manager. I advise you to check the theatre contract specifically regarding how the theatre should be left. Do you need to paint the floor back to black, take the rubbish to a specific place or be out of the venue at a specific time. Don't allow a chaotic get-out to ruin a wonderful show week and be the lasting memory of the production. The excitement of get-in will have evaporated and the cast will likely not be as keen to help and assist. Assigning jobs and making sure everyone pitches in will not only mean the process is quicker but will keep everything positive and collaborative to the very end.

Final Reflection

Amateur theatre can often be a much-misunderstood hobby for those who don't have first-hand experience of it in action. The general public have a view of the exaggerated tropes that have been satirized and joked about in various mediums meaning it can be quite difficult to reframe and defend. It will always feel somewhat inferior to professional theatre and no matter how good it is, fight for a place within the wider theatrical ecosystem. As costs spiral, producing amateur theatre has never been harder and I firmly believe we're at a crunch time for many companies. Audiences haven't fully returned since the Covid-19 pandemic, and as the price of theatre hire, building materials, paint, costume hire and so on has escalated, ticket prices have had to rise accordingly. It's never been riskier or more expensive to produce a musical and companies are finding themselves favouring popular titles to draw in crowds and mitigate against potential losses.

That said, 'show people' are a special kind of resilient. We are experts at making something out of nothing, banding together, painting on a smile and putting on a show. The energy, determination and love that comes from amateur theatre is something that is difficult to describe to those on the outside. I'm often asked 'why' people give up their evenings and weekends against the backdrop of busy lives and jobs to come together to put on a musical. I never really know the answer or most effective way to describe the joy opening night brings or the stomach pain when the curtain falls on the final show. I believe there's a spiritual bond that connects everyone involved that remains indescribable. People coming together as a community for a shared goal, from the people in the fly tower to stage management to the orchestra and leading actors. It's a spark of magic that defies description and can only be experienced. I hope this book inspires you to chase that experience, and have the time of your life whilst doing so.

Glossary

11 o'clock number: traditionally the final new number in a show, usually delivered by the star player. Named due to the time the number was often performed at a time when shows began at 8.30 pm.

Apron: any part of the stage that sits outside of the proscenium and is in front of the tab line.

Audition pack: a set of materials compiled by the creative team that explains the show and includes all details about the production for potential cast members to reference.

Band call: the rehearsal where the cast and band meet for the first time to play through the show.

Book: another word for the script of a musical.

Bookwriter: the author of the script for a musical.

Callback: a second-round audition, also called a recall, where auditionees are seen again for principal roles.

Cast recording: a recording of a musical, usually featuring the original cast.

Charts: a method of drawing out your blocking to keep on file and reference throughout rehearsal.

Committee: a body of people usually tasked with running an amateur theatre group.

Concept musical: broadly described as a non-linear musical that doesn't always have a formal traditional structure.

Costume call: the rehearsal where all cast try on their costumes for the first time.

Costumier: a specialist costume provider or shop that supplies theatre costumes.

Cue-to-cue: a type of run that is interrupted, usually during a technical rehearsal, literally cutting from one technical cue to the next.

Diegetic music: music that exists in the world of the show and is heard by the characters.

Doubling: where actors play more than one role.

Dress rehearsal: the final run through of the show, usually in real time, the day before the first performance and performed in show conditions.

Dry tech: a rehearsal on the stage that uses props and set pieces but doesn't include lights or sound.

Estate: the people tasked with looking after the interests of the creatives involved with each show. Usually their family or other vested party who work with the licensing company.

Gabble: a very fast line-run to cement lines and cues for actors.

Get-in: the process of moving into the theatre, usually involves bringing in all the set and technical apparatus required for the show.

Get-out: a reversal of the process that removes everything to leave the theatre in the condition you found it.

Libretto: the script and book of the show, including the lyrics.

License holder: the company from whom you have acquired the performing licence from.

LX tape: electrical tape frequently used to measure out a stage in rehearsal.

NAs: 'Not available' days for cast and creative team.

NODA: the National Operatic and Dramatic Association – a collective body for amateur theatre.

Non-diegetic music: music that doesn't occur within the world of the show.

Number line: a rehearsal line that measures out the front of the stage. See the section 'Rehearsal Number Line' in Act 2 on how to make your own.

Principals: the lead performers and characters in the show.

Production schedule: the overall schedule for the project that everyone is working from.

Proscenium: the 'frame' of the stage, usually described as 'proscenium arch'.

Rake: the pitch of the stage, usually raked towards the audience on an angle. This differs from stage to stage.

Rehearsal reports: reports that 'minute' the rehearsal process and are distributed to creative team and cast each week.

Rehearsal schedule: the master schedule that instructs everyone when and where rehearsals are happening.

Rig: where the lighting bars sit, usually referred to as the 'lighting rig'.

Round: theatre in the round where audience are situated on all sides.

Sides: pages of script / libretto that are given to auditionees for auditions.

Sitzprobe: often called the 'band call' – the first rehearsal with the band or orchestra where the whole cast assemble and sing through the whole score.

Stagger run: a run where you tentatively work through the whole show.

Table work: the process of sitting at a table and talking about characters and the show with actors as part of rehearsal.

Tabs: the front curtain in a proscenium arch theatre.

Tech rehearsal: the rehearsals where technical elements are added to the show. This can be one rehearsal or a series of them.

Thrust: a type of staging where the audience is usually situated on three sides.

Tracks: the track of each performer that incorporates their full journey throughout the show including every entrance, exit, set change and movement.

Traverse: a type of staging that has audience on two sides like a runway.

Trustee: usually the same as a committee member within amateur theatre, someone who sits on the board of the group and makes decisions.

Vocal call: a type of rehearsal usually led by the musical director that focuses on music.

Youth theatre: a type of group that usually focuses on young people rather than adults.

Bibliography and Further Reading

As I state in the introduction, the best way of learning and refining your skills is by consuming yourself with as much theatre you can, across all mediums. This can range from full productions of different scales to amateur/student theatre and filmed 'pro-shot' versions of shows and even YouTube recordings.

Aside from watching, reading is the best way to develop your skills and learn about different types of theatre making. There are endless numbers of books about theatre practice, many of which are published by the wonderful Methuen Drama, but I've listed some below that I feel are vital to have in your toolkit.

This list is by no means exhaustive, but treat this as my 'desert island disc' selection of books you simply must read.

Musical Theatre History/Understanding

- *The Secret Life of the American Musical: How Broadway Shows Are Built*, by Jack Viertel (2017, Sarah Crichton Books).

- *How Musicals Work: And How to Write Your Own*, by Julian Woolford (2012, Nick Hern Books).

- *Staging Musicals: An Essential Guide*, by Matthew White (2019, Methuen Drama).

Directing Books

- *Theatre Craft: A Director's Practical Companion from A to Z*, by John Caird (2010, Faber).

- *Notes on Directing: 130 Lessons in Leadership from the Director's Chair*, by Frank Hauser and Russell Reich (2018, RCR).

- *Directing: A Handbook for Emerging Theatre Directors*, by Rob Swain (2011, Methuen Drama).

- *The Director's Craft: A Handbook for the Theatre*, by Katie Mitchell (2009, Routledge).

I would encourage you to start collecting a library of musical librettos, which you can read and learn from. Many new musicals get published, but older musicals are harder to find in 'trade' editions. I find the collections below invaluable, and have been used throughout the creation of this book:

- *American Musicals: The Complete Books and Lyrics of Sixteen Broadway Classics: A Library of America Boxed Set* (2014, Library of America).
- *The New American Musical: An Anthology from the End of the 20th Century* (2001, TCG).
- *Ten Great Musicals of the American Theatre* (1973, Chiltern).
- *Great Musicals of the American Theatre Volume 2* (1976, Chiltern).

Index